T0092297

Deep Learning for Chest Radiographs

Primers in Biomedical Imaging Devices and Systems Series

Deep Learning for Chest Radiographs

Computer-Aided Classification

Yashvi Chandola
Department of Computer Science & Engineering
Govind Ballabh Pant Institute of Engineering & Technology
Uttarakhand, India

Jitendra Virmani
CSIR-Central Scientific Instruments Organization (CSIR-CSIO)
Chandigarh, India

H.S Bhadauria
Department of Computer Science & Engineering
Govind Ballabh Pant Institute of Engineering & Technology
Uttarakhand, India

Papendra Kumar
Department of Computer Science & Engineering
Govind Ballabh Pant Institute of Engineering & Technology
Uttarakhand, India

ACADEMIC PRESS
An imprint of Elsevier

ELSEVIER

Academic Press is an imprint of Elsevier
125 London Wall, London EC2Y 5AS, United Kingdom
525 B Street, Suite 1650, San Diego, CA 92101, United States
50 Hampshire Street, 5th Floor, Cambridge, MA 02139, United States
The Boulevard, Langford Lane, Kidlington, Oxford OX5 1GB, United Kingdom

Copyright © 2021 Elsevier Inc. All rights reserved.

No part of this publication may be reproduced or transmitted in any form or by any means, electronic or mechanical,
including photocopying, recording, or any information storage and retrieval system, without permission in writing from
the publisher. Details on how to seek permission, further information about the Publisher's permissions policies and our
arrangements with organizations such as the Copyright Clearance Center and the Copyright Licensing Agency, can be found
at our website: www.elsevier.com/permissions.

This book and the individual contributions contained in it are protected under copyright by the Publisher (other than as may
be noted herein).

Notices
Knowledge and best practice in this field are constantly changing. As new research and experience broaden our
understanding, changes in research methods, professional practices, or medical treatment may become necessary.

Practitioners and researchers must always rely on their own experience and knowledge in evaluating and using any
information, methods, compounds, or experiments described herein. In using such information or methods they should be
mindful of their own safety and the safety of others, including parties for whom they have a professional responsibility.

To the fullest extent of the law, neither the Publisher nor the authors, contributors, or editors, assume any liability for any
injury and/or damage to persons or property as a matter of products liability, negligence or otherwise, or from any use or
operation of any methods, products, instructions, or ideas contained in the material herein.

Library of Congress Cataloging-in-Publication Data
A catalog record for this book is available from the Library of Congress

British Library Cataloguing-in-Publication Data
A catalogue record for this book is available from the British Library

ISBN 978-0-323-90184-0

For information on all Academic Press publications
visit our website at https://www.elsevier.com/books-and-journals

Publisher: Mara Conner
Acquisitions Editor: Sonnini Yura
Editorial Project Manager: Leticia Lima
Production Project Manager: Poulouse Joseph
Cover Designer: Mark Rogers

Typeset by SPi Global, India

Contents

Preface

Medical images are an irreplaceable source of statistical information for the purpose of extensive scientific experimental applications. The imaging modalities that facilitate the capturing of these medical images are evolving speedily, thereby improvising the sophistication in the quality of images. This affects the features associated with different tissues at reasonably subsiding costs. Consequently, in this era of data-driven disciplines, the medical images result in a noteworthy increase in the repository size of the image data. As medical imaging datasets grow grander and become more complicated, the need arises for more advanced machine learning-based methods to analyze and interpret the data. During the past few years, deep learning-based methods have brought a revolution to the field of medical image analysis by introducing novel, efficient solutions to many image analysis problems. These problems are as diverse as computer-aided classification, segmentation of regions of interest, lesion detection, image-guided therapy, and image dataset annotation. Machine learning and deep learning provide a wide range of tools and methods to execute the solutions of this diverse pool of problems.

The principal aim of *Deep Learning for Chest Radiographs: Computer-Assisted Classification* is to describe in detail: (a) the different types of computer-assisted classification systems for chest radiographs; (b) the design of computer-aided classification systems for chest radiographs using end-to-end convolution neural networks; (c) the design of computer-aided classification systems for chest radiographs using end-to-end lightweight convolution neural networks; and (d) the design of computer-aided classification systems for chest radiographs using hybrid approaches like deep feature extraction by convolutional neural network and classification using conventional machine learning classifiers. The authors have created this volume keeping in mind a diverse readership, but the prime target audience are the graduates, undergraduates, academic researchers, research scholars, and industry personnel who are fascinated by the trends in the application of these machine learning and deep learning methods for the design of computer-aided classification systems for medical images in general and chest radiographs in particular. The organization of the book keeps in mind the majority of the readership audience, hence the chapters summarize the basic concepts of deep learning-based convolution neural network-based architectures, machine learning algorithms in medical imaging with prime focus on chest radiographs, the various data augmentation methods, features of medical images that are essential in correct diagnosis of diseases. Each chapter has a set of code snippets as well as illustrations of how to apply these methods focusing on chest radiographs. The topics discussed in this book mirror the persistent progress of deep learning approaches for the analysis of medical images. The authors hope that this book will help the readers understand the current research in medical image analysis and opportunities for developing pioneering computational methods, which will positively accelerate the discoveries of computer-aided classification systems into effective treatments for patients. The authors of this book share the common vision of achieving greater advancements in the field of medical image analysis and are grateful for the opportunity to contribute their knowledge, aptitude, and familiarity with the topic.

Yashvi Chandola
Jitendra Virmani
H.S. Bhadauria
Papendra Kumar

Acknowledgments

This book has been one of the significant academic achievements for all of the contributing authors and has been possible by their combined efforts. We have had the utmost honor and privilege of working with a very professional team at Elsevier, and we are thankful for their timely guidance and support from the initial review of the book proposal to the final copy editing stage and production. With the greatest regards, we acknowledge our heartfelt and sincere thanks to Dr. Nilanjan Dey (series editor) for the critical review of the proposal and for rendering his valuable advice from time to time. The authors are also thankful to Dr. Kriti and Mr. Niranjan Yadav for their support and help in stimulating discussions on different topics covered in this book. The authors are grateful to Mr. V.M. Thakkar, Mr. Bhoopender Chandola, Dr. Jyoti Rawat, and Mrs. Suman Lata Joshi for their constructive suggestions and help rendered in proofreading the manuscript. We extend our utmost gratitude to the participating radiation oncologist Dr. Yamini Bachheti (M.B.B.S, M.D. Radiation Oncology), currently serving as a senior resident at All India Institute of Medical Sciences, Rishikesh, for her valuable inputs during the numerous discussions we had throughout the progress of the work. She made us understand how the differential diagnosis between different classes of chest radiographs is carried out by visual analysis.

Last but not least, we are thankful to our loved ones, family members, and dear friends for their support, patience, and unwavering strength.

Yashvi Chandola
Jitendra Virmani
H.S. Bhadauria
Papendra Kumar

Introduction

1.1 Motivation

The modernism in the field of artificial intelligence (AI), specifically the novelties in deep learning with an eventual growth of annotated datasets associated with medical images, have marked the current period exhilarating for medical image analysis. Pneumonia is an infectious disease mostly caused by bacteria or virus, which leads the alveoli of the lungs to fill up with fluid or mucus. This results in inflammation of the lungs, making it hard to breathe as the air sacs of the lungs cannot fully accommodate the oxygen required by the body. The prime targets of this infectious disease are children below the age of 5 years and elderly above the age of 65 years. These two age groups are the prime targets mostly due to their poor immunity and hence lower rate of recovery. Globally, pneumonia has prevalent footprints and kills more children as compared to any other immunity-based disease that is preventable in nature, causing up to 15% of child deaths per year, especially in developing countries. It is reported to be close to a million children under the age of 5 years that die from this preventable disease each year. Almost 500 million cases of pneumonia are reported every year worldwide. There are multiple known causes of pneumonia, and still, there is no silver bullet to eradicate it, hence it is also referred to as "the silent killer" [1].

The most common bacteria causing pneumonia is streptococcus or pneumococcus; however, other bacteria can also be the prime cause of this disease. These bacteria often live in the throat, but if the immunity of an individual is compromised, then they tend to grow in the lungs. The response of the immune system to this infection causes the air sacs to inflame and fill with pus or fluid. This results in provoked coughing, and the capacity of the lungs to intake air also decreases. When influenza leads to pneumonia, it is popularly known as viral pneumonia. It can also be caused by fungus and other parasites, but this is rare. Vaccines are a tried and tested way to prevent this disease: the pneumococcal conjugate vaccine and Haemophilus influenza type b (Hib) vaccine have been found very effective. A study conducted by the National Statistics Institute (Instituto Nacional de Estadística (INE)) in Spain states that the diseases related to the respiratory system are the third leading cause of death worldwide. This study showed that pneumonia is the leading respiratory system disease causing most frequent deaths [2]. Hence faster diagnosis of pneumonia and timely application of adequate medication can contribute significantly in preventing the downfall of the patient condition. For efficient diagnosis of pneumonia, chest radiographs are considered to be the most suited imaging modality [3]. Bacterial and viral pneumonia are often misclassified, even by trained radiologists due to their similar appearance, which can lead to complications in the treatment. An additional factor motivating the need for carrying out the present work is the lack of resources, especially in the rural areas, which makes designing computer-aided classification (CAC) systems essential for helping the radiologists in early detection of pneumonia.

Deep Learning for Chest Radiographs. https://doi.org/10.1016/B978-0-323-90184-0.00003-5
Copyright © 2021 Elsevier Inc. All rights reserved.

1.2 Introduction to deep learning

AI, in simple words, can be defined as an extensive and prevalent branch of computer science that is interdisciplinary in nature. The basic principle on which AI functions is that human intellect and human behavior can be defined in such a way that the machine could easily mimic it and perform tasks that vary from easy and simple to difficult and complex in terms of implementation. AI focuses on the incorporation of learning, reasoning, and perception into machines with the primary aim to simulate intelligence equivalent to human intelligence.

Over the duration of the past few years, the popularity and media hype around AI has seen revolutionary changes. This has led to a major boom in technology-based publication society resulting in numerous articles proposing self-driving cars, intelligent robots, and application in healthcare such as computer-aided detection systems, CAC systems. At a primary level, AI is majorly of two types, weak AI and strong AI. Weak AI deals with the machines focused on simpler tasks and single task orientations whereas strong AI deals with the designing of machines focused on complex tasks as well as more human equivalent tasks. However, AI mainly comprises of two subsets popularly known as machine learning (ML) and deep learning. Although AI is interdisciplinary, recent advancements and trends in ML and deep learning are the main reasons for the major paradigm shift in virtually every sector associated with technology. Another categorization of AI states that it has, in general, three categories: (a) symbolic approach (rule-based search engine); (b) Bayesian theorem-based approach; and (c) connection-based approach (deep neural networks). The connection-based approach is gaining a lot of attention in relation to solving complex problems [4]. Fig. 1.1 shows the relationship between AI, ML, and DL.

ML is a subset of AI that arises from certain questions: Can a machine go further than what we as humans know about a problem and determine the solution to perform a certain task? Can the machine learn on its own how to perform a specified task? Does a machine have the capability to surprise us? Can a machine automatically learn the data processing rules just by looking at data that are otherwise

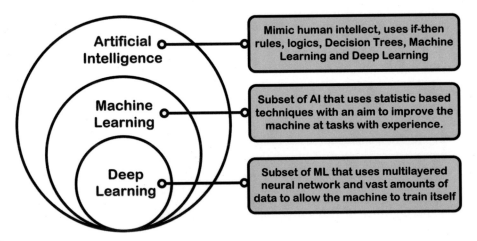

FIG. 1.1

Relationship between artificial intelligence, machine learning, and deep learning. *AI*, artificial intelligence; *ML*, machine learning.

handcrafted by programmers? All of these questions open multiple doors and force the researchers to think and progress toward new paradigms of technology. ML deals with enabling the machines to learn data itself with minimum human intervention with an aim to perform tasks such as to classify categories or predict future or uncertain conditions [5]. As ML is a type of data-driven learning, it is often referred to as nonsymbolic AI, which can perform prediction from unobserved data. It mainly deals with problems associated with regression, classification, detection, segmentation, and so forth. By and large, the dataset consists of training, validation, and test sets. The machine (algorithm) learns characteristics of the data from the training dataset and validates the learned characteristics from the validation dataset. As a final point, one can confirm the accuracy of the algorithm by using the test dataset.

An artificial neural network, popularly referred to as ANN, being a part of ML, is simply defined as an algorithm inspired by the functioning of the human brain. It is a multilayered structure; each layer comprises of interconnected nodes that are simply analogous to neurons in a human brain. A biological neuron is comprised of four key components:

(a) Soma: It is the main processing unit of the neuron and is popularly known as the cell body.

(b) Dendrites: The dendrites are tree-like branched structures that carry the information and signals received from other neurons.

(c) Axon: It is a long tubular structure, through which the neuron communicates information to other neurons.

(d) Synapse: It is the interconnection between the neighboring neurons to facilitate the transmission of signal and information. The synapses are formed by the dendrites of the neurons and the terminal axons.

An ANN is analogous to a biological neural network where the soma of a biological neuron is represented as a node of an artificial neuron, similarly, the dendrites are the same as inputs to the artificial neuron, the synapses are represented as the weighted interconnections between the layers of the ANN, and the axon is the output of the ANN. Fig. 1.2 shows the analogy between biological neuron components and an artificial neuron.

In an ANN, the weights associated with each node are determined by algorithms that facilitate learning such as back propagation. These learning algorithms focus on optimizing the weight associated with each node with an aim to significantly contribute in the reduction of the losses thereby enhancing the overall accuracy of the system. Although ANN training sometimes gets stuck at local minimum, this gives rise to the popular "overfitting" problem. To overcome this, researchers have adopted the concept of deep learning. It can be simply defined as an expansion of ANN into deeper networks by stacking more layers of artificial neurons. This enables the machine to deal with more complex problems. These multilayered networks, popularly called the deep neural networks, have better performance in tasks involving classification and regression as compared to shallow ANN [6]. These networks often improve their performance by implementing the restricted Boltzmann machine (unsupervised) to overcome the problem of overfitting [7].

There are three types of ML methods:

(a) Supervised learning: For supervised learning, the training data has well-labeled outputs for their corresponding input values. This method aims at mapping a mathematical relationship between the input and the well-labeled output. The output data has categorical values in case of classification tasks and has continuous numerical values in case of regression tasks, and depending on the task the output data value type changes. The k-nearest neighbor (k-NN)

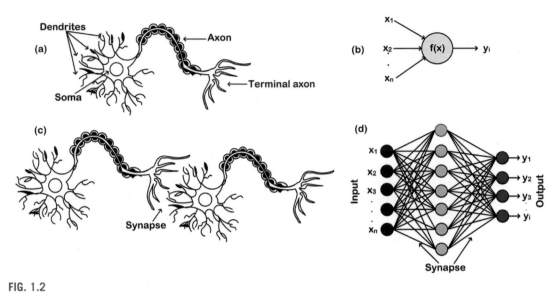

FIG. 1.2

(A) A simple biological neuron, (B) a simple artificial neuron, (C) the synapse between the biological neurons, and (D) an ANN.

algorithm is used for both classification as well as regression tasks [8]. Another popular algorithm used is linear regression, which overcomes the limitation of k-NN with larger datasets (speed decreases) [9, 10]. Support vector machine (SVM), logistic regression, and random forest are popularly used for classification tasks [11], whereas support vector regression and ANNs have shown better results for regression problems [12].

(b) Unsupervised learning: In unsupervised learning the labeled outputs are not available. This learning method determines a functional representation of the hidden characteristics of the input data. It majorly includes the tasks, such as principal component analysis (PCA) and cluster analysis.

(c) Reinforcement learning: Reinforcement learning is primarily concerned with the sequential decision problem. It is not popularly used in medical imaging related problems and tasks, as it learns by trial and error and has a tendency to affect the patient's future treatments with bias [13, 14]. Some other learning types, such as semisupervised (cost-effective, as only small labeled data is used) and ensemble learning (combination of multiple classification based algorithms) [15], are popularly used.

A branch of ML that primarily deals in processing data, trying to mimic the thinking process and develop abstractions by employing algorithms is often defined as deep learning. It makes use of multiple layers of algorithms with an aim to process the data, understanding human speech, and recognize objects visually. The algorithm most popularly is known as convolution neural network (CNN) [16–18]. The basic functional unit of a CNN is the convolution operation. The convolution operation is a mathematical operation over two functions whose result represents the effect of one function on the shape of another.

$$(f * g)(t) = \int_{-\infty}^{\infty} f(x)g(t-x)dx$$

The convolution of functions f and g is denoted by an asterisk (*) symbol. Here f and g are functions having arguments with real values, $f(x)$ is the weighted average of the function, and t is the time. In convolution, one parameter in the equation is the input and the other is the kernel, whereas the output of the convolution is called the feature map.

$$s(t) = (f * g)(t)$$

Here: $s(t)$ is the output of the convolution operation, f is the input argument, g is the kernel. Fig. 1.3 shows a convolution operation performed on a 3×5 input matrix x and 2×2 kernel k. The kernel convolves on the matrix x with a stride of 1 resulting in a 2×4 output matrix.

The convolution controls some essential parameters that help in enhancing the available ML systems. These parameters are as follows:

(a) Sparse interaction: It is often referred to as sparse weights or sparse connectivity, which simply means that the process of calculating the output involves fewer parameters. This is achieved by keeping the size of the kernels smaller than the input size. In this way, only the useful features are detected and stored from an input image or data, unlike the traditional methods that followed matrix multiplication where each output interacts with every input data

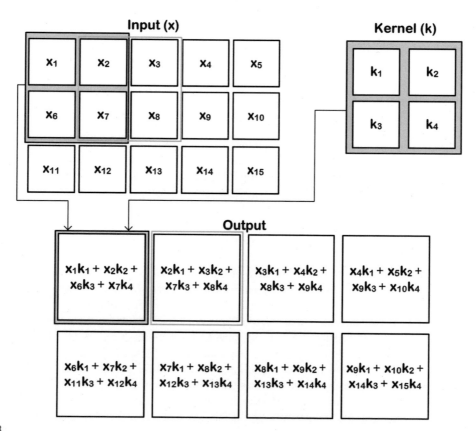

FIG. 1.3

Convolution operation.

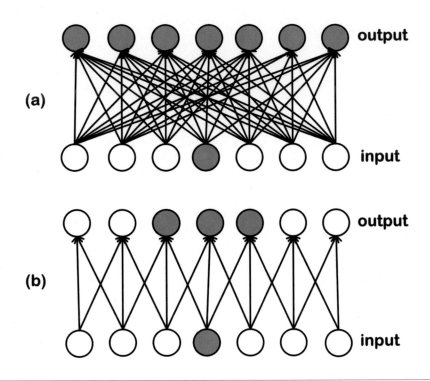

FIG. 1.4

(A) Matrix-matrix multiplication, (B) convolution with a kernel size 3.

point. The sparse connectivity improves the memory requirements as well as the efficiency of the models at large. Fig. 1.4 shows that in matrix multiplication, all the output variables are affected by the single input data point (highlighted nodes), whereas in sparse connectivity, where the convolution of single input variable is performed using a kernel size of 3, only three output variables are affected (highlighted nodes). These highlighted output nodes are called the receptive fields of the particular highlighted input variable. This enables efficient design of complicated connections and interactions among different variables by building smaller, sparse interactions. Fig. 1.4 shows the matrix multiplication and convolution operation. The shaded nodes in (A) and (B) show the receptive field of the input node.

(b) **Sharing of parameters:** This is also referred to as tying of weights in a network, as the weight parameters are shared with different functions in the model. In traditional networks, the weight matrix, which is assigned to each layer, is used only once for calculating the outputs. These weight values are never revisited, whereas in convolution networks they are tied to some other layer where these weight values are reused. The main aim of parameter sharing is that rather than learning new parameters, the convolution network reuses the existing ones. This does not affect the computation time but greatly affects the memory requirements of the network.

(c) **Equivariant representation:** Here equivariance represents that if the input changes, then the output also changes in a similar manner. We can say that a function $f(x)$ is equivariant to function g if:

Table 1.1 Different data formats for CNN.

	1D	2D	3D
Single channel	Audio waveform: measure the amplitude of the waveform by discretizing time	Audio data with Fourier transform	Volumetric data: medical images such as CT scans
Multichannel	Animation data	RGB color images	Color video (time, height, width)

$$f\big(g(x)\big) = g\big(f(x)\big)$$

In processing of time-series data, convolution produces a timeline that shows different features that appear in the input. In this case, it is considered invariant if the event moves in time. Then the same representation would appear in the output later in time. Convolutions are seen to be equivariant in translation but are not by default equivariant to other transformations like scale, rotation, and so on.

(d) Variable size input: Different kinds of data and variable sizes of data cannot be processed by traditional neural networks because these neural networks are defined by a fixed size matrix to perform matrix multiplication. Here convolution-based neural networks come to the rescue and can handle these variable sized inputs having varying spatial extents. The data processed by the CNN is considered to have multiple channels [19]. Table 1.1 shows the different data formats a CNN can work with efficiently.

CNNs have gained popularity for computer vision problems that involve both supervised and unsupervised tasks [20, 21]. The collected information passes through each layer of the network satisfying the temporal dependencies by serving the results of the previous layer as an input to the succeeding layer. The very first layer of the network is known as the input layer, whereas the last layer provides the output, hence it is called the output layer. The layers in between this input and the output are known as hidden layers. Each layer can be defined by an identical, uniform, and unvarying algorithm that simply implements a similar kind of activation function. An additional, popular, and most important trait of deep learning is the technique of feature extraction. This is done by the usage of various algorithms to extract the features automatically with an aim to build significant features of the data essentially for the purpose of training the neural networks or deep networks as well as facilitating efficient and meaningful learning. In Fig. 1.5, (A) shows the structure of a simple neural network and (B) shows a CNN.

A typical structure of CNN primarily includes three layers:

(a) Convolution layer: The primary task of identifying patterns is associated with this layer. Each layer has multiple convolutions that have kernels, which generate features of the image.

(b) Pooling layer: These layers are placed between the convolution layers and the feature maps. Their primary role is to reduce the size of the feature maps.

(c) Fully connected layer: This layer is connected at the end of the CNN architecture and is responsible for providing the decision.

These three layers are stacked to form a multilayered deep structure. In most of the CNN, the convolution layers and the pooling layers are stacked and repeated whereas the fully connected layers are usually present at the end of the network [22].

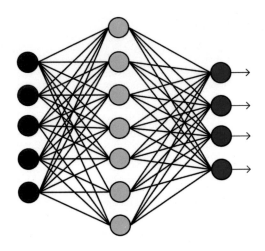

(a) Simple Neural Network

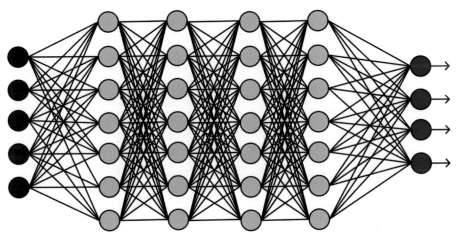

(b) Convolution Neural Network

● Input layer   ● Hidden layer   ● Output layer

FIG. 1.5

(A) Structure of a simple neural network, (B) structure of a convolution neural network.

A repetition of the combination of these three layers results in a complex CNN. The pooling layer plays a vital role in handling varying size input data and downsampling of the complex feature maps obtained from the convolution layers. The pooling layers create a new set of pooled feature maps of the same quantity as the original feature maps by operating on individual feature maps. The size of each feature map after a convolution operation is determined using the formula:

$$w_0 = \frac{w_i - f + 2p}{s} + 1$$

where w_0 is the size of the output feature map, w_i is the size of the input image, f is the size of the kernel, p is the padding, and s is the stride with which the kernel convolves over the input image.

Example: An input image of size $224 \times 224 \times 3$ is convolved using six filters of size 4×4 and stride 2, then the resulting feature map size can be calculated following these steps:

Step 1: Determine the value of parameters: size of the input image (w_i), size of filter (f), padding (p), and stride (s). Fig. 1.6 shows the input and filter parameters that are used to calculate the feature map size.

Here from the previous example, $w_i = 224, f = 4, p = 0, s = 2$, no. of filters $= 6$.

Step 2: Put the values from step 1 in the formula to calculate size of feature map (w_0):

$$w_0 = \frac{w_i - f + 2p}{s} + 1$$

$$w_0 = \frac{224 - 4 + 2 \times 0}{2} + 1$$

$$w_0 = \frac{220}{2} + 1$$

$$w_0 = 111$$

Step 3: The obtained size of the feature map is 111×111. Since six filters are used, six different feature maps are generated.

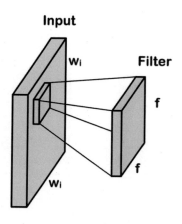

FIG. 1.6

Schematic representation of the input and filter parameters.

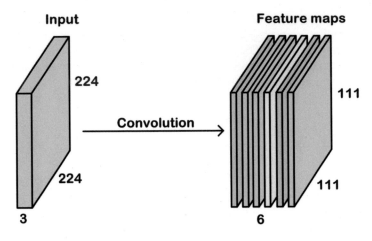

FIG. 1.7

Feature map after convolution.

Fig. 1.7 is the schematic representation of the feature map generated in the previously discussed example. Fig. 1.8A shows a schematic representation of a simple CNN of only three layers, and Fig. 1.8B shows a schematic representation of a complex CNN with stacking layers.

The pooling layer in a CNN functions over each feature map generated by the convolution of the filter over the input and generates new feature maps of reduced size. The motive of the pooling layer is

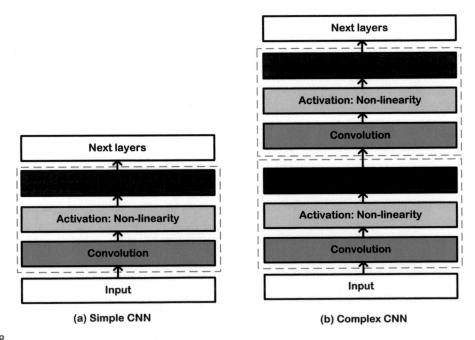

FIG. 1.8

(A) Structure of a simple CNN, (B) structure of a complex CNN.

to reduce the spatial size of the input, resulting in a reduction in the number of parameters; hence the computation size also shrinks. The different types of pooling functions used are as follows:

(a) Average pooling: As the name suggests, it is a function that performs the average mathematical operation. This function calculates the average of the values that lie in the range of the pooling kernel.

(b) Max pooling: This is often known as the maximum pooling and is the function that determines the maximum of the values being compared. This function calculates the maximum of the values that lie in the range of the pooling kernel.

Example: A feature map of 4×4 is subjected to a pooling function of kernel size 2×2 and stride 2, then the feature map is halved and the new feature maps generated are of size 2×2.

The pooling layer introduces invariance of the CNN model to translation, that is, the representations are approximately translation invariant. Hence the small changes in the input do not affect the output of pooling layers; the same pooled value would be generated even if the system undergoes minor translations.

Fig. 1.9 shows the pooling operation performed on a 4×4 input matrix with a kernel size of 2×2 and stride 2. Fig. 1.9A shows the average pooling, and Fig. 1.9B shows the max pooling operation.

Fig. 1.10 gives a schematic representation of a CNN having two convolution layers, two pooling layers, a fully connected layer and a softmax layer. The CNN have shown immense success in image classification tasks [23–25]. They require large amounts of data for training, hence pretrained CNN

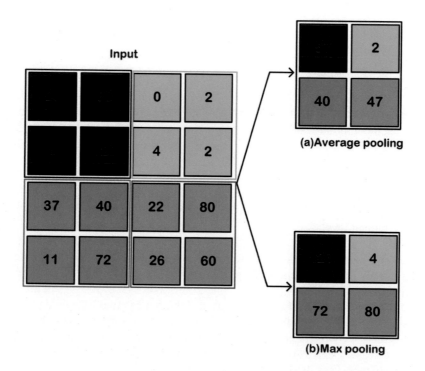

FIG. 1.9

(A) Average pooling with stride 2 and kernel Size 2×2, (B) max pooling with stride 2 and kernel size 2×2.

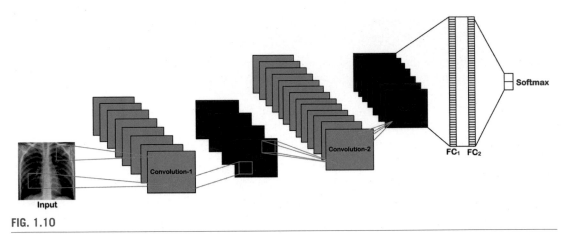

FIG. 1.10

Schematic representation of a simple CNN. *FC*, fully connected layer; *Pool*, pooling layer.

have gained popularity in the process of implementation of deep learning in the field of medicine. The use of pretrained CNN for classification and segmentation tasks is called transfer learning [26–29]. Transfer learning has been successfully used in the diagnosis of breast tumors on mammography, ultrasound, and breast magnetic resonance imaging (MRI) [30, 31].

1.3 Why deep learning in medical image analysis?

Some of the major reasons for which medical image analysis is the hub for application of deep learning techniques are as follows:

- **Large volumes of data:** Medical images play a vital role in diagnosis, and large volumes of data are produced comprising the majority amount of the medical data generated per patient. The amount of medical images that the radiologists have to deal with is overwhelming, as each patient's medical history can take up 200–300 GB of data for around 2000–4000 images. Deep learning aims at reducing the burden of the radiologist by carefully and efficiently sifting the data and helping in analyzing the medical images more efficiently. The most important feature of deep learning is the speed of processing large data along with accuracy and efficiency, which is not possible at the human level.
- **Time efficient:** The most critical factor for medical diagnosis is time. The detection of diseases at an early stage can contribute toward the aim of extending the life of a patient. Deep learning can aid medical practitioners in processing large amounts of data in a reasonable amount of time.
- **Unobserved hidden features:** The phrase "out of sight, out of mind" fits here perfectly; in medical images there are certain features of a tissue that are not observable to human eye and are sometimes missed by the radiologist, although these features may be pivotal in the correct diagnosis of a disease. Deep learning enables the extraction and processing of these deep hidden features for the diagnosis of diseases.

1.4 Medical imaging

The task of attaining visible images, primarily of inner body structures, for scientific, diagnostic, and medical applications as a part of identifying or studying diseases is defined as medical imaging. This technique helps in better identification and management of diseases. A medical image is an essential tool that enables generation of the visual representation of the internals of a body. This plays a vital role in medical analysis and studying the functioning of the internal organs as well as different tissues. It helps in identification of abnormalities by the medical practitioners by picturing the anatomy and the physiology of the organ or tissue as an image.

1.4.1 Features in medical images

The vast amounts of data available from medical images contribute to the efficient disease diagnosis, prognosis, and treatment. The extraction of features from volumes of interest is performed on the basis of the soft tissue with which the disease is associated. These volumes of interest can be tumors, subvolumes of tumors, or diseases of concern. Various tissues have different features that are essential in diagnosis and are broadly classified as texture, shape, and color features [32]. Fig. 1.11 shows the broad classification of these essential features.

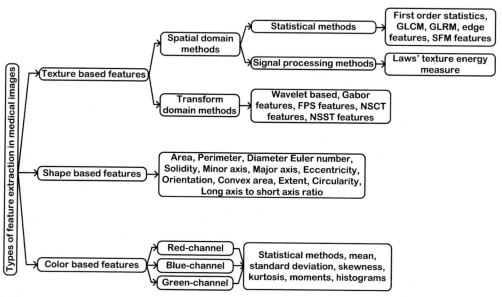

FIG. 1.11

Types of features extracted from medical images. *GLCM*, gray-level cooccurrence matrix; *GLRM*, gray-level run-length matrix; *NGTDM*, neighborhood gray-tone difference matrix; *SFM*, statistical feature matrix; *FPS*, Fourier power spectrum features; *NSCT*, nonsubsampled contourlet transform; *NSST*, nonsubsampled shearlet transform.

1.4.1.1 Texture features

In a broad perspective, texture is defined as a measure of the dissimilarity in a surface that gives information about the spatial organization of the intensities in an image. A high rate of dissimilarity is observed in a rough-textured material as compared to a smooth-textured material. This high rate of dissimilarity is the variation in the high and low points of the surface that is being observed. In radiology, the texture of a medical image refers to differences in the gray-scale that is representing a region of interest (ROI). The medical image of a rough-textured ROI would have a high rate of change between the high and low points of a surface as compared with a smooth-textured ROI. This degree of change measured between the different textured surfaces of the ROI is called the gray-scale value [33–35]. These texture features are able to capture the granularity of the patterns in the ROI.

These texture features or gray-scale variation features find their wide application in pattern recognition tasks. They comprise of first-order statistics, higher-order statistical measures, such as gray-level cooccurrence matrix (GLCM) and gray-level run-length matrix (GLRM), and signal processing-based methods that summarize the local spatial arrangement of intensities. The different parent matrices capturing the spatial intensity distribution comprises of GLCM [36], which is defined as the algorithm counting the voxel pairs with certain gray-values in a predefined direction and a specific distance apart from each other. This generates certain properties about the ROI such as the homogeneity, contrast, and sum variance of the features of the ROI. Another similar spatial domain method is the neighborhood gray-tone difference matrix (NGTDM) and the neighboring gray-level dependence matrix (NGLDM). The NGTDM is based on the variances between each voxel and their neighboring voxels. This results in extraction of features that resemble the human perception of the image in terms of the coarseness, complexity, and texture strength of the ROI [37]. On the other hand, the NGLDM takes into consideration the smoothness of the image instead of image fineness by disregarding the concept of angular dependency between image voxels [38]. The most popular method, the GLRM, takes into account the emphasis of collinear voxels that have the matching gray-level intensities; in simpler words, it calculates the length of pixels having the same gray-values [39]. The gray-level side zone matrix-based (GLSZM-based) features work by focusing on the target groups of connected pixels with same gray-value [40]. The transform domain-based methods include the wavelet decomposition of the original image. It has been employed with an aim to extract intensity and texture features from different frequency bands and to obtain fused texture characteristics [41, 42]. Some of the other transform domain-based feature extraction methods include the nonsubsampled contourlet transform (NSCT), which captures the characteristics of the given signal providing a multidirectional, multiscaled, and shift invariant decomposed image. Another transform domain-based texture feature extraction method is the nonsubsampled shearlet transform (NSST), which is a multiscale, multiresolution analysis method. Fig. 1.12 shows different texture features.

Some of the tissues where only texture features play an essential role in diagnosis are liver, teeth, brain, bone, the soft tissue of the heart, kidney, knee, stomach, and so on. Other tissues are also affected by the texture features, but they co-exist with other features, such as shape and color features, which also contribute highly to the process of efficient diagnosis, prognosis, and treatment. Fig. 1.13 shows a sample of liver ultrasound images available at [43].

Fig. 1.14 shows the 1-DWT and 2-DWT decomposition of brain MRI images available at [44].

Fig. 1.15 shows the 1-DWT and 2-DWT decomposition of a chest X-ray image available at [45].

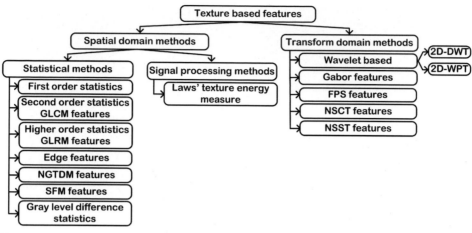

FIG. 1.12

Types of texture features extracted from medical images. *GLCM*, gray-level cooccurrence matrix; *GLRM*, gray-level run-length matrix; *NGTDM*, neighborhood gray-tone difference matrix; *NGTDM*, neighborhood gray-tone difference matrix; *SFM*, statistical feature matrix; *FPS*, Fourier power spectrum features; *NSCT*, nonsubsampled contourlet transform; *NSST*, nonsubsampled shearlet transform; *DWT*, discrete wavelet transform; *WPT*, wavelet packet transform.

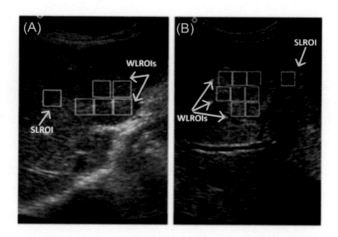

FIG. 1.13

(A, B) Sample images of liver tissue showing the WLROI and SLROI [43]. *WLROI*, within lesion ROI; *SLROI*, surrounding lesion ROI.

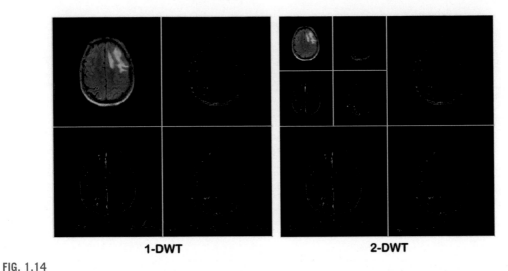

1-DWT   **2-DWT**

FIG. 1.14

Brain MRI 1-DWT and 2-DWT decomposition. *DWT*, discrete wavelet transform.

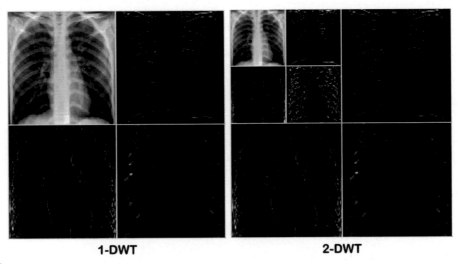

1-DWT   **2-DWT**

FIG. 1.15

Chest X-ray 1-DWT and 2-DWT decomposition. *DWT*, discrete wavelet transform.

1.4.1.2 Shape features

The shape-based features aim to describe the 3D geometrical composition of the segmented ROI. The size includes the volume of the region of interest and its maximal diameter, whereas the shape can be described as the measure of sphericity, compactness, location, and surface-to-volume ratio of the ROI of the specific tissue image [30, 42, 46–49]. Often these shape features are extracted with an aim to describe the aggressiveness of the tumor. Some tumors are described as spiculated, that is, having

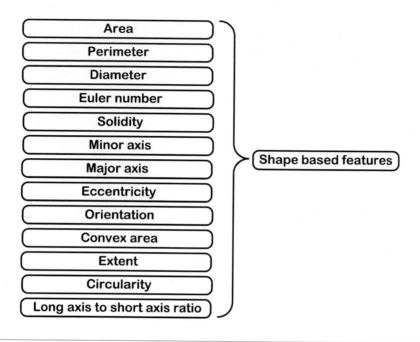

FIG. 1.16

Types of shape-based features extracted from medical images.

ill-defined borders. This spiculated shape indicates the potential of a tumor to spread to contiguous tissues and also indicates the association of the disease with an advanced stage, whereas the benign tumors that have the characteristic quality of being less aggressive in nature are observed to have well-defined margins. The compactness index is also considered another important shape feature to distinguish between benign and malignant tumors, especially in lung nodules [21, 41, 50–55]. Fig. 1.16 shows different shape-based features.

Most of the tissues are influenced by the combination of texture features with shape features for the correct diagnosis of diseases. Some of these tissues include breast, lung, head and neck, ear, fundus, spleen, thyroid, prostate, ovary, urinary bladder, and so forth [30, 42, 46–49, 53]. All these tissues have texture and shape features that are of relevance and are primarily looked at by the radiologists for diagnosis. Fig. 1.17 shows breast ultrasound images having benign and malignant tumors available at [56].

Table 1.2 describes the various shape features and Fig. 1.18 shows the diagramatic representation of these features in a breast ultrasound image.

1.4.1.3 Color features

The color in any image is an essential and absolutely upfront feature that is instantaneously observed by the human eye even at first glance. The human eye is more sensitive to color than it is to the gray-levels. Hence color feature extraction plays a vital role in diagnosis. The color images are composed of three channels, namely red, blue, and green, called the RGB channel. Some other channel compositions of color images are HSV (hue, saturation, value), CMYK (cyan, magenta, yellow, key). Often multiple external injuries to the human body are visible to the eye and are prone to be noticed due to their color. The color of blood is bright red, and rupturing of the skin tissue is immediately noticed due to bleeding;

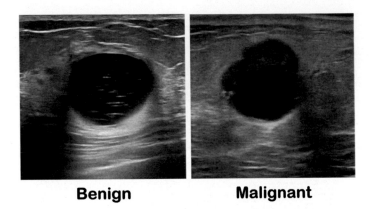

Benign   **Malignant**

FIG. 1.17

Sample breast ultrasound images [56].

Table 1.2 Various shape features and their formula for calculation.

Shape feature	Formula
Area	No. of pixels in tumor ROI
Perimeter	No. of pixels in tumor ROI contour
Convex area	No. of pixels on the convex hull of tumor
Major axis	$L_{major\ axis}$ = No. of pixels on longest axis
Minor axis	$L_{minor\ axis}$ = No. of pixels on shortest axis
Orientation	Angle between horizontal axis and major axis
Eccentricity	$\dfrac{Distance\left(ellipse_{center} \rightarrow ellipse_{focus}\right)}{L_{major\ axis}}$
Circularity	$\dfrac{Perimeter^2}{Area}$
Long axis to short axis ratio	$\dfrac{L_{major\ axis}}{L_{minor\ axis}}$

ROI, region of interest; L; length.

similarly the healing of a ruptured skin tissue injury is observed by the clotting of blood, which often forms a different shade of red (i.e., reddish black). All these color features are visible to the medical practitioners, but the mathematical extraction of these features include the use of feature extraction methods such as first-order statistics, histogram characteristics that reflect the mean value, dispersion, standard deviation, mean absolute deviation, and central moments that include the skewness for the asymmetry and kurtosis for the sharpness and randomness defined by the entropy and uniformity. These methods are applied to individual color channels of the medical image. These images could be the blood smear images that are used to classify leukocytes [57–59]. The blood leukocyte classification involves the observation of all three features, that is, texture, shape, and color of the blood cells.

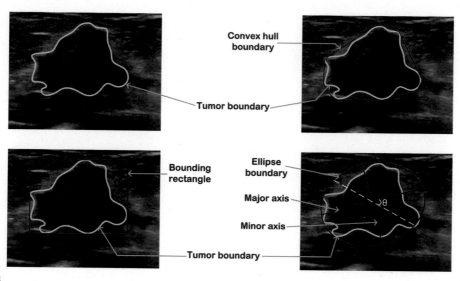

FIG. 1.18

Sample image of breast tissue with shape features.

The infection to skin tissue is identified by swelling, reddish skin rashes, and yellow pus pockets. For other skin tissue-associated disease detection such as melanoma, basal cell carcinoma, squamous cell carcinoma, color, and texture features play a vital role. Fig. 1.19 shows some of the color feature extraction methods.

Fig. 1.20 shows sample blood smear image where texture, shape, and color features are important for diagnosis. These sample images are available at [60].

Fig. 1.21 shows the sample images of skin tissue disease such melanoma, basal cell carcinoma, and squamous cell carcinoma. These sample images are available at [61].

Table 1.3 gives a brief overview of what features are essential for diagnosis of diseases associated with different tissues.

1.4.2 Types of medical imaging modalities for analysis of chest tissue

Medical imaging techniques are either ionizing in nature or nonionizing in nature. The process includes organic imaging as well as radiological imaging that mainly uses X-rays and gamma rays. Some

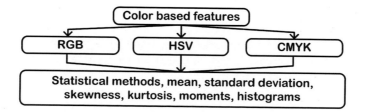

FIG. 1.19

Types of color-based features extracted from medical images. *RGB*, red-green-blue; *HSV*, hue-saturation-value; *CMYK*, cyan-magenta-yellow-key.

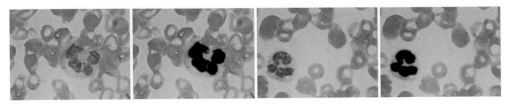

FIG. 1.20

Sample blood smear images [60].

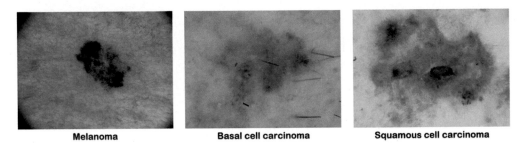

| Melanoma | Basal cell carcinoma | Squamous cell carcinoma |

FIG. 1.21

Sample Images of skin cancer [61].

Table 1.3 Features those are essential for diagnosis corresponding to the tissue.	
Features	**Tissue**
Texture	Liver, brain, teeth, bone, heart, kidney, knee, stomach
Texture + shape	Breast, lung, head & neck, ear, fundus, spleen, thyroid, prostate, ovary, urinary bladder
Texture + color	Skin
Texture + shape + color	Blood

include sonography, magnetic, and thermal imaging. Fig. 1.22 shows the medical imaging modalities used for chest tissues.

Some of the popularly used imaging techniques are: X-ray, computed tomography (CT) scans, MRI, ultrasound, and positron emission tomography (PET) scans, and they can be broadly categorized as follows:

1.4.2.1 Ionizing nature

The imaging modalities that use ionizing radiation for generating images come under this category. The most common ionizing radiation used is X-rays, although nuclear medicine often states the use of small amounts of the gamma rays.

X-ray

They are the most popular and the first ever imaging technique used in medicine. It uses a beam of X-ray to determine and view materials that are nonuniformly composed. The images are popularly

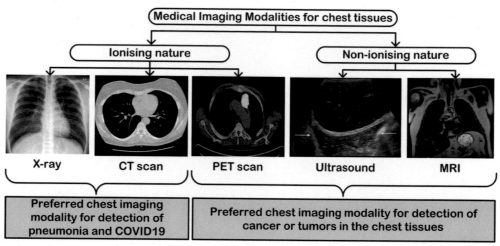

FIG. 1.22

Types of medical imaging modalities for analysis of chest tissue. *CT*, computed tomography; *PET*, positron emission tomography; *MRI*, magnetic resonance imaging.

called radiographic images and are either fluoroscopy based, which uses continuous input of lower doses of X-ray to produce real-time images of internal structures, or projectional radiographs, mainly used for imaging bones. X-rays are ionizing in nature and are therefore avoided for pregnant women [18, 62–66]. On an X-ray the bones appear white and the air appears black, whereas fluids of different density appear in the form of different shades of gray.

The chest X-ray generates an image consisting of the major organs such as the heart and lungs as well as the bones forming the rib cage and the spinal cord. These images help in determining the presence of fluids or air in and around the lungs as the area with fluid present has radio-opacity where the bones appear white and the fluid appears in shades of gray. The image helps the radiologists determine whether the patient has problems associated with the heart, a collapsed lung, pneumonia, broken ribs or bones, emphysema, cancer, or any of several other conditions. Fig. 1.23 shows a sample chest X-ray image that is available at [45]. The chest X-ray is the most popular imaging modality for the detection of pneumonia in lungs.

CT scan

This is considered a series of X-ray scans that is ionizing in nature and is used to diagnose tumors, vascular diseases, heart diseases, and injuries due to trauma [67]. Since CT scans function on the core basics of X-rays, bones appear as white and the air is black on a CT scan similar to that on an X-ray image [68]. The CT scan medical imaging is often preferred for visualization of tissues in the chest cavity, such as the lungs, due to better resolution of lung nodules and detection of even smaller sized lung nodules. CT scan images also help better characterize the morphological features of various lesions. Multiple nodules and regions that are difficult to assess on chest radiographs are better visualized on CT scan images. However, being an expensive imaging modality as compared to X-rays, the CT scans are not the most popular imaging modality for chest tissue analysis. In detection of pneumonia, the CT scan shows attenuation. Nowadays CT scans are more used for detection of COVID-19. Fig. 1.24 shows a sample chest CT scan image available at [69].

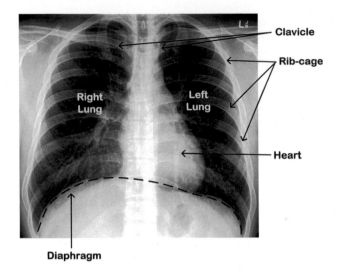

FIG. 1.23

Sample chest X-ray image [45].

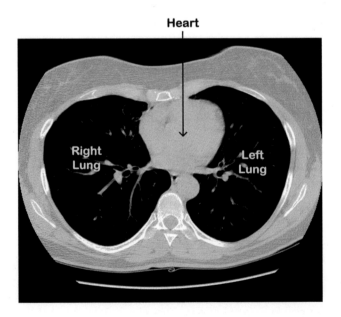

FIG. 1.24

Sample chest CT image [69].

PET scan

This uses a radioactive dye called tracers. These tracers are inhaled, swallowed, or injected in your veins. They help in determining the functioning of the specific organs and tissues. They are mainly used in the diagnosis of seizures, epilepsy, heart diseases, Alzheimer's disease, and Parkinson's disease [16, 17, 51]. PET scans and recently popularized PET-CT scans are found to be more accurate in determining cancer. Although lung tumors are often initially evaluated through a chest X-ray or CT scan, the PET and PET-CT scans are highly accurate at determining whether a lung mass is cancerous or not. A detailed image provided by PET scans is able to accurately distinguish between benign and malignant tumors [52]. However, being a costly imaging modality and given the adverse effects of using dyes and drug allergies of patients, this imaging modality is rarely used for detection of chest abnormalities, especially pneumonia. Fig. 1.25 shows a sample chest PET scan image that is available at [51].

1.4.2.2 Nonionizing nature

The imaging modalities that do not use ionizing radiation for generating the images come under this category. These modalities use high frequency sound waves or radio frequencies. The nonionizing medical imaging modalities are as follows:

Ultrasound

It uses high frequency sound waves that are noninvasive and nonionizing in nature. Although it gives low anatomical details as compared to other imaging modalities, it is still most popular among pregnant women. The high frequency sound waves are reflected by the human tissues forming 3D images. It is used for the diagnosis of breast tumors, gall bladder diseases, prostate-related issues, liver lesions, and monitoring pregnancies [46–48, 70]. This imaging modality is highly organ-specific, and lung ultrasounds are rarely performed. Although the lung ultrasound imaging, if performed, can be used to detect pulmonary changes associated with pneumonia, radiologists detect pneumonia in lung ultrasounds by observing the pleural surface of the lung or the outer lining of the lung tissue. Pneumonia often is

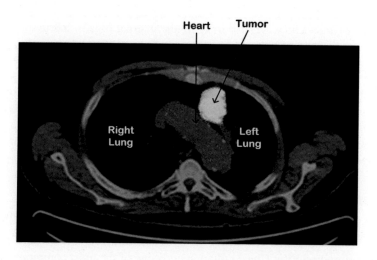

FIG. 1.25

Sample chest PET scan [51].

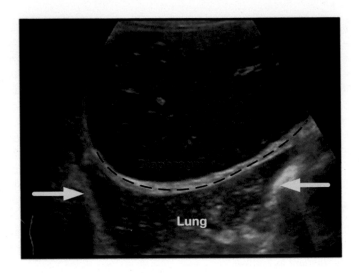

FIG. 1.26

Sample lung ultrasound image [72].

observed to have progressed in stages. Depending on the degree of consolidation and the amount of changes in the ultrasound images, one can identify the extent of the damage to the lung. Some of the most serious damage is the hepatization of the lung due to prolonged consolidation, and ultrasound is beneficial in detection of these indicators. The consolidation and hepatization is quite similar to the ones seen in the liver [71]. However, lung ultrasounds are not highly useful in detection of pneumonia but are actively used for detection of lung tumors. Fig. 1.26 shows a sample lung ultrasound image that is available at [72].

Magnetic resonance imaging

It uses magnetic waves and radio waves for imaging the internal organs and tissues. They do not use X-rays or any ionizing radiations; rather they emit radio frequency pulse equivalent to the resonance frequency of the hydrogen atom so as to excite the hydrogen nuclei in water molecules of the human tissue. It is mainly used for diagnosis of strokes, tumors, spinal cord disorder, and multiple sclerosis [46, 73–79]. As MRI is an expensive imaging modality, it is rarely used for viewing the radiological indications of pneumonia. Additionally, these indications are easily visible in X-ray and CT scans; therefore, the expenditure of an MRI scan for only the diagnosis of pneumonia is a waste of money, time, and resources. MRI scanning is not used for routine clinical procedures and is not popularly used for pneumonia. Fig. 1.27 shows a sample chest MRI image that is available at [68].

1.4.3 Why chest radiographs?

Some of the major reasons for which chest radiographs are preferred over any other imaging modality for diagnosis of pneumonia are as follows:

- **Ubiquitous imaging modality:** Chest radiography is one of the most commonly used imaging modality for screening of abnormalities in the chest cavity. It is an easily available imaging

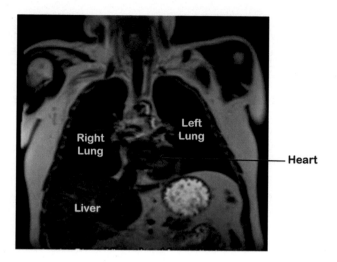

FIG. 1.27

Sample chest MRI image [68].

modality. Even in remote areas, a chest X-ray is the most common type of test and is among the first procedure advised by medical practitioners if they suspect heart- or lung-related disease.

- **Diagnosis of lung diseases:** Chest X-ray images are often used for the detection of diseases associated with the chest cavity, including broken bones such as the rib cage, fractures, infection of the air cavity of lungs or collapsing lungs, and collection of fluid in lung cavity. Chest radiographs are often helpful in detecting chronic lung-associated conditions, complications in conditions such as cystic fibrosis, and more.
- **Cost-effective:** Although chest radiography is an ionizing imaging modality, it is cheaper as compared to other modalities. This cost-effective nature of chest X-rays makes them affordable by the majority of the population in developing countries.
- **Effective evaluation of treatment:** Along with the importance of chest radiographic images in diagnosis, they are of vital use in epidemiology and clinical care as well. Often medical practitioners prefer chest X-ray imaging to keep track of the progress and effectiveness of the treatment given to the patient. Since it is a cheaper imaging modality, more individuals are able to afford it as compared to other modalities.
- **Low doses of radiation:** Although CT provides substantially accurate clinical diagnosis, sometimes it requires the need to inject a drug called Lohexol to highlight the site of disease. This makes CT unsuited for patients having drug allergy. In addition to this, CT subjects the patients to higher doses of radiation as compared to X-ray imaging (radiographs). This clearly makes the use of X-ray imaging one of the most widely preferred imaging modalities [80–85].

1.5 Description of normal and pneumonia chest radiographs

The X-ray imaging modality is one of the vital diagnostic tools that have proved to be of utmost importance in diagnosis of lung and heart diseases. The ability of X-ray imaging to disclose unanticipated changes, those that are pathological and noninvasive in nature, along with low radiation doses, makes it the first choice of diagnosis in pneumonia and other lung-related diseases. Some of the abnormalities that are among the common findings of chest radiographic images are pulmonary infiltrations, abnormality in size of heart, and catheter [3, 71, 80–86].

Pneumonia is typically characterized by pulmonary radiopacity that is focal and segmental in nature, which is sometimes referred to as lobar pulmonary opacity. This opacification, which is often observed in chest radiographs, is termed as ground glass opacity (GGO) and, in layman's terms, is referred to as the hazy lung region. It is often stated as a fairly diffused appearance in which the end of the pulmonary vessels is difficult to observe. It is one of the major diagnostic features of pneumonia. Pneumonia is caused by virus, bacteria, or fungus and is often termed as viral pneumonia, bacterial pneumonia and fungal pneumonia, respectively. Among the three types of pneumonia, cases of viral pneumonia are found in abundance, whereas bacterial pneumonia cases are less common and fungal pneumonia cases are rare. In chest radiographs, it is not possible to differentiate between the bacterial pneumonia and viral pneumonia, since both have similar radiological indicators and appearance on a chest radiograph. A normal chest radiograph mainly shows the rib cage, heart, and two air cavities that form the left and right lungs. Due to high density of bones, X-rays cannot penetrate them and get reflected, which is why bones appear white on a radiograph. Similarly, other soft tissues appear less whitish as compared to bones, fluid appears grayish, and air being the least dense appears black. Pneumonia causes the lungs to fill up with fluid or mucus; hence the key radiological indicator is a hazy appearance due to the presence of fluid in the lungs on a chest radiograph.

Fig. 1.28A shows a normal chest radiograph that has a clear and transparent lung section, Fig. 1.28B shows a pneumonia chest radiograph where the air space can been seen as cloudy or, as stated by the radiologist, "the section of the lung is radio opaque," and Fig. 1.28C shows the appearance of GGO along with shadowing in the nodules, which are among the primary diagnostic characteristics of COVID-19 in chest radiographs.

1.6 Objective of the book

The main objective of this book is to give an idea as to how one can design CAC systems based on deep learning techniques with an aim of efficient analysis and classification of chest radiographic images to determine in an accurate way the visual signs capable of differentiating a case of pneumonia from a normal case. The dataset used provides us with the necessary details for efficient analysis and classification using different CNN model architectures. Some of the specific objectives of the present work are:

- to build an understanding of deep learning-based CNN, concepts of transfer learning, analysis and classification of medical images;
- to study deep learning-based CAC systems for classification of medical images, specifically for chest radiographic images;
- to establish the need for CAC systems with special emphasis on chest radiographic images, description of various features in medical images, and what features are essential for what type of tissue;

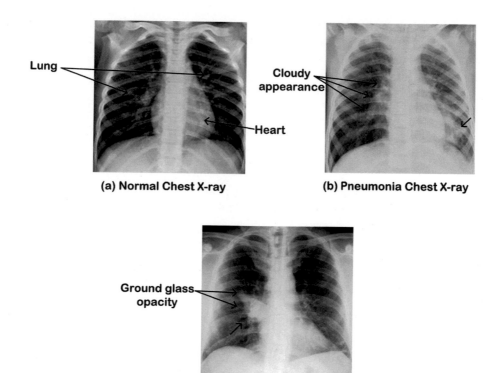

(a) Normal Chest X-ray   **(b) Pneumonia Chest X-ray**

(c) COVID19 Chest X-ray

FIG. 1.28

Sample chest radiographs: (A) normal chest radiograph; (B) pneumonia chest radiograph; (C) COVID-19chest radiograph.

- to provide a brief description of the various datasets of chest radiographs publicly available and the dataset used in the present work, the preprocessing of the radiographs, and augmentation methods applied;
- to offer an insight into how the augmentation techniques are chosen for medical images and details of the hyperparameters of deep learning-based networks;
- to implement details of various experiments carried out using end-to-end pretrained CNN networks, lightweight end-to-end pretrained CNN networks, and different ML classifiers such as ANFC and SVM;
- to give a brief overview of the feature dimensionality reduction and feature selection algorithms such as PCA, linguistic hedges prevalently used with ML classifiers, the concepts of decision fusion, and the techniques used;
- to give an overview to the Deep Learning Toolbox by MATLAB that has been actively used in the implementation of the present work of designing the CAC systems for chest radiographs;

- to elucidate the implementation of design of different CAC system designs through different code snippets with an aim to give an in-depth idea about how the present work can be programmatically implemented; and
- to evaluate the results of the CAC systems designed throughout the work.

1.7 Book chapter outline

The present work has been structured into 10 chapters, each of whose brief description is given as follows:

- Chapter 1 gives a brief introduction to the motivation and objectives of carrying out the proposed work, an overview of the essential features in medical images, the different imaging modalities specific to chest tissues, and the concept of deep learning in medical images that have been used in the present work.
- Chapter 2 gives a background study of the use of ML and deep learning in medical images and the CAC systems designed for the analysis and classification of chest radiographic images.
- Chapter 3 deals with the methodology of the work carried out, dataset description, and a brief overview of the implementation details of the experiments carried out in the later chapters.
- Chapter 4 gives the implementation details of the end-to-end pretrained CNN-based CAC system design for the binary classification of chest radiographic images as well as the architectural details of the CNN networks available in the MATLAB Deep Learning Toolbox that have been used to carry out the proposed experiments.
- Chapter 5 deals with the implementation details of the deep feature extraction of chest radiographic images using GoogLeNet CNN model, feature selection, and classification using an adaptive neuro-fuzzy classifier based on linguistic hedges (ANFC-LH) ML classifier.
- Chapter 6 deals with the deep feature extraction of chest radiographic images using a GoogLeNet CNN model, feature dimensionality reduction and classification using PCA-SVM ML classifier.
- Chapter 7 gives the implementation details of the lightweight end-to-end pretrained CNN-based CAC system design for the binary classification of chest radiographic images.
- Chapter 8 deals with the implementation details of deep feature extraction using a lightweight MobileNetV2 CNN model, feature selection, and classification using ANFC-LH ML classifier.
- Chapter 9 deals with the implementation details of deep feature extraction using a lightweight MobileNetV2 CNN model, feature dimensionality reduction, and classification using a PCA-SVM ML classifier.
- Chapter 10 gives the conclusion of the work carried out throughout the chapters and the future scope.

References

[1] World Health Organization, Revised WHO Classification and Treatment of Pneumonia in Children at Health Facilities: Evidence Summaries, 2014.
[2] Y.G.R. Sánchez, A.L.S. Pérez, I.M. Zacarias, Mortalidad por causas en el estado de México, 2000 y 2015/ Mortality by causes in the state of Mexico, 2000 and 2015, Novedades en Población 14 (28) (2018) 64–78.

[3] World Health Organization, Standardization of Interpretation of Chest Radiographs for the Diagnosis of Pneumonia in Children (No. WHO/V&B/01.35), World Health Organization, 2001.

[4] M. Kim, J. Yun, Y. Cho, K. Shin, R. Jang, H.J. Bae, N. Kim, Deep learning in medical imaging, Neurospine 16 (4) (2019) 657.

[5] K.P. Murphy, Machine Learning: A Probabilistic Perspective, MIT Press, Cambridge, MA, 2012.

[6] K. He, X. Zhang, S. Ren, et al., Deep residual learning for image recognition, in: Proceedings of 2016 IEEE Conference on Computer Vision and Pattern Recognition (CVPR 2016), 27–30 Jun 2016, Las Vegas, NV, USA, Institute of Electrical and Electronics Engineers, Piscataway, NJ, 2016, pp. 770–778.

[7] G.E. Hinton, S. Osindero, Y.W. Teh, A fast learning algorithm for deep belief nets, Neural Comput. 18 (2006) 1527–1554.

[8] N.S. Altman, An introduction to kernel and nearest-neighbor nonparametric regression, Am. Stat. 46 (1992) 175–185.

[9] A.B.A. Hassanat, Two-point-based binary search trees for accelerating big data classification using KNN, PLoS One 13 (2018) e0207772.

[10] A. Schneider, G. Hommel, M. Blettner, Linear regression analysis: part 14 of a series on evaluation of scientific publications, Dtsch. Arztebl. Int. 107 (2010) 776–782.

[11] E. Byvatov, U. Fechner, J. Sadowski, et al., Comparison of sup-port vector machine and artificial neural network systems for drug/nondrug classification, J. Chem. Inf. Comput. Sci. 43 (2003) 1882–1889.

[12] H. Drucker, C.J. Burges, L. Kaufman, et al., Support vector regression machines, in: Advances in Neural Information Processing Systems, Massachusetts Institute of Technology Press, Cambridge, MA, 1997, pp. 155–161.

[13] A. Jonsson, Deep reinforcement learning in medicine, Kidney Dis. 5 (1) (2019) 18–22.

[14] O. Gottesman, F. Johansson, M. Komorowski, et al., Guidelines for reinforcement learning in healthcare, Nat. Med. 25 (2019) 16–18.

[15] S. Amari, The Handbook of Brain Theory and Neural Networks, MIT Press, Cambridge, MA, 2003.

[16] J. Islam, Y. Zhang, Brain MRI analysis for Alzheimer's disease diagnosis using an ensemble system of deep convolutional neural networks, Brain Inform. 5 (2) (2018) 1–14.

[17] N. Gessert, M. Heyder, S. Latus, M. Lutz, A. Schlaefer, Plaque classification in coronary arteries from ivoct images using convolutional neural networks and transfer learning. arXiv preprint arXiv:1804.03904, 2018.

[18] A.K. Jaiswal, P. Tiwari, S. Kumar, D. Gupta, A. Khanna, J.J. Rodrigues, Identifying pneumonia in chest X-rays: a deep learning approach, Measurement 145 (2019) 511–518.

[19] B. Chen, Deep Learning of Invariant Spatio-Temporal Features from Video (Doctoral dissertation), University of British Columbia, 2010.

[20] A. Krizhevsky, I. Sutskever, G.E. Hinton, ImageNet classification with deep convolutional neural networks, in: Advances in Neural Information Processing Systems, Massachusetts Institute of Technology Press, Cambridge, MA, 2012, pp. 1097–1105.

[21] H. Wang, Z. Zhou, Y. Li, et al., Comparison of machine learning methods for classifying mediastinal lymph node metastasis of non-small cell lung cancer from 18F-FDG PET/CT images, EJNMMI Res. 7 (2017) 11.

[22] M.L. Giger, Machine learning in medical imaging, J. Am. Coll. Radiol. 15 (3) (2018) 512–520.

[23] A. Krizhevsky, I. Sutskever, G.E. Hinton, ImageNet classification with deep convolutional neural networks, Adv Neural Inf Process Syst 25 (2012) 1097–1105.

[24] K. Simonyan, A. Zisserman, Very deep convolutional networks for large-scale image recognition. arXiv preprint arXiv:1409.1556.2014, 2014.

[25] C. Szegedy, W. Liu, Y. Jia, et al., Going deeper with convolutions. CoRRabs/1409.4842, 2014.

[26] S.J. Pan, Q. Yang, A survey on transfer learning, IEEE Trans. Knowl. Data Eng. 22 (2010) 1345–1349.

[27] J. Yosinski, J. Clune, Y. Bengio, et al., How transferable are features in deep neural networks? CoRR abs/1411.1792, 2014.

[28] A.S. Razavian, H. Azizpour, J. Sullivan, et al., CNN features off-the-shelf: an astounding baseline for recognition, in: 2014 IEEE Conference on Computer Vision and Pattern Recognition Workshops (CVPRW), IEEE, 2014, pp. 512–519.

[29] J. Donahue, Y. Jia, O. Vinyals, et al., Decaf: a deep convolutional activation feature for generic visual recognition. arXiv preprint arXiv:1310.1531, 2013.

[30] N. Antropova, B.Q. Huynh, M.L. Giger, A deep fusion methodology for breast cancer diagnosis demonstrated on three imaging modalitydatasets, Med. Phys. 44 (2017) 5162–5171.

[31] B. Huynh, H. Li, M.L. Giger, Digital mammographic tumor classification using transfer learning from deep convolutional neural networks, Med Imaging 3 (2016), 034501.

[32] R.J. Gillies, P.E. Kinahan, H. Hricak, Radiomics: images are more than pictures, they are data, Radiology 278 (2) (2016) 563–577.

[33] B.A. Varghese, S.Y. Cen, D.H. Hwang, V.A. Duddalwar, Texture analysis of imaging: what radiologists need to know, Am. J. Roentgenol. 212 (3) (2019) 520–528.

[34] W. Macdonald, P. Campbell, J. Fisher, A. Wennerberg, Variation in surface texture measurements, J. Biomed. Mater. Res. Part B Appl. Biomater. 70 (2) (2004) 262–269.

[35] G. Castellano, L. Bonilha, L.M. Li, F. Cendes, Texture analysis of medical images, Clin. Radiol. 59 (12) (2004) 1061–1069.

[36] R.M. Haralick, K. Shanmugam, I.H. Dinstein, Textural features for image classification, IEEE Trans. Syst. Man Cybern. 6 (1973) 610–621.

[37] M. Amadasun, R. King, Textural features corresponding to textural properties, IEEE Trans. Syst. Man Cybern. 19 (5) (1989) 1264–1274.

[38] C. Sun, W.G. Wee, Neighboring gray level dependence matrix for texture classification, Comput. Graph. Image Process. 20 (3) (1982) 297.

[39] M.M. Galloway, Texture analysis using gray level run lengths, Comput, Graphics Image Process 4 (2) (1975) 172–179.

[40] F. Tixier, C.C. Le Rest, M. Hatt, N. Albarghach, O. Pradier, J.P. Metges, L. Corcos, D. Visvikis, Intratumor heterogeneity characterized by textural features on baseline 18F-FDG PET images predicts response to concomitant radiochemotherapy in esophageal cancer, J. Nucl. Med. 52 (3) (2011) 369–378.

[41] M. Vallières, C.R. Freeman, S.R. Skamene, I. El Naqa, A radiomics model from joint FDG-PET and MRI texture features for the prediction of lung metastases in soft-tissue sarcomas of the extremities, Phys. Med. Biol. 60 (14) (2015) 5471.

[42] H.J. Aerts, E.R. Velazquez, R.T. Leijenaar, C. Parmar, P. Grossmann, S. Carvalho, J. Bussink, R. Monshouwer, B. Haibe-Kains, D. Rietveld, F. Hoebers, Decoding tumour phenotype by noninvasive imaging using a quantitative radiomics approach, Nat. Commun. 5 (1) (2014) 1–9.

[43] Ultrasoundcases.info available at webpage: https://www.ultrasoundcases.info/cases/abdomen-and-retroperitoneum/liver/hepatocellular-carcinoma/.

[44] Kaggle Brain MRI Dataset. https://www.kaggle.com/navoneel/brain-mri-images-for-brain-tumor-detection".

[45] Kaggle Chest X-Ray Dataset, Available from: https://www.kaggle.com/paultimothymooney/chest-xray-pneumonia.

[46] A. Cruz-Roa, H. Gilmore, A. Basavanhally, M. Feldman, S. Ganesan, N.N. Shih, J. Tomaszewski, F.A. González, A. Madabhushi, Accurate and reproducible invasive breast cancer detection in whole-slide images: a Deep Learning approach for quantifying tumor extent, Sci. Rep. 7 (2017) 46450.

[47] Kriti, J. Virmani, R. Agarwal, Effect of despeckle filtering on classification of breast tumors using ultrasound images, Biocybern. Biomed. Eng. 39 (2) (2019) 536–560.

[48] Kriti, J. Virmani, R. Agarwal, Assessment of despeckle filtering algorithms for segmentation of breast tumours from ultrasound images, Biocybern. Biomed. Eng. 39 (1) (2019) 100–121.

[49] V. Kumar, Y. Gu, S. Basu, A. Berglund, S.A. Eschrich, M.B. Schabath, K. Forster, H.J. Aerts, A. Dekker, D. Fenstermacher, D.B. Goldgof, Radiomics: the process and the challenges, Magn. Reson. Imaging 30 (9) (2012) 1234–1248.

[50] L.I. Cervino, J. Du, S.B. Jiang, MRI-guided tumor tracking in lung cancer radiotherapy, Phys. Med. Biol. 56 (13) (2011) 3773.

[51] B. Hochhegger, G.R.T. Alves, K.L. Irion, C.C. Fritscher, L.G. Fritscher, N.H. Concatto, E. Marchiori, PET/CT imaging in lung cancer: indications and findings, J. Bras. Pneumol. 41 (3) (2015) 264–274.

[52] N. Beslic, A. Sadija, R. Milardovic, T. Ceric, S. Ceric, A. Beganovic, S. Kristic, S. Cavaljuga, Advantages of combined PET-CT in mediastinal staging in patients with non-small cell lung carcinoma, Acta Inform. Med. 24 (2) (2016) 99.

[53] T.P. Coroller, P. Grossmann, Y. Hou, E.R. Velazquez, R.T. Leijenaar, G. Hermann, P. Lambin, B. Haibe-Kains, R.H. Mak, H.J. Aerts, CT-based radiomic signature predicts distant metastasis in lung adenocarcinoma, Radiother. Oncol. 114 (3) (2015) 345–350.

[54] J. Wang, X. Liu, D. Dong, J. Song, M. Xu, Y. Zang, J. Tian, Prediction of malignant and benign of lung tumor using a quantitative radiomic method, in: 2016 38th Annual International Conference of the IEEE Engineering in Medicine and Biology Society (EMBC), IEEE, 2016, pp. 1272–1275.

[55] E. Pena, M. Ojiaku, J.R. Inacio, A. Gupta, D.B. Macdonald, W. Shabana, J.M. Seely, F.J. Rybicki, C. Dennie, R.E. Thornhill, Can CT and MR shape and textural features differentiate benign versus malignant pleural lesions? Acad. Radiol. 24 (10) (2017) 1277–1287.

[56] Ultrasoundcases.info available at webpage: https://www.ultrasoundcases.info/metastases-of-non-breast-tumors-5492.

[57] J. Rawat, H.S. Bhadauria, A. Singh, J. Virmani, Review of leukocyte classification techniques for microscopic blood images, in: 2015 2nd International Conference on Computing for Sustainable Global Development (INDIACom), IEEE, 2015, pp. 1948–1954.

[58] S. Mohapatra, D. Patra, S. Satpathi, Image analysis of blood microscopic images for acute leukemia detection, in: 2010 International Conference on Industrial Electronics, Control and Robotics, IEEE, 2010, pp. 215–219.

[59] O. Sarrafzadeh, H. Rabbani, A. Talebi, H.U. Banaem, Selection of the best features for leukocytes classification in blood smear microscopic images, in: Medical Imaging 2014: Digital Pathology, vol. 9041, International Society for Optics and Photonics, 2014, March, p. 90410P.

[60] M. Mohamed, Image Dataset With Ground Truth Images and Code, 2012, Matlab File exchange from https://in.mathworks.com/matlabcentral/fileexchange/36634-an-efficient-technique-for-white-blood-cells-nuclei-automatic-segmentation".

[61] Skin Lesion Dataset. https://www.kaggle.com/nodoubttome/skin-cancer9-classesisic".

[62] W.H. Hsu, F.J. Tsai, G. Zhang, C.K. Chang, P.H. Hsieh, S.N. Yang, S.S. Sun, K. Liao, E.T. Huang, Development of a deep learning model for chest X-ray screening, Med. Phys. Int. 7 (3) (2019) 314.

[63] J.A. Stadler, S. Andronikou, H.J. Zar, Lung ultrasound for the diagnosis of community-acquired pneumonia in children, Pediatr. Radiol. 47 (11) (2017) 1412–1419.

[64] T. Amundsen, G. Torheim, A. Waage, L. Bjermer, P.A. Steen, O. Haraldseth, Perfusion magnetic resonance imaging of the lung: characterization of pneumonia and chronic obstructive pulmonary disease. A feasibility study, J. Magn. Reson. Imaging 12 (2) (2000) 224–231.

[65] V.K. Patel, S.K. Naik, D.P. Naidich, W.D. Travis, J.A. Weingarten, R. Lazzaro, D.D. Gutterman, C. Wentowski, H.B. Grosu, S. Raoof, A practical algorithmic approach to the diagnosis and management of solitary pulmonary nodules: part 1: radiologic characteristics and imaging modalities, Chest 143 (3) (2013) 825–839.

[66] G. Liang, L. Zheng, A transfer learning method with deep residual network for pediatric pneumonia diagnosis, Comput. Methods Programs Biomed. 187 (2020) 104964.

[67] K. Kamnitsas, C. Ledig, V.F. Newcombe, J.P. Simpson, A.D. Kane, D.K. Menon, D. Rueckert, B. Glocker, Efficient multi-scale 3D CNN with fully connected CRF for accurate brain lesion segmentation, Med. Image Anal. 36 (2017) 61–78.

[68] C. Beigelman-Aubry, N. Peguret, M. Stuber, J. Delacoste, B. Belmondo, A. Lovis, C. Rohner, Chest-MRI under pulsatile flow ventilation: a new promising technique, PloS One 12 (6) (2017) e0178807,

https://doi.org/10.1371/journal.pone.0178807. Available from: https://figshare.com/articles/dataset/Chest-MRI_under_pulsatile_flow_ventilation_A_new_promising_technique/5101936".

[69] W. El-Shafai, F. Abd El-Samie, Extensive COVID-19 X-ray and CT chest images dataset, Mendeley Data V3 (2020), https://doi.org/10.17632/8h65ywd2jr.3.

[70] J. Li, M. Fan, J. Zhang, L. Li, Discriminating between benign and malignant breast tumors using 3D convolutional neural network in dynamic contrast enhanced-MR images, in: Medical Imaging 2017: Imaging Informatics for Healthcare, Research, and Applications, 10138, International Society for Optics and Photonics, 2017, p. 1013808.

[71] M. Colombo, G. Ronchi, Focal Liver Lesions – Detection, Characterization, Ablation, Springer, Berlin, 2005, pp. 167–177.

[72] Ultrasoundcases.info available at webpage: https://www.ultrasoundcases.info/pneumonia-and-air-space-consolidation-5358/.

[73] J. Islam, Y. Zhang, Brain MRI analysis for Alzheimer's disease diagnosis using an ensemble system of deep convolutional neural networks, Brain Inform. 5 (2) (2018).

[74] S. Sarraf, G. Tofighi, Classification of Alzheimer's disease using fMRI data and deep learning convolutional neural networks, in: Computer Science Conference Proceedings, 2016, pp. 109–119.

[75] H. Suk, D. Shen, Deep learning-based feature representation for AD/MCI classification, in: Proceedings of Medical Image Computing and Computer-Assisted Intervention, 2013, pp. 583–590.

[76] J.B. Pereira, M. Mijalkov, E. Kakaei, P. Mecocci, B. Vellas, M. Tsolaki, I. Kłoszewska, H. Soininen, C. Spenger, S. Lovestone, A. Simmons, Disrupted network topology in patients with stable and progressive mild cognitive impairment and Alzheimer's disease, Cereb. Cortex 26 (8) (2016) 3476–3493.

[77] A. Ortiz, J. Munilla, Ensembles of deep learning architectures for the early diagnosis of the Alzheimer's disease, Int. J. Neural Syst. 26 (7) (2016) 1650025-1–1650025-23.

[78] J. Rieke, F. Eitel, M. Weygandt, J.D. Haynes, K. Ritter, Visualizing convolutional networks for MRI-based diagnosis of Alzheimer's disease, in: Understanding and Interpreting Machine Learning in Medical Image Computing Applications, Springer, Cham, 2018, pp. 24–31.

[79] J. Islam, Y. Zhang, Alzheimer's Disease Neuroimaging Initiative, Deep convolutional neural networks for automated diagnosis of Alzheimer's disease and mild cognitive impairment using 3D brain MRI, in: International Conference on Brain Informatics, Springer, Cham, 2018, pp. 359–369.

[80] J.A. Stadler, S. Andronikou, H.J. Zar, Lung ultrasound for the diagnosis of community-acquired pneumonia in children, Pediatr. Radiol. 47 (11) (2017) 1412–1419.

[81] T. Amundsen, G. Torheim, A. Waage, L. Bjermer, P.A. Steen, O. Haraldseth, Perfusion magnetic resonance imaging of the lung: characterization of pneumonia and chronic obstructive pulmonary disease. A feasibility study, J. Magn. Reson. Imaging 12 (2) (2000) 224–231.

[82] V.K. Patel, S.K. Naik, D.P. Naidich, W.D. Travis, J.A. Weingarten, R. Lazzaro, D.D. Gutterman, C. Wentowski, H.B. Grosu, S. Raoof, A practical algorithmic approach to the diagnosis and management of solitary pulmonary nodules: part 1: radiologic characteristics and imaging modalities, Chest 143 (3) (2013) 825–839.

[83] D.A. Rosman, R. Duszak Jr., W. Wang, D.R. Hughes, A.B. Rosenkrantz, Changing utilization of noninvasive diagnostic imaging over 2 decades: an examination family–focused analysis of medicare claims using the Neiman imaging types of service categorization system, Am. J. Roentgenol. 210 (2) (2018) 364–368.

[84] S.Y. Ash, R.S.J. Estépar, G.R. Washko, Chest imaging for precision medicine, in: Precision in Pulmonary, Critical Care, and Sleep Medicine, Humana, Cham, 2020, pp. 107–115.

[85] D.M. Tierney, J.S. Huelster, J.D. Overgaard, M.B. Plunkett, L.L. Boland, C.A.S. Hill, V.K. Agboto, C.S. Smith, B.F. Mikel, B.E. Weise, K.E. Madigan, Comparative performance of pulmonary ultrasound, chest radiograph, and CT among patients with acute respiratory failure, Crit. Care Med. 48 (2) (2020) 151–157.

[86] W.H. Hsu, F.J. Tsai, G. Zhang, C.K. Chang, P.H. Hsieh, S.N. Yang, S.S. Sun, K. Liao, E.T. Huang, Development of a deep learning model for chest X-ray screening, Med. Phys. Int. 7 (3) (2019) 314.

Further reading

J. Ashburner, K.J. Friston, Voxel-based morphometry—the methods, NeuroImage 11 (6) (2000) 805–821.

E. Ricci, R. Perfetti, Retinal blood vessel segmentation using line operators and support vector classification, IEEE Trans. Med. Imaging 26 (10) (2007) 1357–1365.

C. Baldauf, A. Bäuerle, T. Ropinski, V. Rasche, I. Vernikouskaya, Convolutional Neural Network (CNN) Applied to Respiratory Motion Detection in Fluoroscopic Frames (Doctoral dissertation), Ulm University, 2019.

K. Kamnitsas, C. Ledig, V.F. Newcombe, J.P. Simpson, A.D. Kane, D.K. Menon, D. Rueckert, B. Glocker, Efficient multi-scale 3D CNN with fully connected CRF for accurate brain lesion segmentation, Med. Image Anal. 36 (2017) 61–78.

Y. Abdallah, S. Mohamed, Automatic recognition of leukemia cells using texture analysis algorithm, Int. J. Adv. Res. 4 (1) (2016) 1242–1248.

Y. Wimalasena, L. Kocierz, D. Strong, J. Watterson, B. Burns, Lung ultrasound: a useful tool in the assessment of the dyspnoeic patient in the emergency department. Fact or fiction? Emerg. Med. J. 35 (4) (2018) 258–266.

P. Atkinson, J. Milne, O. Loubani, G. Verheul, The V-line: a sonographic aid for the confirmation of pleural fluid, Crit. Ultrasound J. 4 (1) (2012) 19.

S. Xiaoming, Z. Ning, W. Haibin, Y. Xiaoyang, W. Xue, Y. Shuang, Medical image retrieval approach by texture features fusion based on Hausdorff distance, Math. Problems Eng. 2018 (2018) 1–12.

E.J. Limkin, S. Reuzé, A. Carré, R. Sun, A. Schernberg, A. Alexis, E. Deutsch, C. Ferté, C. Robert, The complexity of tumor shape, spiculatedness, correlates with tumor radiomic shape features, Sci. Rep. 9 (1) (2019) 1–12.

S.B. Edge, C.C. Compton, The American Joint Committee on Cancer: the 7th edition of the AJCC cancer staging manual and the future of TNM, Ann. Surg. Oncol. 17 (6) (2010) 1471–1474.

A.A. Razek, B.Y. Huang, Soft tissue tumors of the head and neck: imaging-based review of the WHO classification, Radiographics 31 (7) (2011) 1923–1954.

Review of related work

2.1 Introduction

This chapter gives a peek into the work that has recently been carried out by other researchers using chest radiograph datasets. The overview of different computer-aided classification (CAC) systems designed over the years by other researchers for binary classification and multiclass classification of chest radiographs has been discussed in this chapter.

2.2 Overview of the studies based on the classification of chest radiographs

2.2.1 Overview of machine learning-based studies for the classification of chest radiographs

Fig. 2.1 shows the broad distribution of studies related to the classification of medical images specific to chest radiographic images using machine learning-based classifiers. Since the proposed work focuses on the CAC system design for binary classification, the overview of machine learning-based studies for the classification of chest radiographs is discussed in detail only with reference to binary classification-based studies of chest radiographs.

2.2.1.1 Binary classification-based studies of chest radiographs

Binary classification-based studies of chest radiographs refer to the studies carried out by various researchers focused on the two-class classification of chest radiographs. This binary classification includes mainly the class labels Normal/Pneumonia and Normal/Abnormal. Table 2.1 gives a brief overview of the machine learning-based binary classification studies of chest radiographs.

Chapman et al. [1] proposed the binary classification of chest radiographs using rules, Bayesian networks, and decision trees. Chandra and Verma [2] proposed a lung ROI segmentation-based classification of chest X-ray into binary classes Normal and Pneumonia. The authors compared the accuracy of various machine learning classifiers for classification of chest X-rays with segmentation and without segmentation. It is observed that without the lung segmentation, the machine learning classifier achieved the accuracies as follows: multilayer perceptron (Acc.: 92.23%), random forest (Acc.: 90.53%), sequential minimal optimization (Acc.: 89.80%), classification via regression (Acc.: 91.99%), and logistic regression (Acc.: 91.50%). For segmentation-based classification the classifiers achieved the following accuracies: multilayer perceptron (Acc.: 95.38%), random forest (Acc.: 94.41%), sequential minimal optimization (Acc.: 93.68%), classification via regression (Acc.: 94.66%), and logistic regression (Acc.: 95.63%). It is concluded that the proposed method of ROI segmentation of lungs from the chest X-ray achieves the highest accuracy (95.63%) with the

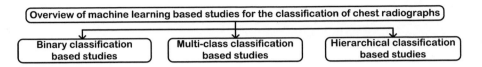

FIG. 2.1

Schematic representation of the type of machine learning-based studies carried out for the classification of chest radiographs.

logistic regression classifier. Al Mamlook et al. [3] proposes the CAC system design using various machine learning classifiers and convolutional neural networks (CNNs) for binary classification of chest X-ray images into Normal and Abnormal. The results reported show that the CNN performs best with an accuracy of 98.46%, and random forest machine learning classifier performs best with an accuracy of 97.61%. Oliveria et al. [4] proposes the design of a system for the binary classification of chest X-ray images using k-NN machine learning classifiers and implementation of Haar wavelet transform for feature extraction. Sousa et al. [5] firstly performed the classification of chest X-ray images using three machine learning classifiers: SVM, k-NN, and naïve Bayes, which reported an accuracy of 77.00%, 70.00%, 68.00%, respectively. They further performed the binary classification of chest X-rays using five machine learning-based classifiers (k-NN, naïve Bayes, multilayer perceptron, decision tree, and SVM) combined with different dimensionality reduction techniques (principle component analysis (PCA), sequential forward elimination, and kernel PCA). The naïve Bayes classifier with kernel PCA yields the highest accuracy of 96.00%. Depeursinge et al. [6] performed classification of chest X-ray images by using five machine learning classifiers (naïve Bayes, k-NN, J48 decision trees, multilayer perceptron, and SVM). The SVM classifier performed best with an accuracy of 88.30%. Yao et al. [7] designed a CAC system using SVM classifiers that yielded an accuracy of 80.00%. Naydenova et al. [8] implemented feature selection techniques to select 47 features of the chest radiographs for the differential diagnosis of Normal and Pneumonia. These extracted features were learned by the combination of SVM and random forest machine learning classifiers and reported an accuracy of 97.80%.

From Table 2.1 it is observed that studies have been carried using a variety of machine learning classifiers, but the most prevalent one is the SVM, whereas no study has used the adaptive neuro-fuzzy classifier. The present work uses both the SVM and the adaptive neuro-fuzzy classifier (ANFC) with feature selection methods and feature dimensionality reduction.

2.2.2 Overview of deep learning-based studies for the classification of chest radiographs

Fig. 2.2 shows the broad distribution of studies related to the classification of medical images specific to chest radiographic images using deep learning-based convolutional neural networks.

2.2.2.1 Binary classification-based studies of chest radiographs

This covers the studies carried out by various researchers focused on the two-class classification of chest radiographs. The two class labels of studies here are mainly Normal/Pneumonia and Pneumonia/COVID-19. The binary classification-based studies are further divided into the following categories:

Table 2.1 Brief review of studies carried out for the machine learning-based binary classification of chest X-ray images.

Investigators	Images	Additional tasks	Classifier
Chapman et al. [1]	292 (Normal, Pneumonia)	–	Rules (AUC: 0.96) Bayesian network (AUC: 0.94) Decision tree (AUC: 0.93)
Chandra and Verma [2]	412 images (Normal, Pneumonia)	Without segmentation With segmentation	Multilayer perceptron (Acc.: 92.23%) Logistic regression (Acc.: 95.63%)
Al Mamlook et al. [3]	5856 images (Normal, Abnormal)	–	Random Forest (Acc.: 97.61%) XGBoost (Acc.: 96.24%) k-NN (Acc.: 92.55%) Decision trees (Acc.: 86.64%) Gradient Boost (Acc.: 96.24%) Adaboost (Acc.: 95.96%)
Oliveria et al. [4]	40 images (Normal, Pneumonia)	(Feature extraction) Haar wavelet	k-NN (Acc.: 97.00%)
Sousa et al. [5]	156 images (Normal, Pneumonia)	– (Feature reduction) Kernel PCA	SVM (Acc.: 77.00%) k-NN (Acc.: 70.00%) Naïve Bayes (Acc.: 68.00%) Naïve Bayes (Acc.: 96.00%)
Depeursinge et al. [6]	843 images (Normal, Pneumonia)	–	SVM (Acc.: 88.30%)
Yao et al. [7]	40 images (Normal, Pneumonia)	–	SVM (Acc.: 80.00%)
Naydenova et al. [8]	1093 images (Normal, Pneumonia)	(Feature selection) Correlation, mRMR, Lasso & Elastic Net (Feature reduction) t-SNE	SVM + RF (Acc.: 97.80%)

k-NN, *k-nearest neighbor;* SVM, *support vector machine;* RF, *random forest;* PCA, *principal component analysis;* mRMR, *minimum redundancy maximum relevance;* t-SNE, *t-distributed stochastic neighbor embedding.*

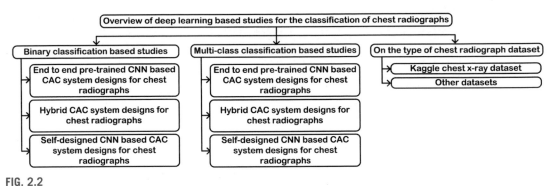

FIG. 2.2

Schematic representation of the type of deep learning-based studies carried out for the classification of chest radiographs.

End-to-end pretrained CNN-based CAC system designs for chest radiographs

This covers the studies carried out by various researchers focused on the two-class classification of chest radiographs using the end-to-end pretrained CNN models. Table 2.2 gives a brief overview of the various studies carried out using the end-to-end pretrained CNN-based CAC systems.

Zech et al. [9] proposed a classification system that efficiently classifies chest radiographs across a variety of data using the DenseNet121 architecture and softmax classifier. The authors collected a variety of data from National Institute of Health (NIH) clinical centers, Mount Sinai Hospital (MSH), and the Indiana University (IU) network for patient care, which resulted in a total of 158,323 chest radiographs. The aim of the authors was to show the generalization power of their designed CAC system, which is why they used such a large dataset obtained from different sources. The AUC of the trained network as reported by the authors is 0.93 for the binary classification of chest radiographs into Normal and Pneumonia. Al Mubarok et al. [10] proposed a CAC system in order to enhance the diagnostic capabilities of radiologists for pneumonia. The authors reported an accuracy of 85.60% for ResNet50 and 78.06% for mask-RCNN. Rahman et al. [11] proposed automatic detection of pneumonia using chest radiographic images. The authors used a dataset of 5247 images on four pretrained CNN models to determine the network's efficiency for classifying the chest X-ray images. The results showed that DenseNet201 yielded an accuracy of 98.00%, which is the maximum when compared with other networks. AlexNet, ResNet18, and SqueezeNet yielded an accuracy of 94.50%, 96.40%, 96.10%, respectively. El Asnaoui et al. [12] conducted a comparative study by using nine different deep learning models to classify chest radiographs into two classes, Normal and Pneumonia. The architectures that the authors used were baseline CNN, Xception, VGG16, and VGG19 showing accuracy of 84.18%, 83.14%, 86.26%, and 85.94%, respectively. Architectures that achieved the highest accuracy for binary classification were InceptionV3, DensNet201, MobileNetV2, InceptionResnetV2, and Resnet50 with a classification accuracy of 94.59%, 93.66%, 96.27%, 96.09%, and 96.61%, respectively. Kermany et al. [13] proposed a CAC system using the InceptionV3 pretrained CNN model that achieved an accuracy of 92.08%. Kermany in 2018 contributed a chest radiograph dataset composed of 5856 images, also known as the Mendeley dataset. The chest X-ray images from this dataset having the two categories (4273 Pneumonia and 1583 Normal) are popularly used under the name of Kaggle chest X-ray dataset. Jakhar and Hooda [14] used a DCNN for predicting big data and extracting features

Table 2.2 Brief review of studies carried out for the deep learning-based classification of chest X-ray images using end-to-end pretrained CNN models.

Investigators	Images	Model	Classifier
Zech et al. [9]	158,323 (Normal, Pneumonia)	DenseNet121	Softmax (AUC: 0.93)
Al Mubarok et al. [10]	26,684 (Normal, Pneumonia)	ResNet Mask-RCNN	Softmax (Acc.: 85.60%) Softmax (Acc.: 78.06%)
Rahman et al. [11]	5247 (Normal, Pneumonia)	DenseNet201 AlexNet ResNet18 SqueezeNet	Softmax (Acc.: 98.00%) Softmax (Acc.: 94.50%) Softmax (Acc.: 96.40%) Softmax (Acc.: 96.10%)
El Asnaoui et al. [12]	Normal: 1583 Pneumonia: 4273	Baseline CNN Xception VGG16 VGG19 InceptionV3 DensNet201 MobileNetV2 InceptionResnetV2 Resnet50	Softmax (Acc.: 84.18%) Softmax (Acc.: 83.14%) Softmax (Acc.: 86.26%) Softmax (Acc.: 85.94%) Softmax (Acc.: 95.59%) Softmax (Acc.: 93.66%) Softmax (Acc.: 96.27%) Softmax (Acc.: 96.09%) Softmax (Acc.: 96.61%)
Kermany et al. [13]	5856 (Normal, Pneumonia)	InceptionV3	Softmax (Acc.: 92.80%)
Jakhar and Hooda [14]	5863 (Normal, pneumonia)	DCNN	Softmax (Acc.: 84.00%)
Rajaraman et al. [15]	5863 (Normal, Pneumonia)	VGG16	Softmax (Acc.: 96.20%)
Ayan and Ünver [16]	5856 (Normal, Pneumonia)	VGG16 Xception	Softmax (Acc.: 87.00%) Softmax (Acc.: 82.00%)
Jain et al. [17]	Viral Pneumonia, COVID-19	ResNet101	Softmax (Acc.: 97.78%)

DCNN, *deep convolution neural network*; CNN, *convolution neural network*; RCNN, *region-based CNN*.

from high-quality X-rays with accuracy of 84.00%. Rajaraman et al. [15] proposed a CAC system for detection of pneumonia in pediatric chest radiographic images. The authors trained the VGG16 with a baseline dataset and cropped ROI dataset to achieve an accuracy of 95.70% and 96.20%, respectively. Ayan and Ünver [16] used VGG16 and Xception network for the classification of the 5856 chest radiographs into Normal and Pneumonia. The authors achieved an accuracy of 87.00% and 82.00% for VGG16 and Xception network, respectively. Jain et al. [17] proposed a hierarchical CAC system that firstly performed a three-class classification of chest X-ray images into Normal, bacterial Pneumonia, and viral Pneumonia using the pretrained ResNet50 network. Then the authors performed a two-class classification using the pretrained ResNet101 network to classify COVID-19 and pneumonia in chest radiographs. The two-class classification achieved an accuracy of 97.78%.

From Table 2.2 it can be seen that a number of studies have been carried out using pretrained CNN networks for designing CAC systems for chest radiographs; however, there is no study using the concept of decision fusion of these pretrained networks. The present work applies the concept of decision fusion of the different pretrained CNN models.

Hybrid CAC system designs for chest radiographs

This covers the studies carried out by various researchers focused on the two-class classification of chest radiographs using hybrid CAC systems. Table 2.3 gives a brief overview of the various studies carried out using the hybrid CAC systems.

Gu et al. [18] proposed a CAC system that aims at classification of the chest radiographs into two classes by firstly segmenting the lung regions using AlexNet-based fully convolutional network

Table 2.3 Brief review of studies carried out for the deep learning-based classification of chest X-ray images using hybrid CAC systems.

Investigators	Images	Model	Classifier
Gu et al. [18]	4513 (Bacterial Pneumonia, Viral Pneumonia)	DCNN	SVM (AUC: 0.82) (Acc.: 80.40%)
Toğaçar et al. [19]	Normal:1583 Pneumonia:4266	AlexNet+VGG16+VGG19	LDA (Acc.: 99.41%) SVM (Acc.: 98.21%)
Varshni et al. [20]	Normal: 1431, Pneumonia: 1431	DenseNet169 DenseNet121 ResNet50	SVM (AUC: 0.80) SVM (AUC: 0.77) SVM (AUC: 0.78)
Dey et al. [21]	Normal, Pneumonia Normal, Pneumonia (threshold filter)	VGG19+Handcrafted features (CWT, DWT, GLCM) VGG19+Handcrafted features (CWT, DWT, GLCM)	Random Forest (Acc.: 95.70%) Random Forest (Acc.: 97.94%)

DCNN, *deep convolution neural network;* SVM, *support vector machine;* LDA, *linear discriminant analysis;* CWT, *continuous wavelet transform;* DWT, *discrete wavelet transform;* GLCM, *gray-level cooccurrence matrix.*

(FCN) and then applying the DCNN for performing feature extraction from the extracted lung regions. Ultimately, the classification is performed by the SVM giving 80.40% accuracy. Toğaçar et al. [19] proposed a CAC system that used the pertained networks AlexNet, VGG16, and VGG19 as feature extractors and implemented the classification of chest radiographs by using the LDA and SVM. The authors used the minimum redundancy and maximum relevance (mRMR) algorithm as a feature reduction technique before applying the machine learning-based classifiers. The linear discriminant analysis (LDA) classifier yields an accuracy of 99.41%, whereas the SVM yields an accuracy of only 98.21%. Varshni et al. [20] proposed a hybrid CAC system that mainly has two modules: feature extraction and classification. The authors performed different experiments for the two-class classification of chest radiographs using pretrained CNN as the feature extractor and performing classification using different machine learning classifiers. The pretrained networks used by the authors for feature learning are Xception, VGG16, VGG19, ResNet50, DenseNet121, and DenseNet169 along with different classifiers, including random forest, k-NN, naïve Bayes and support vector machine (SVM). It was reported by the authors that the CAC system designed using DenseNet169 as feature extractor with SVM as classifier outperformed all the other designed CAC systems achieving an AUC of 0.80. Dey et al. [21] proposed a CAC system for the binary classification of chest radiographs into Normal and Pneumonia using the VGG19 CNN model as deep feature extractor and CWT, DWT, and GLCM handcrafted features. This combination of features is obtained using serial feature fusion that undergoes feature dimensionality reduction using PCA, and then the reduced feature set is fed to the different machine learning-based classifiers such as the SVM, k-NN, decision trees and random forest. The authors performed this with the original chest radiograph data and also the dataset obtained after applying threshold filters to the original dataset. It is reported by the authors that the random forest classifier achieved the best performance yielding 95.70% accuracy for the classification of original chest radiographs and 97.94% accuracy for the filtered chest radiograph dataset.

From Table 2.3, it can be concluded that very few studies have been done on the design of hybrid CAC systems for chest radiographs. The most commonly used machine classifier is SVM, and only two studies use the concept of feature reduction and feature fusion.

Self-designed CNN-based CAC system designs for chest radiographs

This covers the studies carried out by various researchers focused on the two-class classification of chest radiographs using hybrid CAC systems. Table 2.4 gives a brief overview of the various studies carried out using the self-designed CNN-based CAC systems.

Sharma et al. [22] designed a CAC system for the classification of chest radiographs into two classes, Normal and Pneumonia, by performing the feature extraction using the self-designed CNN, one designed with dropout layer and the other designed without dropout layer, and then applying a dense sigmoid classifier. The CAC system designed with dropout layer yielded the highest accuracy of 90.68% over a dataset of 5863 chest radiographic images. Saraiva et al. [23] proposed a CNN that trains the network on the same dataset as Kermany et al. [13] and achieved an accuracy of 95.02%, which is better than the original proposed by Kermany (92.08%). Hashmi et al. [24] proposed a weighted classifier that sums up the predictions of pretrained CNN models ResNet18, DenseNet121, InceptionV3, Xception, and MobileNetV2 to perform final binary classification of the input chest X-ray dataset. The proposed weighted classifier as reported by the authors achieves the maximum accuracy of 98.43%. Li et al. [25] proposed a deep learning-based framework PNet for efficient detection and classification of Pneumonia. The authors trained AlexNet, VGG16, and proposed PNet on 10,784 chest radiographs to compare the accuracy of the networks. The experiments carried out by the authors for training the

Table 2.4 Brief review of studies carried out for the deep learning-based classification of chest X-ray images using self-designed CNN-based CAC systems.

Investigators	Images	Model	Classifier
Sharma et al. [22]	5863 (Normal, Pneumonia)	CNN	Sigmoid (Acc.: 90.68%)
Saraiva et al. [23]	5863 (Normal, Pneumonia)	CNN	Softmax (Acc.: 95.02%)
Hashmi et al. [24]	5856 (Normal, Pneumonia)	ResNet18 + DenseNet121 + InceptionV3 + Xception + MobileNetV2	Weighted classifier (Acc.: 98.43%)
Li et al. [25]	10,784 (Normal, Pneumonia)	PNet	Softmax (Acc.: 92.79%)
Liang and Zheng [26]	5856 (Normal, Pneumonia)	CNN	Sigmoid (Acc.: 90.50%)

DCNN, *deep convolution neural network*; CNN, *convolution neural network*; PNet, *pneumonia network*.

network yielded an accuracy of 90.30%, 90.39%, and 92.79% for AlexNet, VGG16, and PNet, respectively. Liang and Zeng [26] proposed a new deep learning framework to classify the chest radiograph images by combining residual thoughts of the network layers and dilated convolution. The authors used the concept of residual structure to overcome the problem of overfitting whereas the issue of feature space loss is resolved using the concept of dilated convolutions.

From Table 2.4 it is clear that few studies have been carried out using self-designed CNN-based CAC systems, all of which yielded satisfactory performance.

2.2.2.2 Multiclass classification-based studies for chest radiographs

This covers the studies carried out by various researchers focused on the multiclass classification of chest radiographs. The multiclass label studies covered here are mainly simple three-class classification into Normal/Pneumonia/COVID-19 and Normal/bacterial Pneumonia/viral Pneumonia. The multiclass classification-based studies are further divided into following categories:

End-to-end pretrained CNN-based CAC system designs for chest radiographs

This covers the studies carried out by various researchers focused on the multiclass classification of chest radiographs using the end-to-end pretrained CNN-based CAC systems. Table 2.5 gives a brief overview of the various studies carried out using the end-to-end pretrained CNN-based CAC systems.

Table 2.5 Brief review of studies carried out for the deep learning-based classification of chest X-ray images using end-to-end pretrained CNN models.

Investigators	Images	Model	Classifier
El Asnaoui and Chawki [27]	Normal:1583 Pneumonia:2780 COVID-19:1724	InceptionResNetV2 DenseNet201 ResNet50 MobileNetV2 InceptionV3 VGG16 VGG19	Softmax (Acc.: 92.18%) Softmax (Acc.: 88.09%) Softmax (Acc.: 87.54%) Softmax (Acc.: 85.47%) Softmax (Acc.: 88.03%) Softmax (Acc.: 74.84%) Softmax (Acc.: 72.52%)
Apostolopoulos and Mpesiana [28]	Normal, Pneumonia, COVID-19	MobileNet	Softmax (Acc.: 97.40%)
Civit-Masot et al. [29]	396 Normal, Pneumonia, COVID-19	VGG16	Softmax (Acc.: 86.00%)
Jain et al. [17]	1832 Normal, Viral Pneumonia, Bacterial Pneumonia	ResNet50	Softmax (Acc.: 93.01%)

El Asnaoui and Chawki [27] conducted a comparative study of the use of seven different DCNNs (VGG16, VGG19, DenseNet201, InceptionResNetV2, ResNet50, MobileNetV2, InceptionV3) in efficient detection and classification of coronavirus pneumonia. The experiments show that InceptionResNetV2 is better at classification of chest radiographs with an accuracy of 92.18% whereas the DenseNet201 is the second best giving an accuracy of 88.09% among the six pretrained networks. Apostolopoulos and Mpesiana [28] used two types of datasets to test the performance of pretrained networks using VGG19, MobileNetV2, Inception, Xception, Inception, and ResNetV2. The first dataset is comprised of a total of 1427 chest X-ray images (Normal: 504, Bacterial Pneumonia: 700, COVID-19: 224), and the second dataset has the same composition as the first with just the addition of some viral pneumonia chest X-ray images resulting in 1441 chest X-ray images (Normal: 504, Pneumonia: 714, COVID-19: 224). The networks are trained on the first dataset; then the best performing network is trained on the second dataset. The performance of these networks is described by the authors in the form of two types of classification accuracy: (a) three-class accuracy, which focuses on performing classification into three classes (Normal, Pneumonia, and COVID-19); and (b) two-class accuracy, which focuses on classification into two classes. Pneumonia and COVID-19 are considered the same class; hence, misclassification of pneumonia and COVID-19 among each other is not considered. It can be considered as classification into two classes: Normal and Pneumonia/COVID-19. The authors reported that the VGG19 has better accuracy, although the false negatives of MobileNetV2 were way less and were considered the best performing network. Civit-Masot et al. [29] proposed designing CAC system using the pretrained VGG16 network for the single three-class classification of chest radiographs. The CAC system achieves an accuracy of 86.00%. The authors used a dataset comprising of a total of 396 images, each class having 132 images. These are further divided into training and testing sets in the ratio of 80% training and 20% testing, consisting of 105 train images and 27 test images each of Normal and COVID-19 and 106 training images and 27 test images of pneumonia. Jain et al. [17] proposed a hierarchical CAC system that firstly performs a three-class classification of chest X-ray images into Normal, bacterial Pneumonia, and viral Pneumonia using the pretrained ResNet50 network. The three-class classification achieves an accuracy of 93.01%. Then the authors additionally performed a two-class classification using the pretrained ResNet101 network to classify COVID-19 and other diseases in chest radiographs.

From Table 2.5, it is understood that few studies have been carried out for the three-class classification of chest radiographs using an end-to-end pretrained CNN model out of which the maximum is carried out to successfully classify COVID-19.

Hybrid CAC system designs for chest radiographs

This covers the study carried out by the researchers focused on the multiclass classification of chest radiographs using hybrid CAC systems. Table 2.6 gives a brief overview of the study carried out using the hybrid CAC systems.

Table 2.6 Brief review of study carried out for the deep learning-based classification of chest X-ray images using hybrid CAC systems.

Investigators	Images	Model	Classifier
Sethy and Behera [30]	381 Normal, Pneumonia, COVID19	ResNet50	SVM (Acc.: 95.33%)
SVM, *support vector machine*.			

Sethy and Behera [30] proposed the design of a CAC system using deep feature extraction from the different pretrained CNN models. The authors used 13 different pretrained CNN models out of which the ResNet50 pretrained model and SVM as a classifier reported maximum classification accuracy. A dataset of 381 images including 127 images of each class (Normal, Pneumonia, and COVID-19) are used to perform a three-class classification. The designed CAC achieves an accuracy of 95.33%.

As per Table 2.6, only one study has been carried out for the multiclass classification of chest radiographs using the SVM classifier.

Self-designed CNN-based CAC system designs for chest radiographs

This covers the study carried out by researchers focused on the multiclass classification of chest radiographs using self-designed CNN-based CAC systems. Table 2.7 gives a brief overview of the study carried out using the self-designed CNN-based CAC systems.

Ozturk et al. [31] proposed their own DarkCovidNet model for the classification of chest X-ray images into two-class and three-class. The binary classification involved Normal and COVID-19 classes achieving an accuracy of 98.08%, whereas the three-class classification included Normal, Pneumonia, and COVID-19, achieving an accuracy of 87.02%. The dataset used by the authors comprised of 500 Normal, 500 Pneumonia, and 127 COVID-19 images. From Table 2.7, it is clear that only one study has been carried out for the design of a CAC system for multiclass classification of chest radiographs using self-designed CNN model.

2.2.2.3 On the basis of chest radiograph dataset used

The chest X-ray imaging is a ubiquitous medical imaging modality; therefore, a number of chest X-ray image datasets are publicly available. Fig. 2.3 shows the different chest radiograph datasets available online. They are broadly classified on the basis of the presence of pneumonia case images in the dataset. Here the dataset shaded in gray is used in the present work.

Some of the publicly available chest radiograph datasets are as follows:

(1) **JSRT dataset:** This is a publicly available dataset of lung nodules by the Japanese Society of Radiological Technology (JSRT). The standard digital image database was designed by the JRST with the cooperation of the Japanese Radiological Society (JRS) in 1998. The dataset is comprised of 247 images (154 nodule and 93 nonnodule images) of 2048×2048 matrix size. The JSRT database has been used by a number of researchers all over the world for various research purposes such as image processing, CAC, computer-aided diagnosis (CAD), picture archiving and communication system (PACS). The JSRT dataset is available at [32]. Some of the sample images of the JSRT dataset are shown in Fig. 2.4.

Table 2.7 Brief review of study carried out for the deep learning-based classification of chest X-ray images using self-designed CNN-based CAC systems.

Investigators	Images	Model	Classifier
Ozturk et al. [31]	Normal: 500 COVID-19: 127 Pneumonia: 500	DarkCovidNet	Softmax (Acc.: 87.02%)

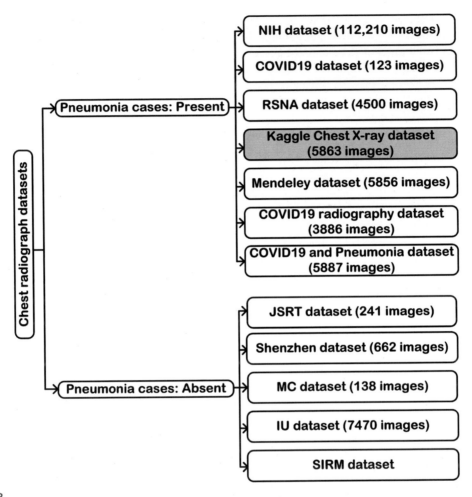

FIG. 2.3

Different chest radiograph datasets. *NIH*, National Institute of Health; *RSNA*, Radiological Society of North America; *JSRT*, Japanese Society of Radiological Technology; *MC*, Montgomery County; *IU*, Indiana University; *SIRM*, Italian Society of Medical Radiology.

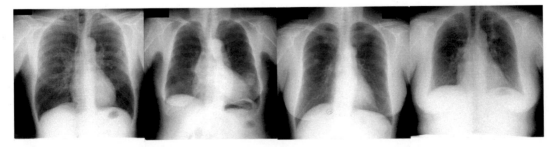

FIG. 2.4

Sample chest X-ray images of the JSRT dataset.

(2) MC dataset: The Montgomery County (MC) dataset has been collected with cooperation of the Department of Health and Human Services, MC, Maryland, United States. The dataset has been collected by Jaeger et al. [33] from a tuberculosis control program, and it contains 138 chest radiographs with class labels as Normal (80 images) and Abnormal (58 images), each varying in size from 4020×4892 to 4892×4020 pixels. The dataset is available at [34]. Some of the sample images of the MC dataset are shown in Fig. 2.5.

(3) Shenzhen dataset: The Shenzhen dataset was collected by Jaeger et al. in collaboration with the Shenzhen No. 3 People's Hospital, Guangdong Medical College, Shenzhen, China. The dataset has 662 chest radiographs comprised of healthy cases (326 images) and tuberculosis cases (366 images). It is available at [35]. Some of the sample images of the Shenzhen dataset are shown in Fig. 2.6.

(4) RSNA dataset: The Radiological Society of North America (RSNA) reached out to the Kaggle community for developing a dataset for pneumonia detection in collaboration with the NIH and MD.ai. It is available for download at [36]. Some of the sample images of the RSNA dataset are shown in Fig. 2.7.

(5) NIH dataset: This is a publicly available dataset of chest radiographs by the NIH. The NIH compiled the dataset of many scans with advanced lung disease. The aim of NIH by offering this free dataset is for academic and research institutions across the country to teach a computer to read and process an extremely large amount of scans, and confirm the results the radiologists have found, and potentially identify some other findings that may have been overlooked. It is available for download at [37]. They published the chest X-ray data for different disease detection competitions. These datasets for different competitions are chest X-ray8 dataset, chest X-ray14 dataset, and so forth. Some of the sample images of the NIH dataset are shown in Fig. 2.8.

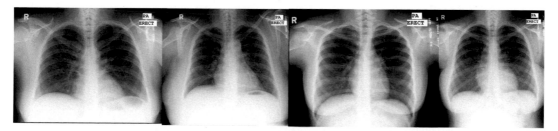

FIG. 2.5

Sample chest X-ray images of the MC dataset.

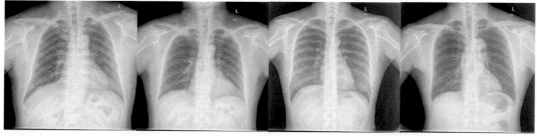

FIG. 2.6

Sample chest X-ray images of Shenzhen dataset.

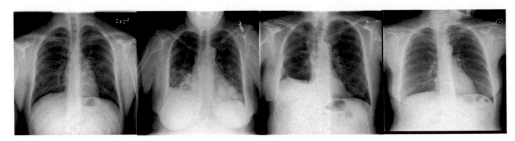

FIG. 2.7

Sample chest X-ray images of the RSNA dataset.

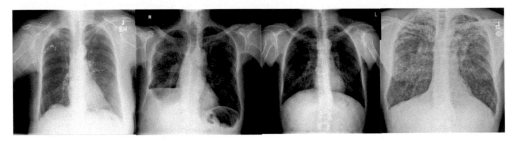

FIG. 2.8

Sample chest X-ray images of the NIH dataset.

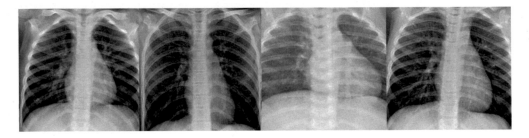

FIG. 2.9

Sample chest X-ray images of the Kaggle chest X-ray dataset.

(6) Kaggle chest X-ray dataset: This widely used open dataset is comprised of chest X-ray images (anterior-posterior) of pediatric patients (1–5 years old) from the Guangzhou Women and Children's Medical Center, Guangzhou, which is publicly made available by Kermany et al. [13]. It is available freely for download at [38]. Some of the sample images of the Kaggle chest X-ray dataset are shown in Fig. 2.9.

(7) SIRM COVID-19 dataset: The Italian Society of Medical Radiology (SIRM) is a medical association of Italian radiologists. The SIRM COVID-19 dataset of chest radiographs is available for download at [39]. Some of the sample images of the SIRM COVID-19 dataset are shown in Fig. 2.10.

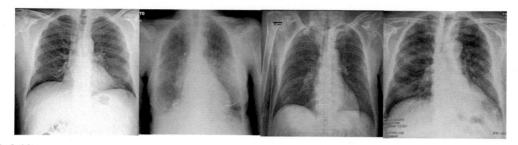

FIG. 2.10

Sample chest X-ray images of the SIRM COVID-19 Dataset.

(8) COVID-19 dataset: This is known as the novel coronavirus 2019 dataset given by Cohen et al. [40]. It is publicly available for download at [41]. Some of the sample images of the COVID-19 image dataset by Cohen et al. [40] are shown in Fig. 2.11.

Some of the other publicly available datasets are: COVID-19 radiography dataset available for download at [42]; the Mendeley dataset, which can be downloaded from [43]; and a COVID-19 and pneumonia dataset available for download at [44]. The two datasets of chest radiographs that are not available publicly but have been used by authors in their work of CAC system designs of chest X-ray images are: the MSH dataset, which is the dataset by Mount Sinai Hospital; and the IU dataset by the Indiana University Network for Patient Care.

On the basis of the datasets used by the researchers to carry out the work for the CAC system design for chest radiographs, the results are given as follows:

(i) Kaggle chest X-ray dataset

Table 2.8 covers the studies carried out using the Kaggle chest X-ray dataset for the CAC system designs.

From Table 2.8, it can be concluded that the most of the researchers have used the Kaggle chest X-ray dataset for the CAC system design. The present work also uses the Kaggle chest X-ray dataset for the design of deep learning-based CAC systems.

(ii) Other datasets

Table 2.9 covers the studies carried out using various other chest X-ray datasets for the CAC system designs.

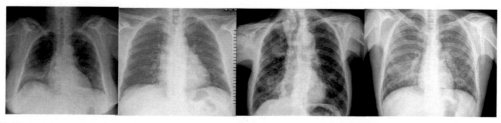

FIG. 2.11

Sample chest X-ray images of the COVID-19 Dataset.

Table 2.8 Brief review of studies carried out for the deep learning-based classification of chest X-ray images using the Kaggle chest X-ray dataset.

Investigators	Images	Model	Classifier
Toğaçar et al. [19]	Kaggle chest X-ray dataset	AlexNet+VGG16+VGG19	LDA (Acc.: 99.41%) SVM (Acc.: 98.21%)
Sharma et al. [22]	Kaggle chest X-ray dataset	CNN	Sigmoid (Acc.: 90.68%)
Rahman et al. [11]	Kaggle chest X-ray dataset	DenseNet201	Softmax (Acc.: 98%)
		AlexNet	Softmax (Acc.: 94.50%)
		ResNet18	Softmax (Acc.:96.40%)
		SqueezeNet	Softmax (Acc.:96.10%)
El Asnaoui et al. [12]	Kaggle chest X-ray dataset	Baseline CNN	Softmax (Acc.: 84.18%)
		Xception	Softmax (Acc.: 83.14%)
		VGG16	Softmax (Acc.: 86.26%)
		VGG19	Softmax (Acc.: 85.94%)
		InceptionV3	Softmax (Acc.: 95.59%)
		DensNet201	Softmax (Acc.: 93.66%)
		MobileNetV2	Softmax (Acc.: 96.27%)
		InceptionResnetV2	Softmax (Acc.: 96.09%)
		Resnet50	Softmax (Acc.: 96.61%)

Author	Dataset	Model	Activation (Accuracy)
Saraiva et al. [23]	Kaggle chest X-ray dataset	CNN	Softmax (Acc.: 95.02%)
Jakhar and Hooda [14]	Kaggle chest X-ray dataset	DCNN	Softmax (Acc.: 84.00%)
Rajaraman et al. [15]	Kaggle chest X-ray dataset	VGG16	Softmax (Acc.: 96.20%)
Ayan and Ünver [16]	Kaggle chest X-ray dataset	VGG16	Softmax (Acc.: 87.00%)
		Xception	Softmax (Acc.: 82.00%)
Jain et al. [17]	Kaggle chest X-ray dataset	ResNet50	Softmax (Acc.: 93.01%)
		ResNet101	Softmax (Acc.: 97.78%)
Hashmi et al. [24]	Kaggle chest X-ray dataset	ResNet18 + DenseNet121 + InceptionV3 + Xception + MobileNetV2	Weighted classifier (Acc.: 98.43%)
Liang and Zheng [26]	Kaggle chest X-ray dataset	CNN	Sigmoid (Acc.: 90.50%)
El Asnaoui and Chawki [27]	Kaggle chest X-ray dataset COVID-19 image dataset	InceptionResNetV2	Softmax (Acc.: 92.18%)
		DenseNet201	Softmax (Acc.: 88.09%)
		ResNet50	Softmax (Acc.: 87.54%)
		MobileNetV2	Softmax (Acc.: 85.47%)
		InceptionV3	Softmax (Acc.: 88.03%)
		VGG16	Softmax (Acc.: 74.84%)
		VGG19	Softmax (Acc.: 72.52%)

Continued

Table 2.8 Brief review of studies carried out for the deep learning-based classification of chest X-ray images using the Kaggle chest X-ray dataset—cont'd

Investigators	Images	Model	Classifier
Sethy and Behera [30]	Kaggle chest X-ray dataset COVID-19 image dataset	ResNet50	SVM (Acc.: 95.33%)
Gu et al. [18]	Kaggle chest X-ray dataset JSRT database MC dataset	DCNN	SVM (AUC: 0.82) (Acc.: 80.40%)
Chowdhury et al. [45]	Kaggle chest X-ray dataset SIRM COVID19 dataset COVID-19 image dataset COVID19 radiography dataset	SqueezeNet DenseNet201	Softmax (Acc.: 98.30%) Softmax (Acc.: 96.10%)
Apostolopoulos and Mpesiana [28]	Kaggle chest X-ray dataset COVID-19 image dataset RSNA SIRM	Mobile Net	Softmax (Acc.: 97.40%)
Dey et al. [21]	Kaggle chest X-ray dataset Kaggle chest X-ray dataset (threshold filter)	VGG19+Handcrafted features (CWT, DWT, GLCM) VGG19+Handcrafted features (CWT, DWT, GLCM)	Random Forest (Acc.: 95.70%) Random Forest (Acc.: 97.94%)

DCNN, deep convolution neural network; SVM, support vector machine; CNN, convolutional neural network; LDA, linear discriminant analysis; CWT, continuous wavelet transform; DWT, discrete wavelet transform; GLCM, gray-level cooccurrence matrix.

Table 2.9 Brief review of studies carried out for the deep learning-based classification of chest X-ray images using other dataset.

Investigators	Images	Model	Classifier
Zech et al. [9]	MSH dataset NIH dataset IU dataset	CNN	Softmax (AUC: 0.93)
Li et al. [25]	Shenzhen dataset	AlexNet VGGNet PNet	Softmax (Acc.: 90.30%) Softmax (Acc.: 90.39%) Softmax (Acc.: 92.79%)
Al Mubarok et al. [10]	RSNA dataset	ResNet Mask-RCNN	Softmax (Acc.: 85.60%) Softmax (Acc.: 78.06%)
Civit-Masot et al. [29]	COVID-19 and Pneumonia scans dataset	VGG16	Softmax (Acc.: 86.00%)
Ozturk et al. [31]	Chest X-ray8 dataset COVID-19 image dataset	DarkCovidNet	Softmax (Acc.: 87.02%)
Varshni et al. [20]	Chest X-ray8 dataset COVID19 image dataset	DenseNet169 DenseNet121 ResNet50	SVM (AUC: 0.80) SVM (AUC: 0.77) SVM (AUC: 0.78)

RCNN, *region-based convolution neural network*; SVM, *support vector machine*; CNN, *convolution neural network*.

From Table 2.9, it is observed that despite the scarce availability of COVID-19 chest radiographs, many researchers have used a combination of chest X-ray datasets for the design of CAC systems. Apart from the popularly used Kaggle chest X-ray dataset, few researchers have used other datasets, such as the SIRM dataset, the Mendeley dataset, and so on, in combination with the prior ones to increase the sample size and achieve higher generalization as well as efficiency in designing the CAC systems for chest radiographs.

Fig. 2.12 gives a schematic representation of the studies carried out for the classification of chest radiographs.

From the summary of the studies carried out for classification of chest radiographs (Table 2.1–2.9), the following can be concluded:

(a) Many studies have been carried out for the binary classification of chest radiographs, and most of them have used the Kaggle dataset alone or in combination with other available chest radiograph datasets. These studies have focused on implementation of end-to-end pretrained CNN networks,

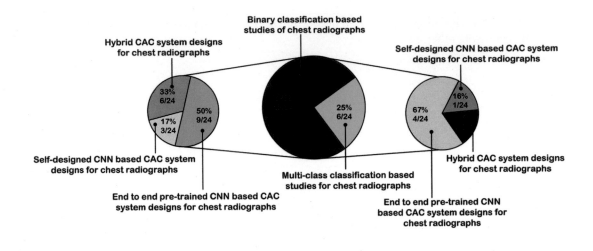

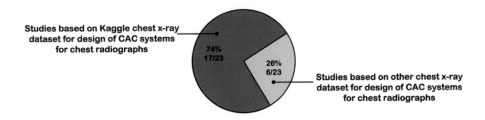

FIG. 2.12

Schematic representation of distribution of deep learning-based studies carried out for the classification of chest radiographs.

few studies are focused on hybrid CNN-based networks, and even fewer studies are based on self-designed CNN-based networks.

(b) For the multiclass classification of chest radiographs, few studies have been carried out using the end-to-end pretrained CNN-based networks whereas one study has been conducted on the self-designed CNN-based networks and one on hybrid CNN-based networks.

(c) Most of the hybrid CNN-based CAC system design studies have implemented SVM machine learning classifier [18–20, 30] whereas only one study has implemented LDA [19]. Other classifiers implemented are weighted classifiers [24] and sigmoid [26] with the self-designed CNN-based CAC systems.

(d) The Kaggle dataset has been widely used in nearly every study carried out whether for the binary classification or the multiclass classification of chest radiographs.

(e) Only one study implements feature reduction using mRMR algorithm for the design of hybrid CAC system for binary classification of chest radiographs [19] while very few studies have used deep feature extraction for the design of CAC systems.

Therefore, the present work performs exhaustive experimentation to design different CAC systems for the binary classification of chest radiographs using end-to-end CNN-based models, hybrid models implementing the SVM and ANFC machine learning classifier and implementing the techniques of decision fusion, deep feature extraction, and feature reduction using a PCA algorithm to design efficient CAC systems.

2.3 Concluding remarks

From the given overview of the related studies that have been conducted in the past for the classification of chest radiographs, it is concluded that most of the studies have been conducted using deep learning-based CNN models and the softmax classifier. Fewer studies have been carried out for the classification of the chest radiographs using the hybrid CAC systems designed using the deep features extraction and machine learning-based classifiers. Hence, the potential of a machine learning-based classifier through deep feature extraction needs to be tested for the classification of the chest radiographs. Therefore, the design of a different CNN-based CAC system for the classification of chest radiographs has been taken up as the next objective of the present work.

References

[1] W.W. Chapman, M. Fizman, B.E. Chapman, P.J. Haug, A comparison of classification algorithms to automatically identify chest X-ray reports that support pneumonia, J. Biomed. Inform. 34 (1) (2001) 4–14.

[2] T.B. Chandra, K. Verma, Pneumonia detection on chest X-ray using machine learning paradigm, in: Proceedings of 3rd International Conference on Computer Vision and Image Processing, Springer, Singapore, 2020, pp. 21–33.

[3] R.E. Al Mamlook, S. Chen, H.F. Bzizi, Investigation of the performance of machine learning classifiers for pneumonia detection in chest X-ray images, in: 2020 IEEE International Conference on Electro Information Technology (EIT), IEEE, 2020, pp. 098–104.

[4] L.L.G. Oliveira, S.A. E Silva, L.H.V. Ribeiro, R.M. de Oliveira, C.J. Coelho, A.L.S. Andrade, Computer-aided diagnosis in chest radiography for detection of childhood pneumonia, Int. J. Med. Inform. 77 (8) (2008) 555–564.

[5] R.T. Sousa, O. Marques, F.A.A. Soares, I.I. Sene Jr., L.L. de Oliveira, E.S. Spoto, Comparative performance analysis of machine learning classifiers in detection of childhood pneumonia using chest radiographs, Procedia Comput. Sci. 18 (2013) 2579–2582.

[6] A. Depeursinge, J. Iavindrasana, A. Hidki, G. Cohen, A. Geissbuhler, A. Platon, P.A. Poletti, H. Müller, Comparative performance analysis of state-of-the-art classification algorithms applied to lung tissue categorization, J. Digit. Imaging 23 (1) (2010) 18–30.

[7] J. Yao, A. Dwyer, R.M. Summers, D.J. Mollura, Computer-aided diagnosis of pulmonary infections using texture analysis and support vector machine classification, Acad. Radiol. 18 (3) (2011) 306–314.

[8] E. Naydenova, A. Tsanas, C. Casals-Pascual, M. De Vos, Smart diagnostic algorithms for automated detection of childhood pneumonia in resource-constrained settings, in: 2015 IEEE Global Humanitarian Technology Conference (GHTC), IEEE, 2015, pp. 377–384.

[9] J.R. Zech, M.A. Badgeley, M. Liu, A.B. Costa, J.J. Titano, E.K. Oermann, Variable generalization performance of a deep learning model to detect pneumonia in chest radiographs: a cross-sectional study, PLoS Med. 15 (11) (2018) e1002683.

[10] A.F. Al Mubarok, J.A. Dominique, A.H. Thias, Pneumonia detection with deep convolutional architecture, in: 2019 International Conference of Artificial Intelligence and Information Technology (ICAIIT), IEEE, 2019, pp. 486–489.

[11] T. Rahman, M.E. Chowdhury, A. Khandakar, K.R. Islam, K.F. Islam, Z.B. Mahbub, M.A. Kadir, S. Kashem, Transfer learning with deep convolutional neural network (CNN) for pneumonia detection using chest X-ray, Appl. Sci. 10 (9) (2020) 3233.

[12] K.E. El Asnaoui, Y. Chawki, A. Idri, Automated methods for detection and classification pneumonia based on x-ray images using deep learning. arXiv preprint arXiv:2003.14363, 2020.

[13] D.S. Kermany, M. Goldbaum, W. Cai, C.C. Valentim, H. Liang, S.L. Baxter, A. McKeown, G. Yang, X. Wu, F. Yan, J. Dong, Identifying medical diagnoses and treatable diseases by image-based deep learning, Cell 172 (5) (2018) 1122–1131.

[14] K. Jakhar, N. Hooda, Big data deep learning framework using Keras: a case study of pneumonia prediction, in: 2018 4th International Conference on Computing Communication and Automation (ICCCA), IEEE, 2018, pp. 1–5.

[15] S. Rajaraman, S. Candemir, I. Kim, G. Thoma, S. Antani, Visualization and interpretation of convolutional neural network predictions in detecting pneumonia in pediatric chest radiographs, Appl. Sci. 8 (10) (2018) 1715.

[16] E. Ayan, H.M. Ünver, Diagnosis of pneumonia from chest X-ray images using deep learning, in: 2019 Scientific Meeting on Electrical-Electronics & Biomedical Engineering and Computer Science (EBBT), IEEE, 2019, pp. 1–5.

[17] G. Jain, D. Mittal, D. Thakur, M.K. Mittal, A deep learning approach to detect Covid-19 coronavirus with X-ray images, Biocybern. Biomed. Eng. 40 (4) (2020) 1391–1405.

[18] X. Gu, L. Pan, H. Liang, R. Yang, Classification of bacterial and viral childhood pneumonia using deep learning in chest radiography, in: Proceedings of the 3rd International Conference on Multimedia and Image Processing, 2018, pp. 88–93.

[19] M. Toğaçar, B. Ergen, Z. Cömert, F. Özyurt, A deep feature learning model for pneumonia detection applying a combination of mRMR feature selection and machine learning models, IRBM 41 (4) (2020) 212–222.

[20] D. Varshni, K. Thakral, L. Agarwal, R. Nijhawan, A. Mittal, Pneumonia detection using CNN-based feature extraction, in: 2019 IEEE International Conference on Electrical, Computer and Communication Technologies (ICECCT), IEEE, 2019, pp. 1–7.

[21] N. Dey, Y.D. Zhang, V. Rajinikanth, R. Pugalenthi, N.S.M. Raja, Customized VGG19 architecture for pneumonia detection in chest X-rays, Pattern Recogn. Lett. 143 (2021) 67–74.

[22] H. Sharma, J.S. Jain, P. Bansal, S. Gupta, Feature extraction and classification of chest X-ray images using CNN to detect pneumonia, in: 2020 10th International Conference on Cloud Computing, Data Science & Engineering (Confluence), IEEE, 2020, pp. 227–231.

[23] A.A. Saraiva, N.M.F. Ferreira, L.L. de Sousa, N.J.C. Costa, J.V.M. Sousa, D.B.S. Santos, A. Valente, S. Soares, Classification of images of childhood pneumonia using convolutional neural networks, in: BIOIMAGING, 2019, pp. 112–119.

[24] M.F. Hashmi, S. Katiyar, A.G. Keskar, N.D. Bokde, Z.W. Geem, Efficient pneumonia detection in chest xray images using deep transfer learning, Diagnostics 10 (6) (2020) 417.

[25] Z. Li, J. Yu, X. Li, Y. Li, W. Dai, L. Shen, L. Mou, Z. Pu, PNet: an efficient network for pneumonia detection, in: 2019 12th International Congress on Image and Signal Processing, BioMedical Engineering and Informatics (CISP-BMEI), IEEE, 2019, pp. 1–5.

[26] G. Liang, L. Zheng, A transfer learning method with deep residual network for pediatric pneumonia diagnosis, Comput. Methods Prog. Biomed. 187 (2020) 104964.

[27] K. El Asnaoui, Y. Chawki, Using X-ray images and deep learning for automated detection of coronavirus disease, J. Biomol. Struct. Dyn. (2020) 1–12.

[28] I.D. Apostolopoulos, T.A. Mpesiana, Covid-19: automatic detection from x-ray images utilizing transfer learning with convolutional neural networks, Phys. Eng. Sci. Med. 43 (2) (2020) 635–640.

[29] J. Civit-Masot, F. Luna-Perejón, M. Domínguez Morales, A. Civit, Deep learning system for COVID-19 diagnosis aid using X-ray pulmonary images, Appl. Sci. 10 (13) (2020) 4640.

[30] P.K. Sethy, S.K. Behera, Detection of coronavirus disease (covid-19) based on deep features, Preprints 2020030300 (2020) 2020.

[31] T. Ozturk, M. Talo, E.A. Yildirim, U.B. Baloglu, O. Yildirim, U.R. Acharya, Automated detection of COVID-19 cases using deep neural networks with X-ray images, Comput. Biol. Med. 121 (2020) 103792.

[32] JSRT dataset. http://db.jsrt.or.jp/eng.php.

[33] S. Jaeger, S. Candemir, S. Antani, Y.X.J. Wáng, P.X. Lu, G. Thoma, Two public chest X-ray datasets for computer-aided screening of pulmonary diseases, Quant. Imaging Med. Surg. 4 (6) (2014) 475.

[34] MC dataset. http://archive.nlm.nih.gov/repos/chestImages.php".

[35] Shenzhen dataset. http://archive.nlm.nih.gov/repos/chestImages.php".

[36] RSNA dataset. https://www.kaggle.com/c/rsna-pneumonia-detection-challenge".

[37] NIH dataset. https://nihcc.app.box.com/v/ChestXray-NIHCC".

[38] Kaggle chest-xray dataset. https://www.kaggle.com/paultimothymooney/chest-xray-pneumonia".

[39] SIRM COVID19 dataset. https://www.sirm.org/en/category/articles/covid-19-database/".

[40] J.P. Cohen, P. Morrison, L. Dao, K. Roth, T.Q. Duong, M. Ghassemi, Covid-19 image data collection: prospective predictions are the future. arXiv preprint arXiv:2006.11988, 2020.

[41] COVID19 dataset. https://github.com/ieee8023/covid-chestxray-dataset".

[42] COVID19 radiography dataset. https://www.kaggle.com/tawsifurrahman/covid19-radiography-database".

[43] Mendeley dataset. https://data.mendeley.com/datasets/rscbjbr9sj/3".

[44] COVID19 and pneumonia dataset. https://public.roboflow.com/classification/covid-19-and-pneumonia-scans.

[45] M.E. Chowdhury, T. Rahman, A. Khandakar, R. Mazhar, M.A. Kadir, Z.B. Mahbub, K.R. Islam, M.S. Khan, A. Iqbal, N. Al-Emadi, M.B.I. Reaz, Can AI help in screening viral and COVID-19 pneumonia? arXiv preprint arXiv:2003.13145, 2020.

Methodology adopted for designing of computer-aided classification systems for chest radiographs

3.1 Introduction

In this chapter a brief overview of the computer-aided classification (CAC) system for chest radiographs designed in this book are given as well as a general overview to the need for CAC systems specifically for chest radiographs, the importance of CAC systems in current scenarios due to the wide spread of COVID-19. The different approaches of designing CAC systems have been discussed with respect to the type of convolution neural network (CNN) used and the number of output classes. This chapter describes the dataset used for designing the CAC systems, the different augmentation techniques, and the motivation for dataset augmentation. The implementation details discussed include the hardware and software requirements, installing the Deep Learning Toolbox, and the various hyper-parameters such as the activation function, epoch, batch size, learning rate, optimizer, and so on that play an important role in learning of a deep learning-based model. The code snippets of the different augmentation techniques aim at giving a better understanding to the programmatic implementation of data augmentation, specifically for chest radiographs.

3.2 What is a CAC system?

A CAC system, as the name suggests, is a computer-based system that facilitates the medical practitioners to take decisions quickly and more efficiently. The medical images have immense amounts of data that the doctors need to assess and evaluate in order to determine the presence of an abnormality. This process is time-consuming whereas the medical practitioners intend at performing the same task in a short span so that timely diagnosis could lead to timely treatment thereby saving the life of critical patients. A CAC system with a purpose to detect abnormalities in medical images includes multiple components such as preprocessing of the input of medical images, the segmentation of the region of interest (ROI), feature extraction, and classification. It is not mandatory that all CAC system designs include every component discussed. The components of any computer-aided system depend on the task they are being designed for. A segmentation-based computer-aided system would focus on segmentation of the ROI whereas a classification-based computer-aided system may or may not perform segmentation. Fig. 3.1 shows some of the basic components of a CAC system.

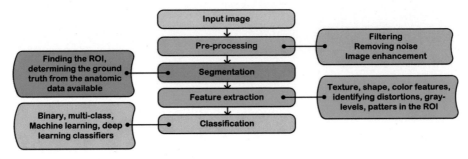

FIG. 3.1

Schematic representation of the components of a computer-aided classification (CAC) system.

3.3 Need for CAC systems

CAC systems in medical imaging have flourished immensely over the span of several years. Ever-improving software as well as hardware specifications and the advancements in the quality of imaging modalities have contributed to the successful design of these CAC systems. Some of the major reasons for the increase in need for CAC systems can be stated as follows:

- **Overcome observational oversights:** One of the major driving forces for the increased need for CAC systems is the aim to overcome observational oversights of the medical practitioners and surpass the limitations of human observers in interpreting medical images.
- **Reduce error in medical image interpretation:** Another limitation is the error and false negative as well as false positive rates of screening different medical images. Hence CAC systems aim at reducing the errors that are not possible to handle at a human end.
- **Increase in detection of diseases:** For disease detection, different medical imaging modalities are used. Each disease has its own characteristic features that are essential for correct diagnosis. However, some of these features may be missed by the human eye. Here the mathematical descriptors are capable of detecting and carefully analyzing these features. This plays an important role in efficient and early diagnosis of diseases.
- **Double reading:** CAC systems often reduce the concept of double reading by another medical practitioner, which is nothing but consulting another radiologist for a second opinion or confirmation on the observation done by the first radiologist. Here CAC systems can reduce the need for double readings.

Although CAC systems cannot substitute medical practitioners, they can ease their work by helping them in becoming better decision makers.

3.4 Need for CAC systems for chest radiographs

The differential diagnosis of chest radiographs is a challenging task even for experienced and skilled radiologists. The appearance of both pneumonia and COVID-19 on a chest radiograph is similar (cloudy appearance or ground glass opacity), and it is difficult for even an experienced radiologist to distinguish between them by simply looking at a chest radiograph. Since COVID-19 is a recent pandemic on which multiple studies are still being conducted with an aim to improve the diagnosis and analyze the key features that can play vital roles in distinguishing COVID-19 from pneumonia. However, the features that are not distinguishable to naked human eye can be easily detected by the mathematical descriptors.

Therefore, there lies significant motivation among the community of researchers with an aim to develop and improve the quality of CAC systems for differential diagnosis between chest radiographs. Some of the major reasons CAC systems are needed for chest radiographs can be stated as follows:

- **Overcome complexity of interpretation of chest radiographs:** The chest radiographs provide immense amounts of information about the health of a patient. Overlying tissues increase the complexity of radiographs making it difficult for medical practitioners to interpret such visually complex information correctly and precisely. This often leads to misdetection and misdiagnosis of diseases even by the most experienced and skilled radiologists. In some cases the contrast between the lesions and the surrounding area is so low that it is invisible to the naked human eye; however, these minor contrast changes can be efficiently detected by mathematical algorithms and descriptors.
- **Similar appearance of pneumonia and COVID-19 on a chest radiograph:** Both pneumonia and COVID-19 appear similar when observed on a chest radiograph even to an experienced radiologist. Both have a cloudy appearance often referred to as ground glass opacity and is commonly called the hazy lung region. Since COVID-19 is spreading worldwide at an immense rate and is a dangerous disease, efficient and early detection plays vital role. Here the CAC systems designed using various machine learning and deep learning algorithms can be highly beneficial.
- **Need of the hour:** The rate at which COVID-19 is spreading and the medium through which it spreads makes it a highly perilous disease. It can be transmitted through droplets in the air or on surfaces, coughing, sneezing, and so forth. Studies are still being carried out to determine the significant features so that the radiologists can correctly diagnose and differentiate between pneumonia and COVID-19 by looking at chest radiographs or CT images. Here CAC systems can be designed and trained on the limited dataset available to help in correctly diagnosing and differentiating between the diseases based on the features extracted by the mathematical descriptors from the chest radiographs that are not visible to the radiologists.

3.5 Types of classifier designs for CAC systems

Computer-aided detection and CAC are often referred to as two different terms where detection focuses on pattern recognition, identifying charts, and guarded features that are not visible to the human eye with an aim to assist radiologists in reducing misdiagnosis, whereas the term computer-aided classification includes all the tasks performed by computer-aided detection with an additional task of predicting the likelihood of a feature that represents a particular disease.

The main aim of any CAC system design is to improve the interpretation of images with significantly reduced amounts of error. The development of CAC systems is not an easy task as the best results are obtained through the analysis carried out by the medical practitioners in real time. Obtaining the reference standard of the truth is highly labor intensive and requires an immense amount of effort

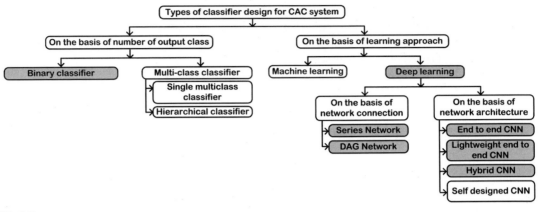

FIG. 3.2

Types of classifier designs for CAC systems.

in data collection and massive investment of time. Different researchers propose different methodologies for designing CAC systems; however, there is no one specific foolproof design paradigm. Some of the common approaches used to design CAC systems are discussed in this section. Fig. 3.2 shows the different types of approaches to designing classifiers for CAC system, the classifier designs in gray are used in the present work.

3.5.1 On the basis of number output classes

CAC systems can be designed on the basis of the numbers of output classes or the number of classes in which the data is divided into and labeled for the task of supervised classification.

(a) Binary classifier: This type of CAC system deals with binary class classification of the images, such as benign/malignant or Normal/Abnormal [1–17]. In the present work the CAC systems are designed based on this approach focusing on the classification of chest radiographs into Normal and Pneumonia. Fig. 3.3 shows the schematic representation of different binary class classifiers.

(b) Multiclass classifier: These types of CAC system designs have more than two class labels. The class labels represent the number of output classes. This can either be a simple three-class classifier dealing with three classifications of the input data or it could be a hierarchical structure. The broad division of a multiclass classifier is discussed as follows:

  (i) Single three-class classifier: This type of CAC systems deals with a simple three-class classification of the images, such as Normal, Pneumonia, and COVID-19 for chest radiographs [9, 18–22]. Fig. 3.4 shows the schematic representation of a simple three-class classifier.

  (ii) Hierarchical classifier: This type of CAC system design first classifies the images into some classes and then further classifies them into subclasses, such as the classification of chest radiographs into Normal/Abnormal then further classifying Abnormal images into Pneumonia/COVID-19. Fig. 3.5 is a schematic representation of a hierarchical classifier where the classifier 1 and classifier 2 can be either a machine learning-based or a deep learning-based classifier.

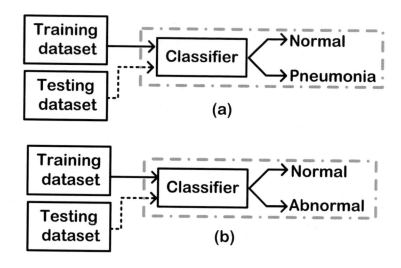

FIG. 3.3

Schematic representation of types of binary classifier.

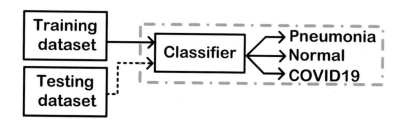

FIG. 3.4

Schematic representation of a three-class classifier.

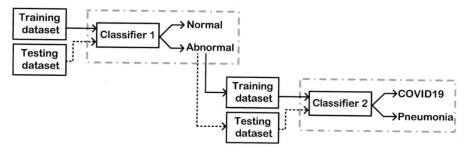

FIG. 3.5

Schematic representation of a hierarchical classifier.

3.5.2 On the basis of learning approach

CAC systems are designed with an aim to search for the same features that a radiologist would look for in a medical image to perform the diagnosis. Each disease has its own unique identifiers that enable the radiologists to correctly diagnose it, such as for diagnosis of pneumonia the radiologist looks at chest radiographs to find opacity of the lungs and see pulmonary densities. For other lung-related diseases features such as sphericity of the lung nodules are searched for [23–29]. Similarly for breast cancer the radiologist looks at mammograms or ultrasound images of breasts for features such as spiculated mass, nonspiculated mass distortion, micro-calcifications, and asymmetries [25, 30, 31]. All of these features can sometimes be unclear or invisible to the human eye, and here various mathematical algorithms play a vital role. These mathematical descriptors or algorithms can identify even minor differences in the images and therefore are highly useful in such cases.

The most popular CAC system design learning approaches are machine learning-based algorithms and deep learning-based algorithms. Both of the approaches are discussed here.

(a) Machine learning: This learning approach is used where the features of the images can be manually mined and fed to the algorithm [32–34]. The machine learning methods are of three types:

  (i) Supervised learning: For supervised learning the training data has well-labeled outputs for their corresponding input values. This method aims at mapping a mathematical relationship between the input and the well-labeled output. The output data has categorical values in case of classification tasks and continuous numerical values in case of regression tasks; depending on the task, the output data value type changes. Some supervised machine learning algorithms are k-NN and support vector machines (SVMs). [35–37].

  (ii) Unsupervised learning: In unsupervised learning the labeled outputs are not available. This learning method determines a functional representation of the hidden characteristics of the input data. Some unsupervised machine learning algorithms are PCA and cluster analysis [34, 38–45].

  (iii) Reinforcement learning: Reinforcement learning is primarily concerned with sequential decision problems. It is not popularly used in medical imaging-related problems and tasks as it learns by trial and error and has a tendency to affect future patient treatments with bias [46, 47].

The machine learning approach is not used for the design of chest radiographs since they depend greatly on the handcrafted features by the experts. This manual extraction of features is not optimal, as the data varies from patient to patient and sometimes many of the otherwise highly useful features for classification are lost.

(b) Deep learning: The deep learning approach is more reliable as compared to machine learning algorithms as it offers automatic feature extraction, and the labor intensive work of manual feature extraction is no more a concern. It is a subsidiary of supervised machine learning algorithms but is most effective and has proven to give promising results [48–52].

A branch of machine learning that primarily deals in processing data, trying to mimic the thinking process and develop abstractions by employing algorithms, is often defined as deep learning. It makes the use of multiple layers of algorithms with an aim to process the data, understanding human speech, and recognize objects visually. The most popularly known algorithms are the CNN and the deep convolution neural network (DCNN). The collected information passes through each layer of the network satisfying the temporal dependencies by serving the results of the previous layer as an input to the succeeding layer. The very first layer of the network is known as the input layer, whereas the last layer provides the output; hence, it is called the output layer. The layers in between the input and the output are known as hidden layers. Each layer can be defined by an identical, uniform, and unvarying algorithm that simply implements similar kinds of activation functions. An additional popular and most important trait of deep learning is the technique of feature extraction. This is done by using various algorithms to extract the features automatically with an aim to build a significant set of features of the input data essentially for the purpose of training the neural networks or deep networks as well as facilitating efficient and meaningful learning.

In the present work for the design of CAC systems for chest radiographs, the deep learning-based approach is chosen as it can extract those features from the X-ray images that are not visible to the human eye.

3.6 Deep learning-based CAC system design

As previously discussed, chest radiographs provide radiologists with huge amounts of information and this information varies from patient to patient, which is sometimes difficult to process manually. Therefore, a deep learning-based approach helps by automating feature extraction and learning those features to perform correct diagnoses. Deep learning-based CAC systems are discussed in this chapter, and the schematic representation of the broad distribution is shown in Fig. 3.6.

3.6.1 On the basis of network connection

(a) Series network: In a series network all the layers forming the network are piled up on each other and arranged one after the other in a contiguous manner. Each layer has an input only from its immediate previous layer and gives output to only its immediate next layer. Here each layer has access parameters of only two layers. Some of the series CNN models are AlexNet, VGG16, VGG19, and DarkNet. Fig. 3.7 gives a schematic representation of series network.

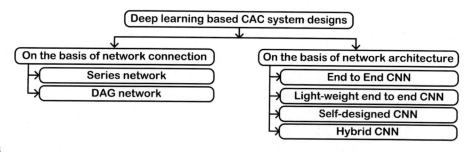

FIG. 3.6

Types of deep learning-based CAC system designs. *CNN*, convolution neural network; *DAG*, directed acyclic graph.

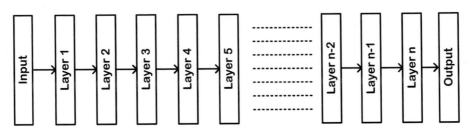

FIG. 3.7

Schematic representation of series network.

(b) DAG network: The DAG network stands for Directed Acyclic Graphs as the arrangement of the layers of the network is similar to directed acyclic graphs. These networks have directed connections to multiple layers. The layers of the network have input from multiple layers and gives **output** to multiple layers. Some of the DAG networks are SqueezeNet, GoogLeNet, ResNet50, ResNet101, ResNet18, InceptionV3, DenseNet201, NASNet-Large, and NASNet-Mobile. Fig. 3.8 gives a schematic representation of a DAG network.

3.6.2 On the basis of network architecture

(a) End-to-end CNN: This type of CAC system is designed by using a single CNN model that can specialize in predicting the output from the inputs. This often results in the development of a complex state-of-the-art system. These end-to-end systems (E2E systems) are very expensive; hence, many industries are unenthusiastic about their use and application. The primary idea of utilizing a single CNN model for performing a specific task has multiple obstacles such as requirement of enormous amounts of training data, inefficient training, and difficulties in performing validation of the CAC system designed. Another major drawback faced while designing the E2E CAC systems is that in worst-case scenarios the network might not learn at all, hence training such systems is inefficient and dicey. Fig. 3.9 shows an E2E CNN-based CAC system design.

(b) Lightweight E2E CNN: Lightweight network architecture has certain properties that are highly desirable: the maximized use of balanced convolutions preferably equivalent to the channel width; analyze the cost of convolutions and the combinations being used; the reduction of degree of fragmentation; and the decrease in the number of element-wise operations. All of these properties combined results in the overall reduction of memory use and an immense increase in processing time. Some of the lightweight CNN models include SqueezeNet, ShuffleNet, MobileNetV2, and NASNet. Fig. 3.10 shows a lightweight E2E CNN-based CAC system design.

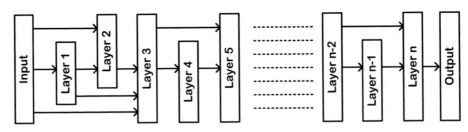

FIG. 3.8

Schematic representation of a DAG network.

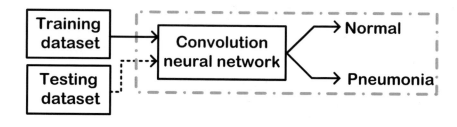

FIG. 3.9

Schematic representation of end-to-end CNN-based CAC.

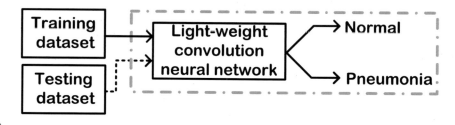

FIG. 3.10

Schematic representation of a lightweight end-to-end CNN-based CAC system.

(c) **Self-designed CNN:** As the name suggests, the CAC systems are designed using the CNN that have been designed by the researcher themselves.

(d) **Hybrid CNN:** The idea behind hybrid CNN-based CAC system is to use machine learning classifiers for performing predictions on the input data. The aim is to use CNN for automatic feature extraction and then feed these deep feature sets to the machine learning classifiers to perform prediction or classification. Another approach is the fusion of the CNN-based deep features and the handcrafted feature from the input data, then feeding this combination to the machine learning classifier. Some of the popularly used machine learning classifiers in hybrid systems are SVMs. The present work also focuses on designing hybrid CAC systems for chest radiographs where the E2e CNN are used as deep feature extractors and then PCA-SVM, ANFC-LH like machine learning algorithms are used to perform the differential binary classification. Fig. 3.11 shows a hybrid CAC system design.

3.7 Workflow adopted in the present work

CAC system designs can be broadly considered of two types: (a) CNN-based CAC system designs, which includes the design of CAC systems using different series and DAG networks as well as lightweight CNN models; and (b) CNN-based CAC systems using deep feature extraction, which includes the CAC system design using the series and DAG networks as deep feature extractors and then applying the machine learning classifiers PCA-SVM and ANFC-LH.

The schematic representation of the workflow adopted in the present work is shown in Fig. 3.12. The workflow primarily includes the dataset generation, which is described in detail further in this

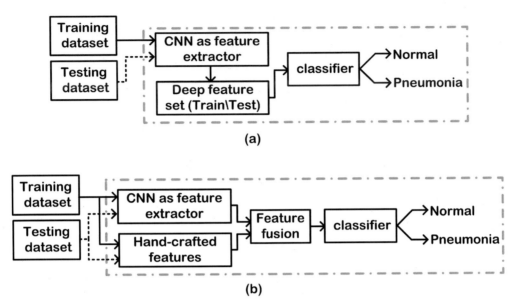

FIG. 3.11

Schematic representation of hybrid CAC: (A) CNN as deep feature extractor; (B) CNN as deep feature extractor and feature fusion with handcrafted features.

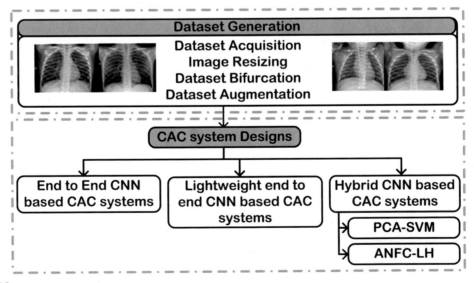

FIG. 3.12

Schematic representation of the workflow adopted in the present work. *CNN,* convolution neural network; *PCA-SVM,* principal component analysis-support vector machine; *ANFC-LH,* adaptive neuro-fuzzy classifier-linguistic hedges.

chapter, followed by the various experiments conducted to design different CNN-based CAC systems explained in detail in the upcoming chapters.

The experiments have been conducted using a comprehensive image dataset of 200 chest radiographs with cases of the image classes: Normal and Pneumonia. The image database comprises of 100 Normal chest radiographs and 100 Pneumonia chest radiographs. Further bifurcation of the dataset is described further in this chapter. The present work focuses on the design of CAC systems for the efficient diagnosis of pneumonia using chest radiographs, which includes the foremost step of dataset generation. The schematic representation of the dataset generated to be used in the design of the CAC systems is shown in Fig. 3.13.

The main task of CAC system design in the present work includes the following experiments: (a) designing CNN-based CAC systems for chest radiographs using AlexNet, ResNet-18, and GoogLeNet to identify the best performing CNN model; (b) designing a hybrid CAC system for chest radiographs using the CNN model with best performance, deep feature extraction, and ANFC-LH classifier; (c) designing a CAC system for chest radiographs using the CNN model with best performance, deep feature extraction, and PCA-SVM classifier, (d) designing lightweight CNN-based CAC systems for chest radiographs using SqueezeNet. ShuffleNet, and MobileNetV2 to identify the best performing lightweight CNN model; (e) designing a CAC system for chest radiographs using the lightweight CNN model with best performance, deep feature extraction, and ANFC-LH classifier; (f) designing a hybrid CAC system

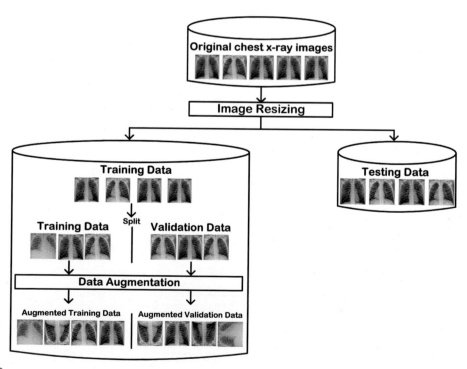

FIG. 3.13

Schematic representation of dataset generation for chest radiographs.

for chest radiographs using the lightweight CNN model with best performance, deep feature extraction, and PCA-SVM classifier. These can be briefly described as follows:

(a) Designing CNN-based CAC systems for chest radiographs using AlexNet, ResNet-18 and GoogLeNet to identify the best performing CNN model: This CAC system design constitutes the first four experiments discussed in detail in Chapter 4. It deals with training the AlexNet, ResNet18, and GoogLeNet CNN models in the transfer learning mode as well as the decision fusion technique for the binary classification of chest radiographs into Normal and Pneumonia class. The CNN model with best performance is then used further in (b) and (c) as a deep feature extractor, which is discussed in detail in Chapters 5 and 6, respectively.

Fig. 3.14 shows the schematic representation of the CNN-based CAC system design for classification of chest radiographs by training AlexNet, GoogLeNet, and ResNet18 to identify the best performing CNN model.

On the basis of the experiments conducted for training the CNN models to design the CAC systems, it is concluded that the GoogLeNet CNN model performs best for the binary classification of chest radiographs with 90.00% accuracy. This GoogLeNet CNN model further acts as a deep feature extractor and is used for designing the CAC system with different machine learning classifiers in (b) and (c).

(b) Designing a CAC system for chest radiographs using the CNN model with best performance, deep feature extraction and ANFC-LH classifier: This CAC system design is the fifth experiment and is discussed in detail in Chapter 5. It deals with using the CNN model with best performance from (a) as a deep feature extractor and then performing the binary classification of the chest radiographs using the ANFC-LH classifier.

Fig. 3.15 shows the schematic representation of designing a CAC system for deep feature extraction using the CNN model with best performance and ANFC-LH machine learning classifier.

On the basis of the experiments conducted in (a), the GoogLeNet CNN model is the best performing CNN for the classification of chest radiographs. Therefore it is used as a deep feature extractor that forms a deep feature set (DFS), which is the input for the feature selection using the correlation-based feature selection technique. This results in a feature set with a limited number of relevant features

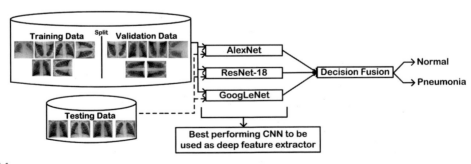

FIG. 3.14

Schematic representation of CNN-based CAC system design for classification of chest radiographs by training AlexNet, ResNet-18, and GoogLeNet to identify the best performing CNN model. *CNN*, convolution neural network.

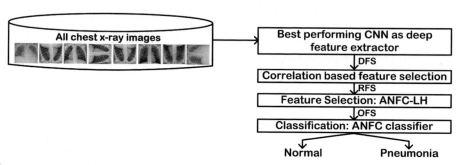

FIG. 3.15

Schematic representation of designing a CAC system for deep feature extraction using the CNN model with best performance and ANFC-LH. *CNN*, convolution neural network; *DFS*, deep feature set; *ANFC-LH*, adaptive neuro-fuzzy classifier-linguistic hedges; *RFS*, reduced feature set; *OFS*, optimal feature set.

called the reduced feature set (RFS), which is additionally subjected to ANFC-LH-based feature selection to further reduce the feature set to the minimum and most relevant features. The resultant optimal feature set (OFS) is projected to the neuro-fuzzy classifier called the ANFC classifier. The CAC system designed yields 93.00% accuracy for the two-class classification of chest radiographs.

(c) **Designing a CAC system for chest radiographs using the CNN model with best performance, deep feature extraction, and PCA-SVM classifier:** This CAC system design forms the sixth experiment and is discussed in detail in Chapter 6. It deals with using the CNN model with best performance from (a) as a deep feature extractor and then performing the binary classification of the chest radiographs using the PCA-SVM classifier.

Fig. 3.16 shows the schematic representation of designing a CAC system for deep feature extraction using the CNN model with best performance and PCA-SVM.

On the basis of the experiments conducted in (a), the GoogLeNet CNN model is the best performing CNN for the classification of chest radiographs. Therefore, it is used as a deep feature extractor that forms a DFS that is the input for the correlation-based feature selection followed by feature

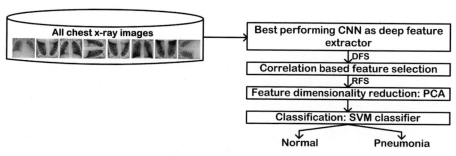

FIG. 3.16

Schematic representation of designing a CAC system for deep feature extraction using the CNN model with best performance and PCA-SVM. *CNN*, convolution neural network; *DFS*, deep feature set; *PCA*, principal component analysis; *SVM*, support vector machine; *RFS*, reduced feature set.

dimensionality reduction by PCA. The resultant feature set is projected to the SVM classifier. The CAC system designed yields 91.00% accuracy for the binary class classification of chest radiographs.

(d) Designing a lightweight CNN -based CAC system for chest radiographs using SqueezeNet, ShuffleNet and MobileNetV2 to identify the best performing lightweight CNN model:
This CAC system design constitutes the seventh to tenth experiment and is discussed in detail in Chapter 7. It deals with training SqueezeNet, ShuffleNet, and MobileNetV2 lightweight CNN models in the transfer learning mode as well as decision fusion technique for the binary classification of chest radiographs into Normal and Pneumonia class. The best performing lightweight CNN model is then used further in (e) and (f) as a deep feature extractor.

Fig. 3.17 shows the schematic representation of a lightweight CNN-based CAC system design for classification of chest radiographs by training SqueezeNet, ShuffleNet, and MobleNetV2 to identify the best performing lightweight CNN model.

On the basis of experiments conducted for training the lightweight CNN models to design the CAC systems it is concluded that the MobileNetV2 lightweight CNN model performs best for the binary classification of chest radiographs into Normal and Pneumonia class with 94.00%. This lightweight MobileNetV2 CNN model further acts as a deep feature extractor for (e) and (f) to design CAC systems using different machine learning-based classifiers.

(e) Designing a hybrid CAC system for chest radiographs using the lightweight CNN model with best performance, deep feature extraction, and ANFC-LH classifier: This CAC system design is the 11th experiment and is discussed in detail in Chapter 8. It deals with using the lightweight MobileNetV2 CNN model from (d) as a deep feature extractor and then performing the binary classification of the chest radiographs using the ANFC-LH classifier.

Fig. 3.18 shows the schematic representation of designing a CAC system for deep feature extraction using the lightweight MobileNetV2 CNN model and ANFC-LH classifier.

On the basis of the experiment carried out in (d), the lightweight MobileNetV2 CNN model acts as a deep feature extractor to design a CAC system using the ANFC-LH classifier. The DFS is formed by the MobileNetV2 CNN model, which on application of CFS forms the RFS. This RFS acts as an input

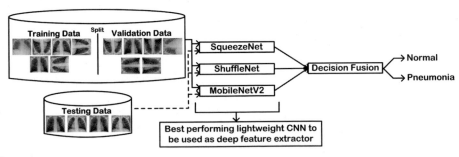

FIG. 3.17

Schematic representation of lightweight CNN-based CAC system design for classification of chest radiographs by training SqueezeNet, ShuffleNet, and MobileNetV2 to identify the best performing lightweight CNN model.

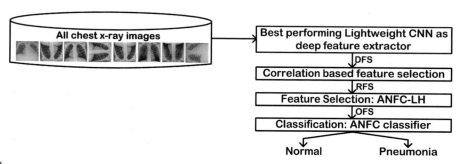

FIG. 3.18

Schematic representation of designing a CAC system for deep feature extraction using the best performing lightweight CNN model and ANFC-LH. *CNN*, convolution neural network; *DFS*, deep feature set; *ANFC-LH*, adaptive neuro-fuzzy classifier linguistic hedges; *RFS*, reduced feature set; *OFS*, optimal feature set.

to the feature selection performed by ANFC-LH resulting in an OFS. The binary classification of chest radiographs is performed by the ANFC classifier and yields 95.00% accuracy.

(f) Designing a CAC system for chest radiographs using the lightweight CNN model with best performance, deep feature extraction, and PCA-SVM classifier: This CAC system design is the final experiment and is discussed in detail in Chapter 9. It deals with using the lightweight MobileNetV2 CNN model from (d) as a deep feature extractor and then performing the binary classification of the chest radiographs using the PCA-SVM classifier.

Fig. 3.19 shows the schematic representation of designing a CAC system for deep feature extraction using the lightweight MobileNetV2 CNN model and PCA-SVM.

On the basis of the experiment carried out in (d), the lightweight MobileNetV2 CNN model acts as a deep feature extractor to design a CAC system using the SVM classifier. The DFS is formed by the MobileNetV2 CNN model, which on application of CFS forms the RFS. This RFS acts as an input for feature dimensionality reduction performed by PCA. The binary classification of chest radiographs is performed by the SVM classifier and yields 95.00% accuracy.

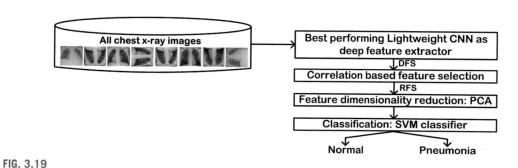

FIG. 3.19

Schematic representation of designing a CAC system for deep feature extraction using the best performing lightweight CNN model and PCA-SVM. *CNN*, convolution neural network; *DFS*, deep feature set; *PCA*, principal component analysis; *SVM*, support vector machine; *RFS*, reduced feature set.

3.8 Implementation details

This includes a description of the hardware and software requirements for carrying out the present work.

3.8.1 Hardware and software specifications

The present work has been implemented on an HP Z4G4 PC functioning on a Windows operating system with Intel Xeon W-series, octa-core processor, NVIDIA Quadro P620 2GB GPU. The system has a 2TB hard drive with 128 GB RAM. The software used for the successful implementation of the present work was MATLABR2020a and the MATLAB Deep Learning Toolbox.

3.8.2 MATLAB Deep Learning Toolbox

The MATLAB Deep Learning Toolbox offers a framework that enables the users to implement deep neural networks, Pre-trained networks, and different deep learning-based algorithms. This toolbox offers various built-in features to make the implementation of deep learning efficient. After installing this toolbox, one can easily implement CNNs, time-series based deep networks, GAN networks, and more. It offers easy design of deep neural networks by using the network designer application called the Deep Network Designer. Another important feature is the downloading of packages to implement Pre-trained networks. Installing MATLAB automatically installs the Deep Learning Toolbox; in the event it does not install automatically, one can install it manually by following some simple steps. The steps for installation of Deep Learning Toolbox are as follows:

Step 1: Open the MATLABR2020a application installed on your system.
Step 2: Go to the Add-On Explorer. Fig. 3.20 shows the "Add-On Explorer" symbol in the MATLABR2020a task bar.

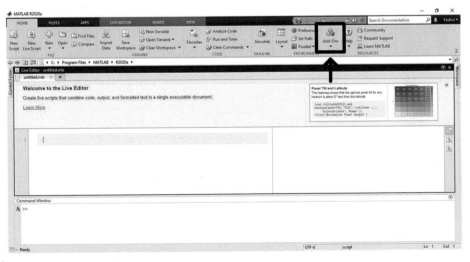

FIG. 3.20

Screenshot showing the Add-On Explorer.

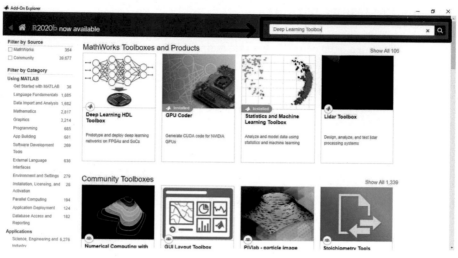

FIG. 3.21

Screenshot showing the search for the Deep Learning Toolbox.

Step 3: Search for "Deep Learning Toolbox." Fig. 3.21 shows the search bar of MATLABR2020a. **Step 4: Download** and install the Deep Learning Toolbox by MathWorks. Fig. 3.22 shows the installed Deep Learning Toolbox in MATLABR2020a.

In case of any problems in following these steps, then one can search in the "Search documentation" tab or the Help tab to obtain instructions on how to install and use the required packages and toolboxes. MATLAB provides detailed documentation that can be accessed by anyone and are just a search away.

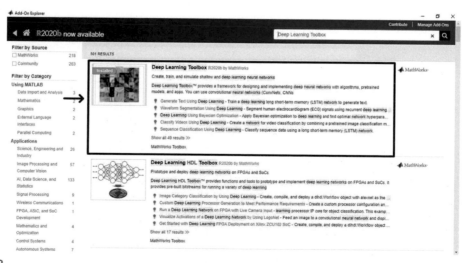

FIG. 3.22

Screenshot showing the successful install of Deep Learning Toolbox.

3.8.3 Installing Pre-trained networks

The present work uses the Pre-trained series and DAG networks for designing the CAC systems. In order to use these Pre-trained deep neural networks, their packages need to be installed separately. The generalized steps to install a Pre-trained CNN are given as follows:

Step 1: Open the MATLABR2020a application installed on your system.
Step 2: Go to the Add-On Explorer as shown previously while installing the Deep Learning Toolbox.
Step 3: Search for the Pre-trained network you wish to install and use.
Step 4: Download and install the network package provided by the MathWorks Deep Learning Toolbox Team.

Example: The steps to download Pre-trained AlexNet CNN model is as follows:

Step 1: Open the MATLABR2020a application installed on your system.
Step 2: Go to the Add-On Explorer.
Step 3: Search for "AlexNet." Fig. 3.23 shows the search bar of MATLABR2020a to search for AlexNet CNN model.
Step 4: Download and install the network package provided by the MathWorks Deep Learning Toolbox Team titled "Deep Learning Toolbox Model for AlexNet Network by MathWorks Deep Learning Toolbox Team." Fig. 3.24 shows the installed AlexNet CNN model in MATLABR2020a.

You can check whether the network package has been successfully installed or not by typing the Pre-trained network name in the command window of MATLAB2020a. If the network has been installed successfully, it shows the details of the network architecture. Otherwise, it shows a prompt to go to the Add-On Explorer to install the package. One can install the package by following the steps or through the command window. After installing all the packages, you are ready to implement your work on MATLAB2020a. Fig. 3.25 shows how one can check whether the model is installed through command prompt of MATLABR2020a.

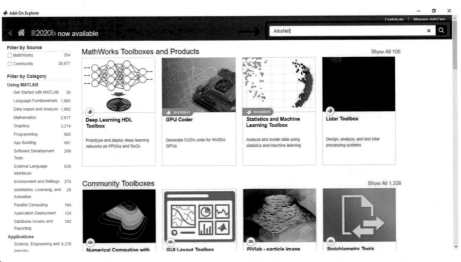

FIG. 3.23

Screenshot showing the search for Pre-trained AlexNet CNN model.

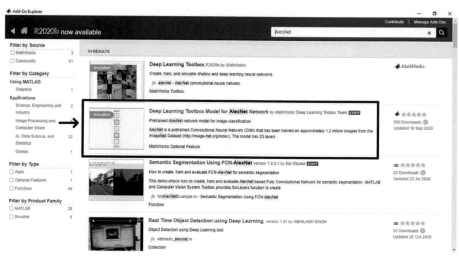

FIG. 3.24

Screenshot showing the successful download of Pre-trained AlexNet CNN model.

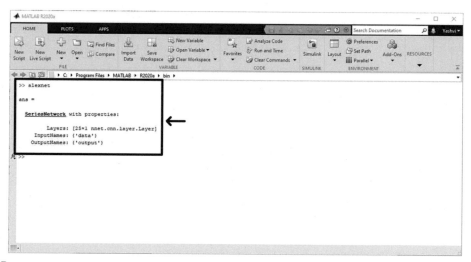

FIG. 3.25

Screenshot showing the successful download of Pre-trained AlexNet CNN Model through command window.

3.8.4 Key hyperparameters of deep learning-based networks

A hyperparameter is defined as a configuration that cannot be estimated from the data. It is to be specified by the user prior to training the network. Since the best value of hyperparameters are not known, one has to iterate through a large number of combinations. These trials may result in application of rule of thumb or brute force methods to gain the values of hyperparameters that give best results. The key hyperparameters of deep learning-based networks include the learning rate, activation function, epochs, batch size, and number of hidden layers [53]. Fig. 3.26 shows the key hyperparameters.

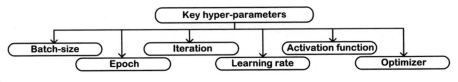

FIG. 3.26

Types of key hyperparameters.

Some of the hyperparameters that are crucial in training a network are discussed as follows:

(a) Batch size

The batch size is simply defined as the numbers of data samples that have to be processed before the internal network parameters get updated. In other words, the number of training samples present in a single (forward + backward pass). Another approach of understanding a batch size is to consider it analogous to a for-loop that is iterating over a single sample or multiple samples and making predictions. At the end of each batch, the predictions are compared with the expected outputs and an error is calculated. This error is back-propagated to update the model parameters and improve the predictions. A training dataset is divided into one or more batches depending on the total number of training samples. Each batch is sometimes called a mini-batch.

The batch size is a carefully chosen numerical value that can evenly divide the training dataset into multiple batches of same size. Selection of the batch size in such a way makes sure that no training sample is left, the batches do not have uneven number of samples, and the network is trained efficiently without any bias.

Example: If a dataset has 10,000 images that have been split into mini-batches of size 1000 images each, then the total number of batches is 10.

The batch size is of three types depending on the number of samples in each batch:

(i) Batch gradient descent: When the entire training dataset forms one single batch, the learning algorithm is called batch gradient descent.

Batch size = All the training samples

(ii) Stochastic gradient descent: When the batch is the size of one sample, the learning algorithm is called stochastic gradient descent.

Batch size = 1

(iii) Mini-batch gradient descent: When the batch size is more than one and less than the size of the training dataset, the learning algorithm is called mini-batch gradient descent.

(Batch size > 1) & (Batch size < All the training samples)

What if the training dataset is not evenly divisible by the batch size?

This does happen very often when training a deep learning model. It simply means that either the final batch has fewer samples than the other batches or some of the data samples are left and thereby not contributing to the process of training the network. To overcome this one can do the following:

Case 1: Final batch has fewer samples: In this scenario where the final batch has fewer samples as compared to other batches, one must change the batch size to a number that evenly divides the entire dataset to equal-sized batches or add more samples using the data augmentation techniques.

Case 2: Some samples are unused: In this scenario one can remove some samples from the dataset manually to match the batch size, add more samples using data augmentation, or change the batch size as in Case 1.

Often choosing a very large batch size results in the division of the training dataset into less batches, which is not optimal as the network may not attain generalization and might be poorly trained. On the other hand, choosing a very small batch size would result in too many batches and consume resources, such as time and memory. Both of these situations are not desirable; therefore, the batch size should be selected with utmost precision and care.

(b) Epoch

An epoch is defined as the number of times the entire dataset passes through the network and has the opportunity to update the network parameters. The number of epochs is another important hyperparameter that determines the number of times that the learning algorithm will work through the entire training dataset. One can consider an epoch analogous to for-loop that iterates over the batch size. The number of epochs is often chosen in a multiple of 10 to ease the plotting of line plots for the training progress. These line plots have the x-axis as the number of epochs and the y-axis as the training error or loss. These plots tend to hint at whether the network is overfitting, underfitting, or suitably fit for the desired task. Unlike batch size, the number of epochs can vary from one to infinity. One can run the algorithm for as long as desired and can also stop it as desired or using some criteria such as early-stopping (when there is no change in learning or a lack of change).

(c) Iteration

Iteration is defined as the number of times the parameters of the algorithm are updated. Here a single iteration is the number of passes that result in the gradient update. Each pass consists of the forward propagation of weights/input and backward propagation of error. The iterations are equivalent to the number of mini-batches. The completion of these iterations results in the finishing of a single epoch only.

Example: If a dataset has 10,000 images that have been split into mini-batches of size 1000 image each, then it takes 10 iterations to complete a single epoch.

(d) Learning rate

The learning rate is another essential hyperparameter that determines the amount of change to the model in response to the back-propagated error. It determines how slow or fast the network learns. If one chooses a value of learning rate that is too small, then the training could get stuck in one place. If one chooses a value of learning rate that is too large, then the model training might be unstable and nonoptimal. Hence, choosing an optimal learning rate is a trial-and-error process. Every individual has to adopt hit and trial as analytically calculating an optimal learning rate is not possible. However the range of values for choosing the learning rate lies between 10^{-6} and 1. The learning rate must not exceed 1 and should not be less than 10^{-6} [54]. Another approach could be to initially keep the learning rate large and then linearly decrease it and study the changes in the training of the model [22].

(e) Activation function

An activation function is a mathematical equation associated with each neuron that acts like a gate between the input and the output. It is used to determine the output of an artificial neural network. An activation function acts as a "firing" threshold for each neuron by determining whether a neuron should be activated or not based on the inputs of the neuron and the relevance of the input to the model predictions. They also play an important role by normalizing the output of each neuron thereby facilitating smooth predictions. They normalize the value of each prediction in between (1, 0) or (− 1, 1), depending on the type of activation function used. Fig. 3.27 shows the different types of activation functions.

There are three types of activation functions:

(i) Binary step activation function

As the name suggests, it is a binary function, that is, it performs binary class or two-class predictions and does not allow multivalue predictions. It is a threshold-based function where the neuron fires only if the input value is greater or smaller than the specified threshold. Fig. 3.28 shows the graphical representation of the binary step function.

(ii) Linear activation function

The only advantage that the linear function offers over the binary step function is that they allow multiclass predictions. They generate an output proportional to the input data. However, the linear activation function lacks the back propagation of the gradient, which is crucial for training the network. This activation function does not really contribute as the entire neural network can be simply replaced by just a single layer as the linear combination of all the linear function in different layers results in a linear function only. Fig. 3.29 shows the graphical representation of the linear activation function.

(iii) Nonlinear activation function

They are the most widely used type of activation function as they provide multiclass classification and facilitate the training model to generate complex mapping between the input and the output. The nonlinear activation function overcomes the issues faced with the other two activation functions, namely binary step function and linear activation function. The nonlinear activation function facilitates back propagation, and multiple hidden layers contribute to the learning of datasets loaded with complex information and make predictions with greater accuracies. Some of the popularly used nonlinear activation functions are as follows:

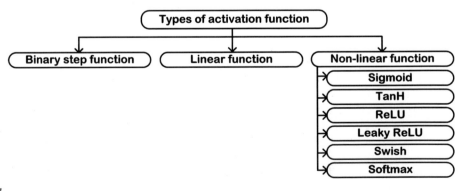

FIG. 3.27

Types of activation functions. *TanH*, hyperbolic tangent; *ReLU*, rectified linear unit.

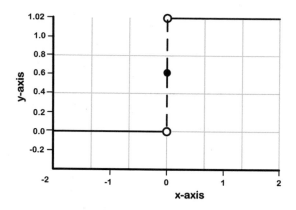

FIG. 3.28

Binary step function.

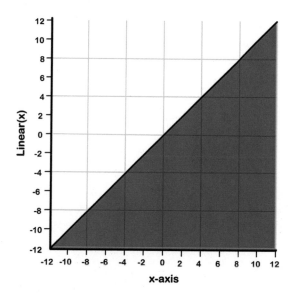

FIG. 3.29

Linear activation function.

(1) Sigmoid activation function: This is often referred to as the logistic activation function and generates the output values between (0, 1). This means that the sigmoid activation function normalizes the output of each neuron between 0 and 1. This nonlinear activation function is often not used due to its computational expense and the problem of vanishing gradient. The vanishing gradient is caused when the network refuses to learn extremely high or low input values or there is nearly no degree of change in the result of predictions. This function is also not symmetric around zero or the origin, that is, the sign of the output of each neuron is same. The mathematical expression of sigmoid function is given as:

$$f(x) = \frac{1}{\left(1+e^{-x}\right)}$$

Fig. 3.30 shows the graphical representation of the logistic function.

(2) **"tanh" activation function**: This is known as the hyperbolic tangent nonlinear activation function and is similar to sigmoid nonlinear activation function with the only difference being that it is symmetric around origin. The mathematical expression of tanh function is given as:

$$\tanh(x) = \frac{2}{\left(1+e^{-2x}\right)} - 1$$

$$\tanh(x) = \frac{\left(e^x - e^{-x}\right)}{\left(e^x + e^{-x}\right)}$$

Fig. 3.31 shows the graphical representation of the tanh function.

(3) **ReLU activation function**: This activation function is the most popular among all the nonlinear activation functions, especially for CNN. It is computationally highly efficient and does not have the problem of the vanishing gradient or any other problems associated with the symmetry around the origin. The mathematical expression of ReLU function is given as:

$$f(x) = \max(0,x)$$

The ReLU activation function works by predicting 0 for all negative input values and predicting the input itself for the positive input values. This results in a problem called dying ReLU, where the

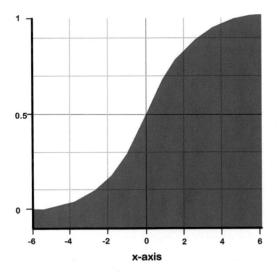

FIG. 3.30

Logistic activation function.

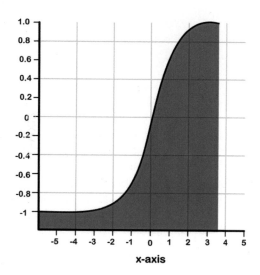

FIG. 3.31

"tanh" activation function.

negative values have 0 as the output, this 0 output causes some of the neurons to die completely and hence back propagation is not possible, resulting in the inability of the network to learn. Sometimes ReLU encounters the problem of exploding activations as the upper limit depends on the positive input value that can vary up to infinity. This results in highly unstable neurons or nodes. Fig. 3.32 shows the graphical representation of the ReLU function.

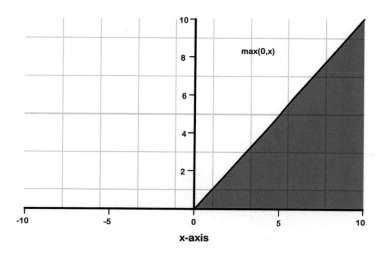

FIG. 3.32

ReLU activation function.

(4) Leaky ReLU activation function: This variation of the ReLU activation function overcomes the problem of dying ReLU. This is carried out by including another hyperparameter called α, which is mostly given a value near about 0.01. The leaky ReLU is mathematically given as:

$$f(x) = \max(\alpha x, x)$$

However in a case if $\alpha = 1$, then the leaky ReLU also behaves as normal ReLU. Therefore in leaky ReLU, α is never set to any value that is too close to 1.To overcome this issue, parametric ReLU is used. In parametric ReLU the value of α is given for each neuron and is often referred to as PReLU. Fig. 3.33 shows the graphical representation of the leaky ReLU function.

(5) **Swish activation function**: This is one of the recently discovered nonlinear activation functions by the researchers at Google. It is a self-gated activation function that performs slightly better than ReLU [55]. The mathematical expression for Swish activation function is given as:

$$f(x) = x \times \text{sigmoid}(x)$$

$$f(x) = x \times \frac{1}{\left(1 + e^{-x}\right)}$$

(6) **Softmax activation function**: This is used for classifying the inputs to multiple categories and is mostly used as the output layers of the CNN. It is often used as a multiclass classifier as it gives

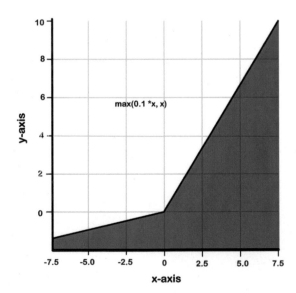

FIG. 3.33

Leaky ReLU activation function.

the probability of each input value being in a particular class. The mathematical expression of softmax activation function is given as:

$$S(x_i) = \frac{e^{x_i}}{\sum_{j=1}^{n} e^{x_j}}$$

(f) Optimizer

The optimizers determine the way the model makes updates to the network weights and the learning rate with an aim to reduce the errors and losses. The optimization algorithms are greatly responsible for reducing the errors as well as the losses and, consequently, provide much more accurate results. Fig. 3.34 shows the types of optimizers.

Some of the commonly used optimizers in deep learning-based model training are as follows:

(i) **Gradient descent optimizer:** This is one of the most used optimization algorithms because it is easy to implement, compute, and understand. The gradient descent is the most basic optimization algorithm popularly used in linear regression problems. The process of back propagation also implements the same algorithm. This algorithm functions on the first-order derivative of the loss function and is often termed first-order optimization algorithm. One of the major drawbacks is that the gradient descent sometimes gets stuck at the local minima and is not suited for larger datasets since the weights are changed after the error on the entire dataset is calculated.

(ii) **Stochastic gradient descent (SGD) optimizer:** This is a variation of the gradient descent algorithm with the ability to update the model parameters after the computation of loss on each of the training samples. The SGD converges more rapidly as compared to its predecessor, the gradient descent, and it has the ability to reach new minimas. The issue lies with the large amount of variance brought to the training model due to the SGD optimizer algorithm.

(iii) **Momentum optimizer:** This optimization algorithm overcomes the issues of high variance in SGD by increasing the convergence into meaningful direction and deflecting from the irrelevant directions. As a result it converges even faster than SGD. This optimization algorithm is often referred to as SGD with momentum (SGDM).

(iv) **AdaGrad optimizer:** In the previously discussed optimization algorithms, the learning rate remains constant throughout the training process. The AdaGrad optimizing algorithm focuses on manipulating the learning rate. This results in a second-order optimization algorithm [56] and is designed to swiftly optimize convex problems. Since the learning rate keeps decreasing, the training process is slower. The speed of the convergence of AdaGrad comes at the expense of computation, which is a costly tradeoff.

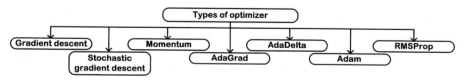

FIG. 3.34

Types of optimizer. *RMSProp,* root mean square propagation.

   (v) AdaDelta optimizer: This is an advancement to the AdaGrad optimization algorithm to overcome the issue of the decay of learning rate. This is done by restricting the number of previously accumulated gradients to a fixed size "w." This results in the elimination of the decay problem; however, it becomes computationally expensive.

   (vi) Adam optimizer: Adam stands for adaptive moment estimation, and it functions on the concept of performing a careful search while reducing the velocity and maintaining the momentum. Similar to AdaDelta, it stores the average of exponentially decaying previous square of gradients and the average of the decaying gradients. It results in formation of both first-order and second-order momentums. This results in high speed convergence and elimination of the problem of vanishing gradient [57].

   (vii) RMSProp optimizer: This is a modification of the AdaGrad adaptive learning optimizer with aim to optimize nonconvex problems. It is named root mean squared propagation (RMSProp) because it keeps moving the average of the squared gradients for each weight and then divides the gradient by the square root of the mean square, resulting in the gradient as an exponentially weighted moving average [58].

3.8.4.1 The problem of overfitting

Overfitting is often referred to as the problem of generalization where the trained model corresponds too closely to a specific set of data and may not be fit to predict future observations reliably. The primary reason for such behavior of the trained model is usually that the model learns some residual variations (i.e., noise). In machine learning or deep learning we aim at achieving a model that correctly estimates the data or accurately describes the data. The process involves building models that learn the representation from the training data with an aim that the trained model would generalize to the unseen test data. Underfitting is when the trained model is unable to grasp the state of complexity of the training data and is unable to learn the data representation to its fullest. It is referred to as a model with a high bias as the trained model is inclined toward having less variance in its predictions and more bias in the direction of misclassifications. On the other hand, overfitting involves training the model such that it memorizes specific training data representations. It is referred to as a model with high variance as the trained model is inclined toward having more variance in its predictions. The aim is to achieve a balance between the two and result in an ideal-fit model that is not too complex so that it memorizes the training representation and has the ability to perform generalizations when encountered with new data samples, usually the test samples. The ideal-fit models have low bias and high variance. Fig. 3.35 shows the different fittings of a trained model to the data.

   The task of detecting overfitting is highly skillful and essential. Multiple solutions for overfitting have been proposed over the years, including cross-validation, increasing the size of the training dataset, applying feature selection, and regularization.

3.8.4.2 Overcoming the problem of overfitting: Regularization

One of the solutions to the problem of overfitting is regularization. It includes a broad range of techniques that force the model to simplify its learning. Many times regularization is considered a hyperparameter since the regularization methods have to be decided by the user beforehand. Fig. 3.36 shows the different types of regularization methods.

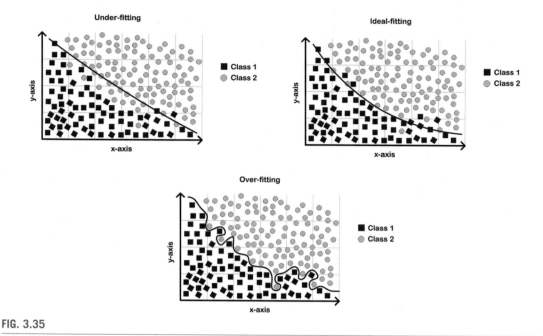

FIG. 3.35

Schematic representation of underfitting, ideal-fitting, and overfitting.

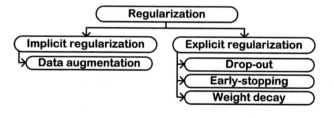

FIG. 3.36

Types of regularization.

The task of regularization can be implicitly applied using data augmentation or explicitly using various methods such as drop-out, early-stopping, and weight decay. The data augmentation has been further discussed in this chapter. Some of the regularization methods to overcome overfitting are discussed as follows:

(a) Drop-out: This refers to the process of dropping off the units of a model that can be hidden or visible. Here the term "units" refers to neurons or connections. When the drop-out term is used, it usually refers to neurons being ignored or neglected. Whereas when the connections are dropped, it is called drop-connect. Here the term "ignore" translates to the key concept of not including the units of the network in the training process (forward or backward pass). The main aim of applying drop-out is that it forces the network to learn more robust features, consequently overcoming the problem of overfitting. Fig. 3.37 shows a network with drop-out.

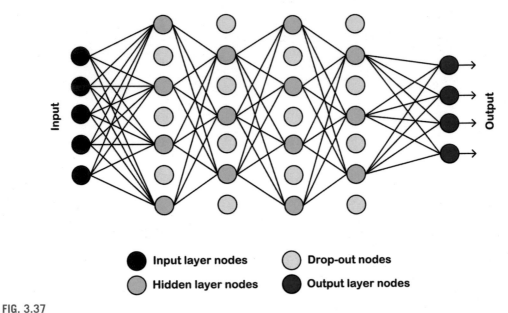

FIG. 3.37

Schematic representation of drop-out.

(b) Early-stopping: This refers to the point in the training process after which the model starts to overfit. The model training is required to be stopped before it reaches that point. This ideal-fit point of the model can be considered a threshold point before which the model is underfitted. If the model training crosses that point, then it is overfitted. Fig. 3.38 shows the process of early-stopping.

FIG. 3.38

Schematic representation of early-stopping.

The present work applies the concept of early-stopping whenever required while training the models. The MATLABR2020a Deep Learning Toolbox provides the users with a stop button on the GUI that enables the users to stop the training process whenever necessary.

(c) Weight decay: This includes the regularization methods whose key task is to change the way the weight decay occurs while training the model. These methods include the L1 **and** L2 regularization that function on the key concept of penalizing the weight values of the network to improve the learning of the model.

(i) L1-regularization: The L1-regularization is referred to as the Lasso-regression (least absolute shrinkage and selection operator) that penalizes with the absolute value of weight in the training model. This method is basic and simpler in nature, quite similar to feature selection as it shrinks the coefficients of the less essential features, thereby removing them. This method of regularization is highly robust when outliners are present in the data. The regularization parameter λ is manually tuned ($\lambda > 0$). Here the regularization term is called the penalty and is popularly known as the Laplacian penalty.

$$L1\left(\text{regularization term}\right) = \lambda \sum_{j=0}^{m} \left|W_j\right|$$

$$\text{Cost function} = \sum_{i=0}^{n} \left(y_i - \sum_{j=0}^{m} x_{ij} W_j \right)^2 + \lambda \sum_{j=0}^{m} \left|W_j\right|$$

(ii) L2-regularization: The L2-regularization is referred to as the Ridge-regression that penalizes with the sum of square values of weight in the training model. It enables the model to learn and interpret complex patterns in the data but is not robust to the outliners present in the data. The regularization parameter λ is manually tuned ($\lambda > 0$). Here the regularization term is called the penalty and is popularly known as the Gaussian penalty.

$$L2\left(\text{regularization term}\right) = \lambda \sum_{j=0}^{m} W_j^2$$

$$\text{Cost function} = \sum_{i=0}^{n} \left(y_i - \sum_{j=0}^{m} x_{ij} W_j \right)^2 + \lambda \sum_{j=0}^{m} W_j^2$$

3.8.5 Key hyperparameters of deep learning-based convolution neural networks used in the present work

In the present work the training dataset comprises of 16,290 chest X-ray images (Normal + Pneumonia), each class having 8145 chest X-ray images. In order to calculate the mini-batch size the authors determined the numerical factors of the size of training dataset so that it could be divided evenly. From the various factors of 16,290, the authors performed hit and trial and came to the conclusion that a batch size of 45 evenly divides the training dataset into 362 batches and also yields satisfactory results. The number of epochs is chosen in the power of 10, as discussed before. Here the authors decided to keep the number of epochs as 10 (keeping in mind the computational resources available). Hence the total number of iterations per epoch would be 362, that is, the same as the number of batches discussed before. The total number of iteration for 10 epochs would then be (number

Table 3.1 Hyperparameters used in the present work.

Hyperparameter	Formula	Value in present work
Training dataset	Total number of training images	16,290 images (Normal + Pneumonia)
Batch size	Factor of the number of training images	45
Number of batches	$\dfrac{\text{Training dataset}}{\text{Batch} - \text{size}}$	362
Epoch	10^x $x = 1, 2, \ldots, \infty$	10 $x = 1$
Iterations for 1 epoch	batch − size	362
Total iterations	epoch × batch − size	3620
Learning rate	(Learning rate < 1) & (Learning rate > 10^{-6})	10^{-4}
Activation function	Nonlinear	ReLU
Optimizer	–	SGDM, RMSProp, Adam
Regularization	–	Early-stopping

ReLU, rectified linear unit; SGDM, stochastic gradient descent with momentum; RMSProp, root mean squared propagation.

of epoch × number of batches), that is, $(10 \times 362) = 3620$ iterations. The learning rate used by the authors is 10^{-4} and the optimizers used are Adam, RMSProp, and SGDM. The details of the hyperparameters used in the present work are shown in Table 3.1.

3.9 Dataset: Kaggle chest X-ray dataset

Kaggle is a data science platform and online community of data scientists and machine learning practitioners. It is a part of Google LLC and the brain child of Anthony Goldbloom. The primary objective of Kaggle is to bring large amounts of open-source data to the masses through crowdsourcing. According to Anthony Goldbloom, Kaggle has an aim of uniting data scientists and businesses in a meaningful way. It not only allows users to find and publish datasets but also helps them explore and build models in a web-based data-science environment. It makes working with other data scientists and machine learning engineers much easier and efficient and encourages them to enter competitions to solve data science challenges. Some of the major services offered by Kaggle are: (a) finding and publishing datasets, (b) exploring and building models in a web-based data-science environment, (c) working with other data scientists and machine learning engineers, and (d) participating in competitions to solve data science challenges.

For conducting the proposed work of designing the CAC systems for binary classification of chest radiographs, these chest radiograph images have been obtained from the dataset published by Kermany et al. [4], publicly available for download at Kaggle [59]. The dataset is organized into three folders (train, test, val) and contains subfolders for each image category (Normal and Pneumonia). There are a total of 5863 chest X-ray images in JPEG format for the two categories (Normal and Pneumonia). The description of the dataset as given by the original authors state

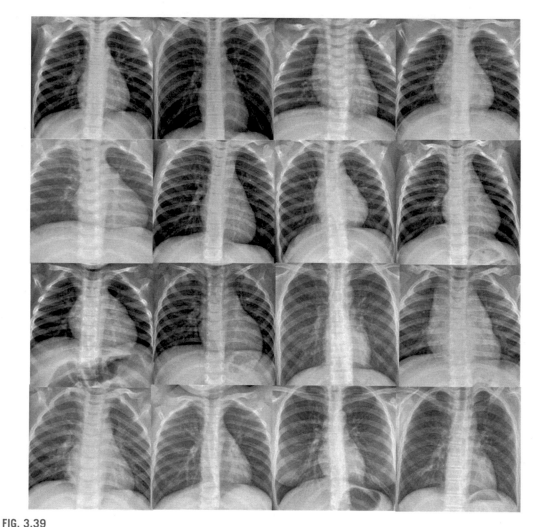

FIG. 3.39

Sample chest X-ray images in the Kaggle chest X-ray dataset of Normal class.

that, "The Chest radiographs (anterior-posterior) were selected from retrospective cohorts of pediatric patients of one to five years old from Guangzhou Women and Children's Medical Center, Guangzhou. All Chest X-ray imaging was performed as part of patients' routine clinical care. For the analysis of Chest X-ray images, all Chest radiographs were initially screened for quality control by removing all low quality or unreadable scans. The diagnoses for the images were then graded by two expert physicians before being cleared for training the AI system. In order to account for any grading errors, the evaluation set was also checked by a third expert" [4]. Figs. 3.39 and 3.40 show the Normal and Pneumonia sample images of the Kaggle chest X-ray dataset used in the present work, respectively, available at [59].

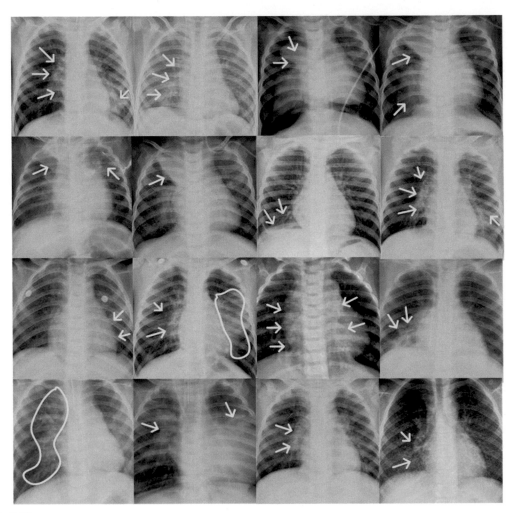

FIG. 3.40

Sample chest X-ray images in the Kaggle chest X-ray dataset of Pneumonia class.

3.10 Dataset description

The original Kaggle chest X-ray dataset published by Kermany et al. [4] consists of 5863 chest radiographs. All of these images are not used in the present work, rather only 100 images of each class Normal and Pneumonia have been selected after discussions with the participating radiation oncologist. A brief overview of the dataset that has been used to carry out the present work is demonstrated in Fig. 3.41.

A total of 200 chest radiograph images consisting of 100 Normal chest X-ray images and 100 Pneumonia chest X-ray images have been considered for analysis. The resolution (both horizontal and vertical) of each chest radiograph image in the present dataset used is of 96 dpi. The 200 selected images

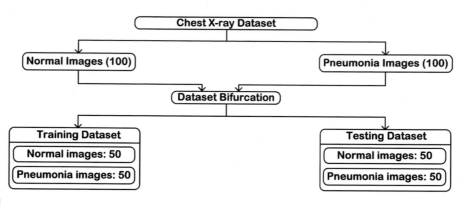

FIG. 3.41

Image dataset description for binary class chest radiograph classification and its bifurcation.

are bifurcated into training dataset and testing dataset. From here the training dataset is augmented to meet the basic demand of deep learning (large amount of data), and the testing data is kept aside to perform final testing of the designed CAC systems.

3.11 Dataset generation

The experiments have been conducted using a comprehensive image dataset of 200 chest radiographs with cases of the image classes: Normal and Pneumonia. The image database is comprised of 100 Normal chest radiographs and 100 Pneumonia chest radiographs. The present work focuses on the design of CAC systems for the efficient diagnosis of Pneumonia disease using chest radiographs, which includes the foremost step of dataset generation.

The dataset generation is simply divided into three modules namely:

(a) Preprocessing module: This deals with the image resizing and cropping to the required size of the experiment.
(b) Dataset bifurcation: This aims at dividing the dataset generated into training, validation, and testing sets.
(c) Augmentation module: This deals with increasing the size of the dataset by applying geometrical transformations (rotation, translation, and flipping).

The steps followed for the dataset generation for the task of classification and deep feature extraction of chest radiograph images is shown in Fig. 3.42.

3.11.1 Preprocessing module: Image resizing

The deep learning-based networks that are Pre-trained have a fixed input size of the images. Hence in order to train the network on the desired data, the images are resized to match the fixed input size of these Pre-trained networks. Hence before training the networks on the desired dataset, these images are resized to the appropriate sizes matching the predefined desired acceptable input sizes of the networks.

Chest x-ray Images

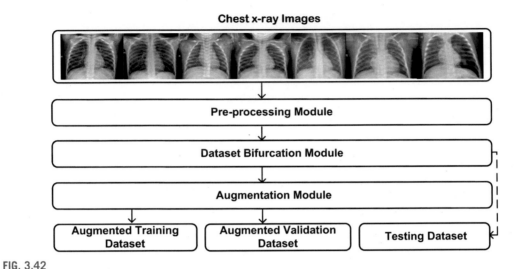

FIG. 3.42

Image dataset generation workflow.

For the characterization of chest radiograph images, it is significant to know that the shape (morphology) of the lung in the chest radiograph image is considered significant in the process of diagnosis of Pneumonia. Therefore resizing the image directly with an aim to get the acceptable network input image size and thereby not focusing on preserving the aspect ratio of the image sometimes results in distortion of the shape of the lung when compared to the original chest radiographic image. The schematic representation of the preprocessing module is shown in Fig. 3.43.

In the present work to preserve the shape of the lung in the resized chest radiograph images, the original images have been resized by preserving their aspect ratio keeping in mind the aim of getting the acceptable network input image size of the network architecture. The process for the image resizing followed in the present work is demonstrated in Fig. 3.44.

Chest x-ray Images

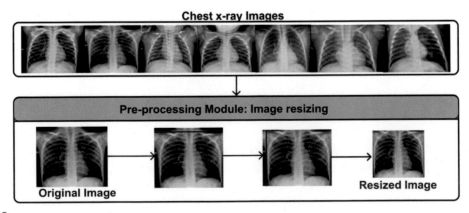

FIG. 3.43

Schematic representation of image resizing.

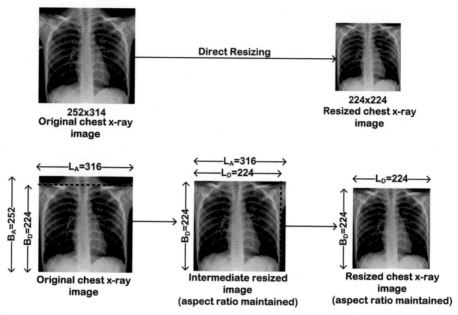

FIG. 3.44

Process of image resizing. L_A, actual length of image; B_A, actual breadth of image; L_D, desired length of image; B_D, desired breadth of image.

The first step of resizing the chest radiographs to the desired size includes the generation of images that are square in shape while maintaining the aspect ratio. This is carried out by scaling the minor side of the original radiographic image to the size of the desired side.

Here the minor side refers to the side that is shorter in the original image. Henceforth, from the resulting intermediate image with an aim to get the final desired image, a random crop of the desired size is taken. This random crop marks the concluding step of getting the final desired sized image. Let original chest radiographic image have size $L_A \times B_A$, with $L_A > B_A$, then according to the first step of resizing, the minor side, which is the breadth of the original radiographic image (B_A), is scaled to the desired breadth size B_D. This results in the formation of an intermediate chest radiographic image having the size $L_A \times B_D$ (where only the minor edge is similar to the desired side). Then, according to the steps of image resizing, from this intermediate chest radiographic image the length L_A needs to be cropped to the desired length of L_D. This final cropping of the length generates the desired resized square image having the image size $L_D \times B_D$.

The following code snippets show how the image resizing is performed using MATLABR2020a to carry out the present work. Code Snippet 3.1 gives the syntax of how to access the chest radiographs from the folder in your computer.

Once the chest radiographs are read successfully, the next step is to determine the color channels of the images. Code Snippet 3.2 gives the syntax of how to determine the individual red, green, and blue color channels of the images. After determining the color channels, the next step is to obtain the actual size of the input chest radiograph. The predefined size() function of MATLAB is used here.

Code Snippet 3.1 Reading original images

```
%% Reading original images from the folder %%
for i=1:50
    Im{i}=['H:\DataChestX-ray\Original Images\Normal\',
          sprintf('%d.jpg',i)];
    CXR=imread(Im{i});
end
```

Code Snippet 3.2 Determining the RGB channel and size of original image

```
%% Determining the rgb colour channels of original image %%
CXR_red=CXR(:,:,1);
CXR_green=CXR(:,:,2);
CXR_blue=CXR(:,:,3);

%% Determining the size of original image%%
CXR_size=size(CXR);
```

After obtaining the actual size of the inputimage, the next step is to calculate the aspect ratio so that the image can be preserved during resizing. Code Snippet 3.3 gives the syntax of how to calculate the aspect ratio of the original image.

Here after calculating the aspect ratio and initializing the desired size of the image, the process of resizing begins. Code Snippet 3.4 gives the syntax of performing image resizing. After resizing the resultant image is the intermediate image as discussed before. To this image random cropping is applied to obtain the final resized image.

To obtain the final resized image, the last step of random cropping is given in Code Snippet 3.5.

Code Snippet 3.3 Calculating the aspect ratio of the image

```
%% Calculating the aspect ratio of the image %%
aspect_ratio=(CXR(2))/(CXR(1));

%% Initializing the desired size of the image %%
desired_size=227;
```

3.11.2 Dataset bifurcation

The schematic representation of the bifurcation of resized chest radiographs dataset into training, validation, and testing datasets before the data augmentation is shown in Fig. 3.45.

The dataset used in the present work has been primarily divided into training, validation, and testing sets. From whole dataset, half of the data (i.e., 50%) is randomly selected to form the testing dataset. The remaining half forms the training dataset, which is further divided into a ratio of 90% training data and 10% validation data. To these final training and validation datasets multiple data augmentation

Code Snippet 3.4 Resizing the original image while maintaining the aspect ratio

```
%% Resizing the original image while maintaining the aspect ratio %%
if(CXR(1)<CXR(2))
    resized_CXR_red=imresize(CXR_red,[desired_size,aspect_ratio*desired_size]);
    resized_CXR_green=imresize(CXR_green,[desired_size,aspect_ratio*desired_size]);
    resized_CXR_blue=imresize(CXR_blue,[desired_size,aspect_ratio*desired_size]);
else
    resized_CXR_red=imresize(CXR_red,[desired_size/aspect_ratio,desired_
    size]);resized_CXR_green=imresize(CXR_green,[desired_size/ aspect_ratio,
    desired_size]);
    resized_CXR_blue=imresize(CXR_blue,[desired_size/ aspect_ratio,desired_size]);
end

resized_CXR=cat(3,resized_CXR_red, resized_CXR_green, resized_CXR_blue);
```

Code Snippet 3.5 Random cropping

```
%% Random cropping of the resized intermediate image %%
CXR_crop=imcrop(resized_CXR,[1,1,226,226]);

%% Writing the final desired image to the destination folder %%
imwrite(CXR_crop, 'H:\DataChestX-ray\Original Images\Normal\CXR_1.jpg');
```

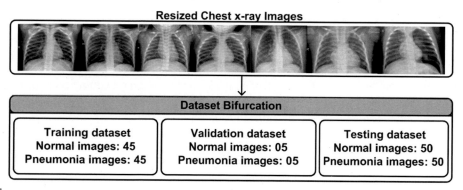

FIG. 3.45

Schematic representation of division of resized images.

techniques (as further discussed in this chapter) were applied as an attempt to increase the number of representative cases in a balanced manner so that the number of augmented Normal chest radiograph images are equivalent to the number of Pneumonia chest radiograph images. The schematic representation of the dataset division is shown in Fig. 3.46.

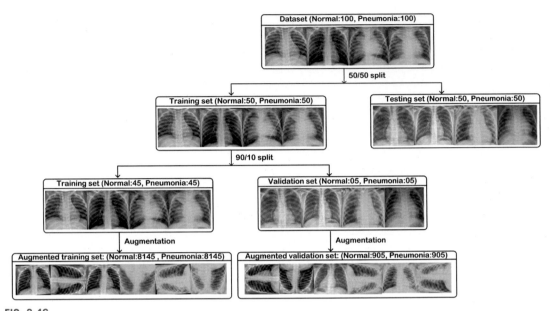

FIG. 3.46

Image dataset bifurcation for binary class classification of chest radiograph images.

Another important factor that was taken care of while allocating the data and forming two sets of training and validation was that for an individual image, the original as well as all the versions formed after augmentation of that chest radiograph were the part of the same set, either training or validation.

3.11.3 Augmentation module: Dataset augmentation

The deep learning-based CAC systems are state-of-the-art and require a huge amount of labeled training data to gain high accuracy and build efficient systems. Data augmentation deals with increasing the diversity of the data, thereby enabling the researchers to train their models more efficiently with diversified data without actually collecting it. The performance of deep learning techniques has high dependency on the amount of data available. Therefore, to compensate the lack of data availability, various data augmentation techniques are utilized with an aim to drastically increase the number of images available [60–63]. Hence, it can be simply understood as an essential technique that virtually increases the sample size by utilizing the actual data available.

3.11.3.1 Motivation for data augmentation

Data augmentation is pivotal in cases where the actual data is very limited and procuring new samples of the ground truth data is an expensive and time-intensive task. These problems are often faced while working with data related to medical images where there is scarcity of data. In such cases data augmentation is a highly beneficial technique for increasing the sample size. Some of the major reasons that have led to the immense use of data augmentation techniques are given as follows:

- **Data unavailability:** One of the major motivations of using data augmentation is the unavailability of data for training deep learning models, specifically medical images. Acquiring access to patient medical records is a time-draining, tedious task that results in very few datasets being available for medical image analysis. The generation of medical datasets requires agreement on the patients' behalf, and patient data security and patient privacy are other concerns. Data augmentation helps researchers increase the quantity of available data while maintaining the quality similar to the original images and fulfilling the requirements of training the deep learning models.

- **Class imbalance:** Another one of the benefits of data augmentation is to overcome class imbalance. One can apply various data augmentation techniques to any particular class of the dataset or to the entire dataset to balance the numbers equally and perform the required task of prediction or classification on the augmented dataset.
- **Variation in data:** Data augmentation not only increases the number of samples but also brings about variation in data as it increases the sample of unseen data for the deep learning model. Variation in data helps toward generalizability of the model, which is highly aspired while training the deep learning model. Some of the techniques, such as feature space augmentation, GAN networks, and neural style transfer are popular for introducing maximum variation in existing dataset.
- **Ease the work of researchers and cost-effectiveness:** Data augmentation increases the sample space virtually without the labor intensive work of manually collecting the data, which is cost-effective in terms of both money and time. In the case of medical imaging, substantial domain specific expertise is required to generate well-labeled and well-annotated datasets. Here augmentation saves the need for medical experts and plays an important role in generating well-labeled datasets.
- **Implicit regularization:** The various deep learning-based models in the absence of appropriate regularization often result in overfitting of the training data. Hence with an aim to significantly reduce the problem along with simultaneously increasing the classification and prediction performance of the model on the test data (unseen data), multiple data augmentation techniques are applied. The data augmentation aids in increasing the generalizability of the deep learning model.

3.11.3.2 Why augment only the training dataset?
Augmentation is applied with an aim to increase the sample size of the available dataset. The large size of the dataset is desirable to facilitate generalized training of the designed CAC system or network to achieve robust training and reduce overfitting. Hence larger sample space is required for the purpose of training the system. Whereas the purpose of a test dataset is to determine the error in the system designed that it will face in real time. Hence test data should be kept as close to real cases as possible. There remains no motivation for increasing the sample size of the test dataset as the required optimal model parameters are already available and it would just be a waste of time and resources to perform augmentation without any motivation. Often augmentation of test sets result in change of class labels and may adulterate the prediction accuracy of the trained model. These reasons support that data augmentation is beneficial in most cases when being applied only to the training datasets.

3.11.3.3 How to choose data augmentation technique for medical images
The data augmentation techniques for medical images are chosen in such a way that the class labels and the features that are diagnostically important to a specific tissue are preserved. The augmentation

approaches used for natural images may not work for medical images as a lot of medical images are a top-down solved problem, not bottom-up like natural images. For different tissues there are different features that are considered clinically significant and pivotal for diagnosis. The features that are diagnostically important are texture, shape, and color features. For brain tumor and examination of liver ultrasounds, the texture features are primarily taken into consideration by the radiologists [64–68]. Whereas for chest radiographs, breast ultrasound, and fundus image analysis, the texture and shape features are diagnostically essential [30, 31, 68–74]. For histopathology images, the color and texture information are considered the key features for clinical diagnosis [20, 21]. For blood smear images, the features that are of prime concern are texture, color, and shape; all the three features are significant in diagnosis [75–77]. The key features of medical images have already been discussed in Chapter 1.

3.11.3.4 *Types of data augmentation techniques*

The recent growth in the field of radiological medical imaging techniques and digitization of records have made medical image analysis a hub for application of deep learning-based models. However, the need for large amounts of data to train these deep learning models is a challenge. The design of medical image datasets is a complex task involving the need for medical experts, time for annotation of the datasets, and some concerns such as consensus of the patient, patient privacy, and data security. Here data augmentation plays an instrumental role in generating new well-labeled data based on the existing data to increase the sample space for training the models and achieve generalizability while maintaining high performance.

For data augmentation purposes, a number of techniques have been utilized that include affine or geometrical transformation, random cropping, intensity-based methods, adding noise, color jittering, and so forth [5–9, 19]. The data augmentation techniques can broadly be of two types:

(a) White-box techniques: These techniques are generic in nature and focus on transforming the original images in such a way that their labels are preserved. They include the following methods:
- **Geometrical transformations:** This is the utmost generic type of augmentation performed and is most popular, often known as affine transformations. It includes cropping, scaling, shearing, rotation, translation, random crop, and so forth.
- **Photometric transformation:** This is another one of the generic augmentation methods but is to be used carefully as it is applicable to color images and may be detrimental to the features of medical images. It includes transformations such as color jittering, fancy PCA, sharpening, and blurring of images.
- **Other transformations:** These include the addition of noise, image stitching, random erasing, and more.

(b) Black-box techniques: These techniques are more complex and focus on generation of synthetic data and adding it to the original image dataset. These include techniques such as:
- **Neural style transfer:** This is a data generation technique in which the style of one image is blended with the content from another image with a motive to generate the input image as content image but generated in the style of the reference style image.
- **Adversarial training:** This makes the use of generative adversarial networks popularly called the GAN.

The traditional data augmentation techniques, also known as the white-box method, include the geometrical transformations, intensity (color)-based transformation, and mixing of image pixels and techniques such as random erasing. Deep learning-based augmentation techniques, also known as the black-box techniques, mainly include adversarial networks and their use for data augmentation and techniques such as meta learning and neural style transfer are all considered under this. Fig. 3.47 shows the broad classification of various data augmentation techniques where the techniques shaded in gray are used in the present work. The types of data augmentation techniques on the basis of the time at which augmentation is performed on the data samples are classified as online and offline augmentation. In online augmentation the data is augmented just before the data is to be fed to the network and is called augmentation on the go. It is usually preferred for larger datasets. The second one is the offline data augmentation in which the data is augmented beforehand. This augmentation is used for smaller datasets as they can be easily managed manually. Fig. 3.48 shows the different geometrical transformation that can be applied to the breast ultrasound image.

Similarly Fig. 3.49 shows the different geometrical transformations that can be applied to chest radiographs.

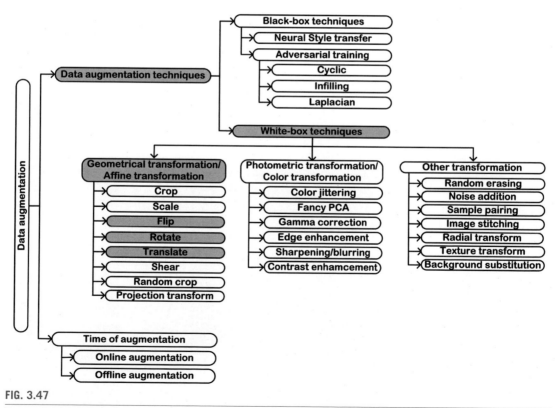

FIG. 3.47

Types of data augmentation techniques. *PCA,* principal component analysis.

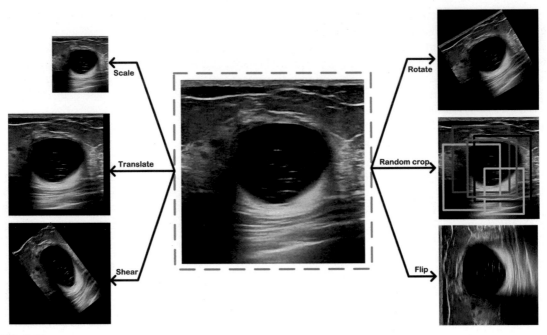

FIG. 3.48

Schematic representation of the data augmentation techniques on breast ultrasound image.

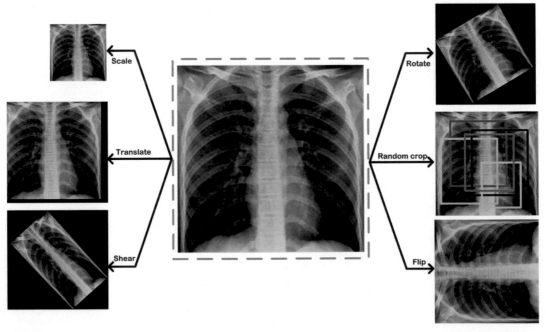

FIG. 3.49

Schematic representation of the data augmentation techniques on chest X-ray image.

The augmentation technique to be applied on medical images exceedingly depends on the type of tissue being used as the underlying features should be preserved and should not be lost in the process of increasing the size of the dataset. For chest radiograph images the texture and shape feature are to be preserved; hence for the present work the augmentation techniques used are rotation, translation, and flipping. Fig. 3.50 shows the schematic representation of the data augmentation module used in the present work.

In the present work the same augmentation techniques are applied to both Normal and Pneumonia chest radiograph images. The original dataset is composed of 100 images (Normal: 50, Pneumonia: 50) in training and 100 images (Normal: 50, Pneumonia: 50) in testing. The training dataset of 100 images is augmented to a total of 18,100 images. Each image is at first rotated and translated resulting in 36 images and 24 images each, respectively.

These rotated and translated images are then flipped (horizontal flip and vertical flip) resulting in 108 images after rotation and flipping, similarly resulting in 72 images after translation and flipping. In total each image is augmented to result in 181 images.

Fig. 3.51 shows the data augmentation techniques applied to the dataset used in the present work. The augmentation techniques applied in the present work are as follows:

(a) Rotation: This is a geometrical augmentation technique that is among the most commonly and widely used techniques, especially in medical images. The image is rotated at a certain angle except in those cases where the features of the image are highly dependent on the orientation of the object. It is performed by rotating the image right or left of the axis at angle of θ. It applies the affine transformation that follows the given equation:

$$A = \begin{pmatrix} \cos\theta & -\sin\theta \\ \sin\theta & \cos\theta \end{pmatrix}$$

Where θ is varied between 5 and 180 degrees with an interval of 5 degrees each. The rotation operation results in a total of 36 images from a single original image in the present work.

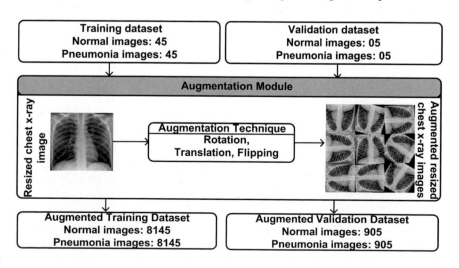

FIG. 3.50

Schematic representation of the data augmentation module.

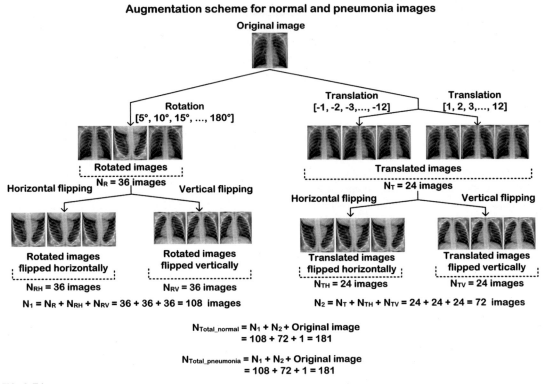

FIG. 3.51

Image dataset augmentation.

Figs. 3.52 and 3.53 show rotation of original Normal chest radiograph images and original Pneumonia chest radiograph images, respectively.

Code Snippet 3.6 shows the syntax of how to access the chest radiographs from the folder in your computer. Here the chest radiographs are stored at the path "H:\DataChestX-ray\Original Images\ Normal\." This path corresponds to the Normal chest radiographs. Similarly for Pneumonia chest radiographs the path "H:\DataChestX-ray\Original Images\Pneumonia\" is accessed in the present work.

Once the images have been read from the folders they are subjected to rotation using the "imrotate" predefined function by MATLAB between angles 5 and 180 degrees with an interval of 5 degrees each. Here Code Snippet 3.7 shows the rotation of the chest X-ray radiographs between angles 5 and 45 degrees with an interval of 5 each. The rotated images are then stored to the path specified in the variable "filename1," which is "H:\DataChestX-ray\Augmented Images\Normal\."

(b) Translation: This is the shifting of pixels of the image to the right, left, up, or down the axis. This method helps in introducing positional variation in the dataset, thereby avoiding the positional bias in the data. As most of the original images are centered, a model will train for perfectly centered images. Therefore, increasing the robustness of the system translation plays a major role. When the original images are translated, the remaining space is filled with a constant

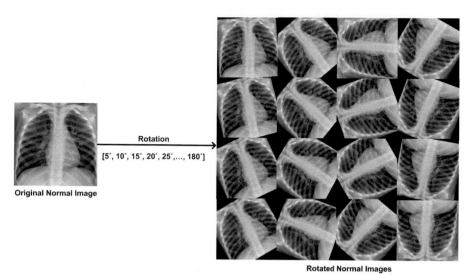

FIG. 3.52

Rotation on Normal chest radiograph image.

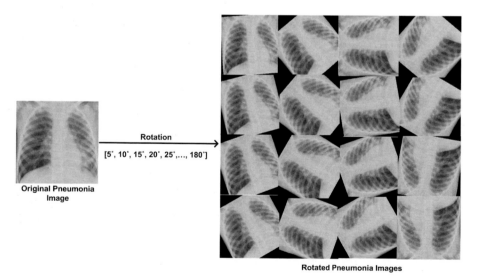

FIG. 3.53

Rotation on Pneumonia chest radiograph image.

value between 0 and 255 or random Gaussian noises are added. This helps in preserving the postaugmentation spatial dimensions of the image. This augmentation technique has been applied in the present work. Fig. 3.54 shows the Normal chest radiograph images translated from [1, 2, 3, ..., 12] and [−1, −2, −3, ..., −12]. Fig. 3.55 shows the Pneumonia chest radiograph images translated from [1, 2, 3, ..., 12] and [−1, −2, −3, ..., −12].

Code Snippet 3.6 Reading images from the folder

```
%% Reading original images from the folder %%
for i=1:50
    Im_OB{i}=['H:\DataChestX-ray\Original Images\Normal\',
            sprintf('%d.jpg',i)];
    CXR_O=imread(Im_OB{i});
end
```

Code Snippet 3.7 Rotation of images

```
%% Rotation of the images %%
f= [5 10 15 20 25 30 35 40 45]; %angle of rotation
for j=1:length(f)
    CXR_O=imrotate(CXR_O,f(j),'crop');
    Filename1= (['H:\DataChestX-ray\Augmented
                Images\Normal\',num2str(i)'_R_'num2str(f(j)
                ),'.jpg']);
    imwrite(CXR_O,Filename1)
end
```

Code Snippet 3.6 shows the syntax of how to access the chest radiographs from the folder in your computer. Here the chest radiographs are stored at the path "H:\DataChestX-ray\ Original Images\Normal\." Once the images have been read from the folders they are subjected to translation using the "imtranslate" predefined function by MATLAB between pixel values ± 12 as shown in Code Snippet 3.8. The translated Normal chest images are then stored to the path specified in the variable "filename1," which is "H:\DataChestX-ray\Augmented Images\Normal\." Similarly the Pneumonia chest images after translation are stored at "H:\DataChestX-ray\Augmented Images\Pneumonia\." The values for translation are passed in pairs of two representing the x- and y-axis values [x y]. Here in Code Snippet 3.8 the value of translation $f=[11\ 12]$, representing 11 pixel translation in x-direction and 12 pixel translation in y-direction. The negative values of x and y would indicate the negative of the axis w.r.t quadrant representation.

(c) **Flip:** This geometrical transformation deals with flipping of the image on the horizontal axis or the vertical axis. It is often referred to as mirroring and is one of the most commonly used and easiest augmentation techniques. This augmentation technique preserves the labels of the original data while the samples generated are entirely new for the deep learning model and widely used. In some scenarios where the features are highly dependent on the position of objects in the original image, such as features of unilateral organs, this technique is not preferred. These are those organs that are present on only one side of the human body and their change of position would affect the annotations of the original data such as the spleen and pancreas. In the present work both horizontal flip and vertical flips are applied to rotated and translated images. Some other medical images on which flipping is applied are skin images.

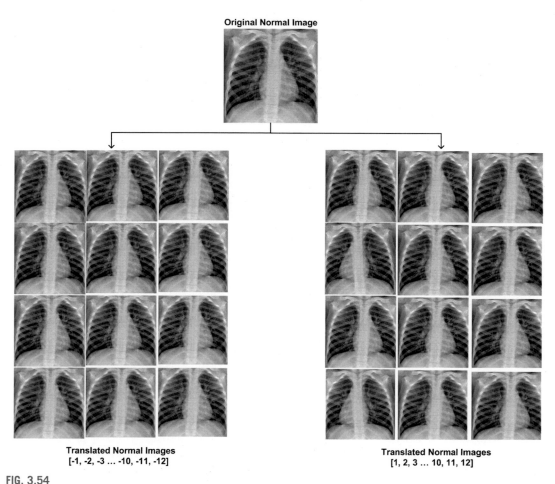

Original Normal Image

Translated Normal Images
[-1, -2, -3 ... -10, -11, -12]

Translated Normal Images
[1, 2, 3 ... 10, 11, 12]

FIG. 3.54

Translation on Normal chest radiograph image.

Figs. 3.56 and 3.57 show horizontal flipping and vertical flipping of the original Normal image and original Pneumonia images, respectively.

Code Snippets 3.9 and 3.10 give the syntax of how to perform horizontal and vertical flipping on the rotated images. The images are read in the same manner as seen in Code Snippet 3.6 and then flipping is performed using the "flip" predefined function of MATLAB where the argument of the function determines the type of flip. If the argument of flip function is 1, then it is horizontal flipping, and if the argument value passed is 2, then it represents vertical flipping.

In the present work for each augmentation, the hyperparameters are varied such as the value of θ in rotation, the translation value, and the flipping axis to generate a final augmented dataset consisting of 18,100 chest radiograph images. The augmentation was performed only on the original training dataset of 100 images, and the testing data was left unaugmented.

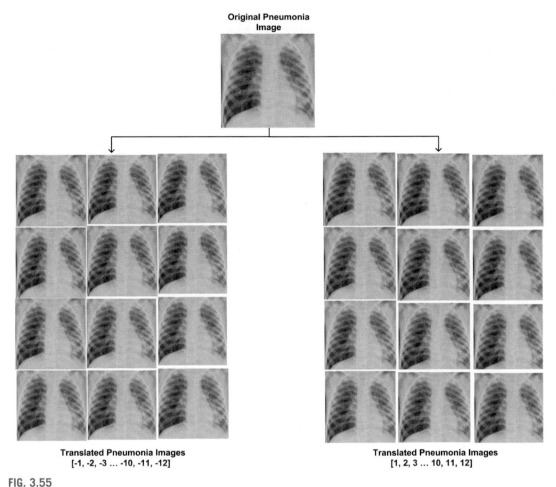

FIG. 3.55

Translation on Pneumonia chest radiograph image.

Code Snippet 3.8 Translation of images

```
%% Translation of the images %%
f= [11 12];
for j=1:length(f)
    CXR_O=imtranslate(CXR_O,f,'FillValues',255,'OutputView',
    'same');
    Filename1= (['H:\DataChestX-ray\Augmented
                Images\Normal\',num2str(i) '_T_'
                num2str(f(j)),'.jpg']);
    imwrite(CXR_O,Filename1)
end
```

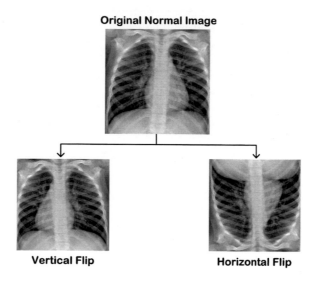

FIG. 3.56

Flipping on Normal chest radiograph image.

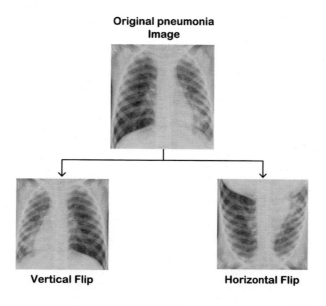

FIG. 3.57

Flipping on Pneumonia chest radiograph image.

Code Snippet 3.9 Horizontal flipping of images

```
%% Horizontal flipping of the rotated images %%
for j=1:length(f)
    CXR_H=flip(CXR_O,1);
    Filename2 = (['H:\DataChestX-ray\Augmented
                   Images\Normal\',num2str(i) '_R_'
                   num2str(f(j)),'_H.jpg']);
    imwrite(CXR_H,Filename2)
end
```

Code Snippet 3.10 Vertical flipping of images

```
%% Vertical flipping of the rotated images %%
for j=1:length(f)
    CXR_H=flip(CXR_O,2);
    Filename3 = (['H:\DataChestX-ray\Augmented
                   Images\Normal\',num2str(i) '_R_'
                   num2str(f(j)),'_V.jpg']);
    imwrite(CXR_V,Filename3)
end
```

3.12 Concluding remarks

The methodology adopted to carry out the present work on CNN-based CAC system design for chest radiographs are presented in this chapter. This chapter explains in detail the image dataset that has been used to conduct the different experiments for designing the CNN-based CAC systems in the present work as well as the methodology adopted for data augmentation, the hardware and software requirements to carry out the present work, and the hyperparameters in deep learning. The next chapter deals with the experiments conducted that focus on designing the CNN-based CAC systems for chest radiographs. The architecture of the different CNN models, the feature selection, and feature space dimensionality reduction along with different machine learning classifiers used in the present work are discussed in subsequent chapters.

References

[1] J.R. Zech, M.A. Badgeley, M. Liu, A.B. Costa, J.J. Titano, E.K. Oermann, Variable generalization performance of a deep learning model to detect pneumonia in chest radiographs: a cross-sectional study, PLoS Med. 15 (11) (2018) e1002683.

[2] A.F. Al Mubarok, J.A. Dominique, A.H. Thias, Pneumonia detection with deep convolutional architecture, in: In 2019 International Conference of Artificial Intelligence and Information Technology (ICAIIT), IEEE, 2019, pp. 486–489.

[3] T. Rahman, M.E. Chowdhury, A. Khandakar, K.R. Islam, K.F. Islam, Z.B. Mahbub, M.A. Kadir, S. Kashem, Transfer learning with deep convolutional neural network (CNN) for pneumonia detection using chest X-ray, Appl. Sci. 10 (9) (2020) 3233.

[4] D.S. Kermany, M. Goldbaum, W. Cai, C.C. Valentim, H. Liang, S.L. Baxter, A. McKeown, G. Yang, X. Wu, F. Yan, J. Dong, Identifying medical diagnoses and treatable diseases by image-based deep learning, Cell 172 (5) (2018) 1122–1131.

[5] K. Jakhar, N. Hooda, Big data deep learning framework using Keras: a case study of pneumonia prediction, in: 2018 4th International Conference on Computing Communication and Automation (ICCCA), IEEE, 2018, pp. 1–5.

[6] S. Rajaraman, S. Candemir, I. Kim, G. Thoma, S. Antani, Visualization and interpretation of convolutional neural network predictions in detecting pneumonia in pediatric chest radiographs, Appl. Sci. 8 (10) (2018) 1715.

[7] E. Ayan, H.M. Ünver, Diagnosis of pneumonia from chest X-ray images using deep learning, in: 2019 Scientific Meeting on Electrical-Electronics & Biomedical Engineering and Computer Science (EBBT), IEEE, 2019, April, pp. 1–5.

[8] K.E. El Asnaoui, Y. Chawki, A. Idri, Automated methods for detection and classification pneumonia based on x-ray images using deep learning, arXiv preprint arXiv:2003.14363, 2020.

[9] G. Jain, D. Mittal, D. Thakur, M.K. Mittal, A deep learning approach to detect Covid-19 coronavirus with X-ray images, Biocybern. Biomed. Eng. 40 (4) (2020) 1391–1405.

[10] W.W. Chapman, M. Fizman, B.E. Chapman, P.J. Haug, A comparison of classification algorithms to automatically identify chest X-ray reports that support pneumonia, J. Biomed. Inform. 34 (1) (2001) 4–14.

[11] T.B. Chandra, K. Verma, Pneumonia detection on chest X-ray using machine learning paradigm, in: Proceedings of 3rd International Conference on Computer Vision and Image Processing, Springer, Singapore, 2020, pp. 21–33.

[12] R.E. Al Mamlook, S. Chen, H.F. Bzizi, Investigation of the performance of machine learning classifiers for pneumonia detection in chest X-ray images, in: 2020 IEEE International Conference on Electro Information Technology (EIT), IEEE, 2020, pp. 098–104.

[13] L.L.G. Oliveira, S.A. e Silva, L.H.V. Ribeiro, R.M. de Oliveira, C.J. Coelho, A.L.S. Andrade, Computer-aided diagnosis in chest radiography for detection of childhood pneumonia, Int. J. Med. Inform. 77 (8) (2008) 555–564.

[14] R.T. Sousa, O. Marques, F.A.A. Soares, I.I. Sene Jr., L.L. de Oliveira, E.S. Spoto, Comparative performance analysis of machine learning classifiers in detection of childhood pneumonia using chest radiographs, Procedia Comput. Sci. 18 (2013) 2579–2582.

[15] A. Depeursinge, J. Iavindrasana, A. Hidki, G. Cohen, A. Geissbuhler, A. Platon, P.A. Poletti, H. Müller, Comparative performance analysis of state-of-the-art classification algorithms applied to lung tissue categorization, J. Digit. Imaging 23 (1) (2010) 18–30.

[16] J. Yao, A. Dwyer, R.M. Summers, D.J. Mollura, Computer-aided diagnosis of pulmonary infections using texture analysis and support vector machine classification, Acad. Radiol. 18 (3) (2011) 306–314.

[17] E. Naydenova, A. Tsanas, C. Casals-Pascual, M. De Vos, Smart diagnostic algorithms for automated detection of childhood pneumonia in resource-constrained settings, in: 2015 IEEE Global Humanitarian Technology Conference (GHTC), IEEE, 2015, pp. 377–384.

[18] K. El Asnaoui, Y. Chawki, Using X-ray images and deep learning for automated detection of coronavirus disease, J. Biomol. Struct. Dynam. (2020) 1–22.

[19] I.D. Apostolopoulos, T.A. Mpesiana, Covid-19: automatic detection from x-ray images utilizing transfer learning with convolutional neural networks, Phys. Eng. Sci. Med. 43 (2) (2020) 635–640.

[20] T. Ozturk, M. Talo, E.A. Yildirim, U.B. Baloglu, O. Yildirim, U.R. Acharya, Automated detection of COVID-19 cases using deep neural networks with X-ray images, Comput. Biol. Med. 121 (2020) 103792.

[21] P.K. Sethy, S.K. Behera, Detection of coronavirus disease (covid-19) based on deep features, Preprints 2020030300 (2020) 2020.

[22] J. Civit-Masot, F. Luna-Perejón, M. Domínguez Morales, A. Civit, Deep learning system for COVID-19 diagnosis aid using X-ray pulmonary images, Appl. Sci. 10 (13) (2020) 4640.

[23] T.P. Coroller, P. Grossmann, Y. Hou, E.R. Velazquez, R.T. Leijenaar, G. Hermann, P. Lambin, B. Haibe-Kains, R.H. Mak, H.J. Aerts, CT-based radiomic signature predicts distant metastasis in lung adenocarcinoma, Radiother. Oncol. 114 (3) (2015) 345–350.

[24] V. Kumar, Y. Gu, S. Basu, A. Berglund, S.A. Eschrich, M.B. Schabath, K. Forster, H.J. Aerts, A. Dekker, D. Fenstermacher, D.B. Goldgof, Radiomics: the process and the challenges, Magn. Reson. Imaging 30 (9) (2012) 1234–1248.

[25] E.J. Limkin, S. Reuzé, A. Carré, R. Sun, A. Schernberg, A. Alexis, E. Deutsch, C. Ferté, C. Robert, The complexity of tumor shape, spiculatedness, correlates with tumor radiomic shape features, Sci. Rep. 9 (1) (2019) 1–12.

[26] J. Wang, X. Liu, D. Dong, J. Song, M. Xu, Y. Zang, J. Tian, Prediction of malignant and benign of lung tumor using a quantitative radiomic method, in: 2016 38th Annual International Conference of the IEEE Engineering in Medicine and Biology Society (EMBC), IEEE, 2016, pp. 1272–1275.

[27] R.J. Gillies, P.E. Kinahan, H. Hricak, Radiomics: images are more than pictures, they are data, Radiology 278 (2) (2016) 563–577.

[28] F. Homayounieh, S. Ebrahimian, R. Babaei, H. Karimi Mobin, E. Zhang, B.C. Bizzo, I. Mohseni, S.R. Digumarthy, M.K. Kalra, CT Radiomics, radiologists and clinical information in predicting outcome of patients with COVID-19 pneumonia, Radiol. Cardiothorac. Imaging 2 (4) (2020) e200322.

[29] T. Zhang, M. Yuan, Y. Zhong, Y.D. Zhang, H. Li, J.F. Wu, T.F. Yu, Differentiation of focal organising pneumonia and peripheral adenocarcinoma in solid lung lesions using thin-section CT-based radiomics, Clin. Radiol. 74 (1) (2019) 78–e23.

[30] Kriti, J. Virmani, R. Agarwal, Effect of despeckle filtering on classification of breast tumors using ultrasound images, Biocybern. Biomed. Eng. 39 (2) (2019) 536–560.

[31] Kriti, J. Virmani, R. Agarwal, Assessment of despeckle filtering algorithms for segmentation of breast tumours from ultrasound images, Biocybern. Biomed. Eng. 39 (1) (2019) 100–121.

[32] R. Caruana, A. Niculescu-Mizil, An empirical comparison of supervised learning algorithms, in: Proceedings of the 23rd International Conference on Machine Learning, 2006, June, pp. 161–168.

[33] T.O. Ayodele, Types of machine learning algorithms, in: New Advances in Machine Learning, vol. 3, 2010, pp. 19–48.

[34] N.S. Gill, H. Yadav, M. Bagga, Overview of machine learning and artificial intelligence, Int. J. Progress. Res. Sci. Eng. 1 (3) (2020) 78–79.

[35] L. Wang (Ed.), Support Vector Machines: Theory and Applications, vol. 177, Springer Science & Business Media, 2005.

[36] A. Pradhan, Support vector machine—a survey, Int. J. Emerging Technol. Adv. Eng. 2 (8) (2012) 82–85.

[37] O. Harrison, Machine learning basics with the k-nearest neighbors algorithm, Towards Data Science (2018). September, 10.

[38] J. Virmani, V. Kumar, N. Kalra, N. Khandelwal, PCA-SVM based CAD system for focal liver lesions using B-mode ultrasound images, Defence Sci. J. 64 (5) (2013) 478–486.

[39] M. Khanum, T. Mahboob, W. Imtiaz, H.A. Ghafoor, R. Sehar, A survey on unsupervised machine learning algorithms for automation, classification and maintenance, Int. J. Comput. Appl. 119 (13) (2015).

[40] R. Gentleman, V.J. Carey, Unsupervised machine learning, in: Bioconductor Case Studies, Springer, New York, NY, 2008, pp. 137–157.

[41] I.T. Jolliffe, J. Cadima, Principal component analysis: a review and recent developments, Philos. Trans. Royal Soc. A Math. Phys. Eng. Sci. 374 (2065) (2016) 20150202.

[42] M. Brems, A one-stop shop for principal component analysis, Medium Towards Data Science 17 (2017).

[43] V. Powell, L. Lehe, Principal Component Analysis Explained Visually, 2015, DISQUS, Available: http://setosa.io/ev/principal-componentanalysis/. (Accessed 11 July 2016).

[44] S.J. Roberts, Parametric and non-parametric unsupervised cluster analysis, Pattern Recogn. 30 (2) (1997) 261–272.

[45] V. Roman, Unsupervised machine learning: clustering analysis, Towards Data Science (2019).

[46] A. Jonsson, Deep reinforcement learning in medicine, Kidney Dis. 5 (1) (2019) 18–22.

[47] O. Gottesman, F. Johansson, M. Komorowski, et al., Guidelines for reinforcement learning in healthcare, Nat. Med. 25 (2019) 16–18.

[48] J. Virmani, V. Kumar, N. Kalra, N. Khandelwal, Neural network ensemble based CAD system for focal liver lesions from B-mode ultrasound, J. Digit. Imaging 27 (4) (2014) 520–537.

[49] A. Bashar, Survey on evolving deep learning neural network architectures, J. Artif. Intell. 1 (02) (2019) 73–82.

[50] N. O'Mahony, S. Campbell, A. Carvalho, S. Harapanahalli, G.V. Hernandez, L. Krpalkova, D. Riordan, J. Walsh, Deep learning vs. traditional computer vision, in: Science and Information Conference, Springer, Cham, 2019, pp. 128–144.

[51] M. Robinson, A. Whelan, S. Burton, B. Bolon, H. Ellis, Deep Learning Course, 2020.

[52] CS230 Deep Learning Course. https://cs230.stanford.edu/.

[53] J. Leonel, Hyperparameters in machine/deep learning. Online, April, 2019.

[54] M.F. Hashmi, S. Katiyar, A.G. Keskar, N.D. Bokde, Z.W. Geem, Efficient pneumonia detection in chest xray images using deep transfer learning, Diagnostics 10 (6) (2020) 417.

[55] P. Ramachandran, B. Zoph, Q.V. Le, Searching for activation functions, arXiv preprint arXiv:1710.05941, 2017.

[56] J. Duchi, E. Hazan, Y. Singer, Adaptive subgradient methods for online learning and stochastic optimization, J. Mach. Learn. Res. 12 (7) (2011).

[57] D.P. Kingma, J. Ba, Adam: a method for stochastic optimization, arXiv preprint arXiv:1412.6980, 2014.

[58] G. Hinton, N. Srivastava, K. Swersky, Neural networks for machine learning, Coursera, video lectures, 264(1), 2012.

[59] Kaggle Chest X-Ray Dataset. https://www.kaggle.com/andrewmvd/pediatric-pneumonia-chest-xray.

[60] C. Shorten, T.M. Khoshgoftaar, A survey on image data augmentation for deep learning, J. Big Data 6 (1) (2019) 60.

[61] B. Hu, C. Lei, D. Wang, S. Zhang, Z. Chen, A preliminary study on data augmentation of deep learning for image classification, arXiv preprint arXiv:1906.11887, 2019.

[62] A. Mikołajczyk, M. Grochowski, Data augmentation for improving deep learning in image classification problem, in: 2018 International Interdisciplinary PhD Workshop (IIPhDW), IEEE, 2018, pp. 117–122.

[63] L. Perez, J. Wang, The effectiveness of data augmentation in image classification using deep learning, arXiv preprint arXiv:1712.04621, 2017.

[64] J. Islam, Y. Zhang, Brain MRI analysis for Alzheimer's disease diagnosis using an ensemble system of deep convolutional neural networks, Brain Inform. 5 (2) (2018) 2.

[65] S. Amari, The Handbook of Brain Theory and Neural Networks, MIT Press, Cambridge, MA, 2003.

[66] J. Virmani, V. Kumar, N. Kalra, N. Khandelwal, Characterization of primary and secondary malignant liver lesions from B-mode ultrasound, J. Digit. Imaging 26 (6) (2013) 1058–1070.

[67] J. Virmani, V. Kumar, N. Kalra, N. Khandelwal, Prediction of liver cirrhosis based on multiresolution texture descriptors from B-mode ultrasound, Int. J. Conv. Comput. 1 (1) (2013) 19–37.

[68] M. Colombo, G. Ronchi, Focal Liver Lesions – Detection, Characterization, Ablation, Springer, Berlin, 2005, pp. 167–177.

[69] J. Li, M. Fan, J. Zhang, L. Li, Discriminating between benign and malignant breast tumors using 3D convolutional neural network in dynamic contrast enhanced-MR images, in: Medical Imaging 2017:

Imaging Informatics for Healthcare, Research, and Applications, vol. 10138, International Society for Optics and Photonics, 2017, March, p. 1013808.

[70] E. Ricci, R. Perfetti, Retinal blood vessel segmentation using line operators and support vector classification, IEEE Trans. Med. Imaging 26 (10) (2007) 1357–1365.

[71] Y. Abdallah, S. Mohamed, Automatic recognition of leukemia cells using texture analysis algorithm, Int. J. Adv. Res. 4 (1) (2016) 1242–1248.

[72] A.K. Jaiswal, P. Tiwari, S. Kumar, D. Gupta, A. Khanna, J.J. Rodrigues, Identifying pneumonia in chest X-rays: a deep learning approach, Measurement 145 (2019) 511–518.

[73] W.H. Hsu, F.J. Tsai, G. Zhang, C.K. Chang, P.H. Hsieh, S.N. Yang, S.S. Sun, K. Liao, E.T. Huang, Development of a deep learning model for chest X-ray screening, Med. Phys. Int. 7 (3) (2019) 314.

[74] V.K. Patel, S.K. Naik, D.P. Naidich, W.D. Travis, J.A. Weingarten, R. Lazzaro, D.D. Gutterman, C. Wentowski, H.B. Grosu, S. Raoof, A practical algorithmic approach to the diagnosis and management of solitary pulmonary nodules: part 1: radiologic characteristics and imaging modalities, Chest 143 (3) (2013) 825–839.

[75] J. Rawat, H.S. Bhadauria, A. Singh, J. Virmani, Review of leukocyte classification techniques for microscopic blood images, in: 2015 2nd International Conference on Computing for Sustainable Global Development (INDIACom), IEEE, 2015, pp. 1948–1954.

[76] S. Mohapatra, D. Patra, S. Satpathi, Image analysis of blood microscopic images for acute leukemia detection, in: 2010 International Conference on Industrial Electronics, Control and Robotics, IEEE, 2010, pp. 215–219.

[77] O. Sarrafzadeh, H. Rabbani, A. Talebi, H.U. Banaem, Selection of the best features for leukocytes classification in blood smear microscopic images, in: Medical Imaging 2014: Digital Pathology, vol. 9041, International Society for Optics and Photonics, 2014, p. 90410P.

Further reading

[78] X. Gu, L. Pan, H. Liang, R. Yang, Classification of bacterial and viral childhood pneumonia using deep learning in chest radiography, in: Proceedings of the 3rd International Conference on Multimedia and Image Processing, 2018, pp. 88–93.

[79] M.E. Chowdhury, T. Rahman, A. Khandakar, R. Mazhar, M.A. Kadir, Z.B. Mahbub, K.R. Islam, M.S. Khan, A. Iqbal, N. Al-Emadi, M.B.I. Reaz, Can AI help in screening viral and COVID-19 pneumonia? arXiv preprint arXiv:2003.13145, 2020.

[80] M. Toğaçar, B. Ergen, Z. Cömert, F. Özyurt, A deep feature learning model for pneumonia detection applying a combination of mRMR feature selection and machine learning models, IRBM 41 (4) (2020) 212–222.

[81] Z. Li, J. Yu, X. Li, Y. Li, W. Dai, L. Shen, L. Mou, Z. Pu, PNet: an efficient network for pneumonia detection, in: 2019 12th International Congress on Image and Signal Processing, BioMedical Engineering and Informatics (CISP-BMEI), IEEE, 2019, pp. 1–5.

[82] H. Sharma, J.S. Jain, P. Bansal, S. Gupta, Feature extraction and classification of chest X-ray images using CNN to detect pneumonia, in: 2020 10th International Conference on Cloud Computing, Data Science & Engineering (Confluence), IEEE, 2020, pp. 227–231.

[83] A.A. Saraiva, N.M.F. Ferreira, L.L. de Sousa, N.J.C. Costa, J.V.M. Sousa, D.B.S. Santos, A. Valente, S. Soares, Classification of images of childhood pneumonia using convolutional neural networks, in: BIOIMAGING, February, 2019, pp. 112–119.

[84] G. Liang, L. Zheng, A transfer learning method with deep residual network for pediatric pneumonia diagnosis, Comput. Methods Prog. Biomed. 187 (2020) 104964.

[85] D. Varshni, K. Thakral, L. Agarwal, R. Nijhawan, A. Mittal, Pneumonia detection using CNN based feature extraction, in: 2019 IEEE International Conference on Electrical, Computer and Communication Technologies (ICECCT), IEEE, 2019, pp. 1–7.

[86] J.P. Cohen, P. Morrison, L. Dao, K. Roth, T.Q. Duong, M. Ghassemi, Covid-19 image data collection: prospective predictions are the future, arXiv preprint arXiv:2006.11988, 2020.

[87] M. Gadermayr, A.K. Dombrowski, B.M. Klinkhammer, P. Boor, D. Merhof, CNN cascades for segmenting whole slide images of the kidney, arXiv preprint arXiv: 1708.00251, 2017.

[88] V. Makde, J. Bhavsar, S. Jain, P. Sharma, Deep neural network based classification of tumourous and non-tumorous medical images, in: International Conference on Information and Communication Technology for Intelligent Systems, Springer, Cham, 2017, March, pp. 199–206.

[89] V.B. Kolachalama, P. Singh, C.Q. Lin, D. Mun, M.E. Belghasem, J.M. Henderson, J.M. Francis, D.J. Salant, V.C. Chitalia, Association of pathological fibrosis with renal survival using deep neural networks, Kidney Int. Rep. 3 (2) (2018) 464–475.

[90] J.W. Choi, Y. Ku, B.W. Yoo, J.A. Kim, D.S. Lee, Y.J. Chai, H.J. Kong, H.C. Kim, White blood cell differential count of maturation stages in bone marrow smear using dual-stage convolutional neural networks, PLoS One 12 (12) (2017) e0189259.

[91] T. Glasmachers, Limits of end-to-end learning, arXiv preprint arXiv:1704.08305, 2017.

[92] Y. Bengio, Practical recommendations for gradient-based training of deep architectures, in: Neural Networks: Tricks of the Trade, Springer, Berlin, Heidelberg, 2012, pp. 437–478.

[93] I. Goodfellow, Y. Bengio, A. Courville, Y. Bengio, Deep Learning (Vol. 1, No. 2), MIT Press, Cambridge, 2016.

[94] D.A.B. Oliveira, M.P. Viana, Lung nodule synthesis using cnn-based latent data representation, in: International Workshop on Simulation and Synthesis in Medical Imaging, Springer, Cham, 2018, pp. 111–118.

[95] Q. Yang, An introduction to transfer learning, in: ADMA, October, 2008, p. 1.

[96] M. Raghu, C. Zhang, J. Kleinberg, S. Bengio, Transfusion: understanding transfer learning for medical imaging, 2019. arXiv preprint arXiv:1902.07208.

[97] J. Virmani, V. Kumar, N. Kalra, N. Khandelwal, SVM-based characterization of liver ultrasound images using wavelet packet texture descriptors, J. Digit. Imaging 26 (3) (2013) 530–543.

[98] J. Virmani, V. Kumar, N. Kalra, N. Khandelwal, Prediction of cirrhosis from liver ultrasound B-mode images based on Laws' mask analysis, in: Proc. 2011 International Conference on Image Information Processing, 2011.

[99] J. Virmani, V. Kumar, N. Kalra, N. Khandelwal, A comparative study of computer-aided classification systems for focal hepatic lesions from B-mode ultrasound, J. Med. Eng. Technol. 37 (4) (2013) 292–306.

[100] J. Virmani, V. Kumar, N. Kalra, N. Khandelwal, Prediction of cirrhosis based on singular value decomposition of gray level co-occurrence matrix and a neural network classifier, in: Proc. Developments in E-Systems Engineering (DeSE), 2011.

[101] J. Virmani, V. Kumar, N. Kalra, N. Khandelwal, SVM-based characterization of liver cirrhosis by singular value decomposition of GLCM matrix, Int. J. Artif. Intell. Soft Comput. 3 (3) (2013) 276–296.

[102] J. Virmani, V. Kumar, N. Kalra, N. Khandelwal, A rapid approach for prediction of liver cirrhosis based on first order statistics, in: Proc. 2011 International Conference on Multimedia, Signal Processing and Communication Technologies (IMPACT-2011), 2011.

[103] A. Cruz-Roa, H. Gilmore, A. Basavanhally, M. Feldman, S. Ganesan, N.N. Shih, J. Tomaszewski, F.A. González, A. Madabhushi, Accurate and reproducible invasive breast cancer detection in whole-slide images: a Deep Learning approach for quantifying tumor extent, Sci. Rep. 7 (2017) 46450.

[104] Y. LeCun, Y. Bengio, G. Hinton, Deep learning, Nature 521 (7553) (2015) 436–444.

End-to-end pre-trained CNN-based computer-aided classification system design for chest radiographs

4.1 Introduction

This chapter gives an exhaustive description of the experiments carried out for the design of end-to-end pre-trained convolutional neural network-based (CNN-based) computer-aided classification (CAC) systems for chest radiographs. It explains in detail the concepts of transfer learning, pre-trained networks, series network, directed acyclic graph (DAG) network, and architectural description of the pre-trained CNN model AlexNet. GoogLeNet and ResNet18 were used for carrying the experiments. The code snippets of the different experiments aim at giving a better understanding of the programmatic implementation of designing these CAC systems.

4.2 Experimental workflow

A total of four experiments are conducted to design four different CAC systems for chest radiographs. These experiments are carried out using the pre-trained source models available in the MATLAB Deep Learning Toolbox. These source models are originally trained on ImageNet data and then made available for use to other researchers under the term "pre-trained network." These pre-trained networks are retrained and fine-tuned over smaller desired datasets. The smaller datasets are the target datasets for which the researcher desires to design the CAC system. The pre-trained networks used to carry out the experiments in this chapter are AlexNet, GoogLeNet, and ResNet18 CNN models. The experimental workflow followed for analyzing the best-performing pre-trained CNN for classification of chest radiograph images into Normal class and Pneumonia class is shown in Fig. 4.1.

4.3 Transfer learning-based convolutional neural network design

Over the span of recent times, the CNN-based CAC systems have found a major role in medical image analysis [1–13]. CNNs are layered structures whose architecture represents a high level of abstraction in data. These layers usually are: convolution layer, activation layer, pooling layer, fully connected layer, and softmax layer. Each layer of a CNN makes use of a set of filters in an attempt to capture the dependencies in an image that mainly relate to either spatial dependencies or temporal dependencies [14–16]. The CNN focuses on learning the features of an image through the process of training. These

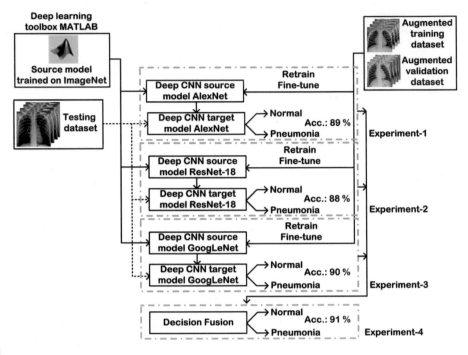

FIG. 4.1

Experimental workflow of end-to-end pre-trained CNN-based CAC system design for classification of chest radiograph images.

features of an image can be local or global in nature. The process of training enables the CNN to identify the patterns in an input image and automatically makes an attempt to classify the testing data into the defined image classes. The main aim is the efficient training of the CNN so that the CAC system designed delivers the best test results, the efficient training can be achieved through: (a) the task of transfer learning, (b) the process of fine-tuning, and (c) training the network from scratch. However the training of a CNN or a deep neural network from scratch can take many days or even weeks, especially on larger datasets. An alternative to this lengthy process of training the network is to reuse the model weights of pre-trained networks that have been trained on benchmark datasets. The most commonly used benchmark dataset for training deep neural networks for computer vision and recognition tasks is the ImageNet dataset. In simple words, the learned weights of the trained network are used to train a new network on a new dataset. The original task or the network can be considered as a base network, which has been trained on a base dataset for performing a base task. The learned weights of this base network are transferred to a second network, called the target network, with an aim to efficiently and quickly train the network for a new task dealing with a target dataset [17–19]. These pre-trained networks can be downloaded and then used by any individual to train the network for their own problems. The next popular training technique is fine-tuning where the new dataset is utilized for adjusting the parameters of a pre-trained network taking into consideration that the two datasets, that is, the original and the new dataset, are similar to each other. Mainly due to the deficiency of wide-ranging and well-explained datasets, this method of training a CNN is not popular in designing the CAC systems for classification of medical images. Among the three techniques of training a CNN, transfer learning as well as fine-tuning are the most popular training techniques. The transfer learning technique has been widely used for designing efficient CAC systems for classification of various medical images [1–13].

Some of the features of transfer learning that make this technique most popular can be stated as follows:

- It enables the reuse of model weights and can be considered analogous to a teacher-student relationship where the teacher transfers knowledge to the student through experience of teaching and learning over the years.
- Transfer learning facilitates the training of networks even for smaller datasets thereby enabling the design of solution to problems that often face data unavailability.
- One of the most important features is the flexible nature, thus making it a versatile learning technique that often achieves superior model performance.
- It allows direct use of pre-trained networks as feature extractors and design of hybrid systems using the machine learning classifiers for prediction purposes.
- This learning technique as compared to the traditional method of training from scratch is more efficient in terms of time and computational costs.

The present work uses transfer learning wherein a preexisting CNN model that has been designed and trained for a specific task is used again for the task of binary classification of chest radiographs. The schematic representation of the concept of transfer learning is shown in Fig. 4.2.

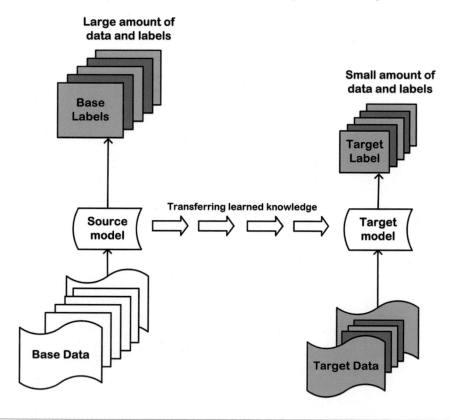

FIG. 4.2

Schematic representation of transfer learning.

4.4 Architecture of end-to-end pre-trained CNNs used in the present work

The basic architectures of CNN models are either series networks that are stacked layers in a contiguous manner or DAG networks where the output of one layer is an input to multiple layers at different levels. Fig. 4.3 shows the different types of pre-trained networks available in the MATLAB Deep Learning Toolbox where the networks shaded in gray are used in the present work.

4.4.1 Series end-to-end pre-trained CNN model: AlexNet

A CNN marked the breakthrough in deep learning by winning the ImageNet Large Scale Visual Recognition Challenge (ILSVRC) 2012, and it was introduced by Alex Krizhevsky et al. in the year 2012 [20]. AlexNet is a 25-layer network comprising of eight deep layers formed by convolutional layers (five layers) and fully connected layers (three layers), and the remaining layers consist of max pooling layers, normalization layers, rectified linear unit (ReLU) activation layers, and dropout layers. AlexNet was the first deep CNN to use ReLU as the activation function, which is considered to be the reason for the massive boost in the accuracy of the network. In addition to ReLU activation, Krizhevsky applied the normalization and dropout layers along with heavy data augmentation with an attempt to improve the general performance. The convolutional layers of AlexNet are of different sizes, such as 11×11, 5×5, 3×3, each having different strides and padding. The ReLU activation is applied after every convolutional layer followed by the normalization and the max pooling layers. Fig. 4.4 shows the basic architecture of AlexNet. The network has an input size of $227 \times 227 \times 3$. All the layers are piled up on each other or arranged one after the other; hence, AlexNet is often referred to as a type of series network [20]. In AlexNet, each of convolutional layer aims at automatic feature

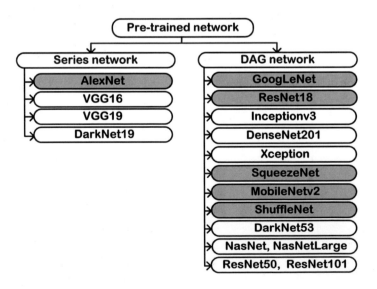

FIG. 4.3

Types of pre-trained networks.

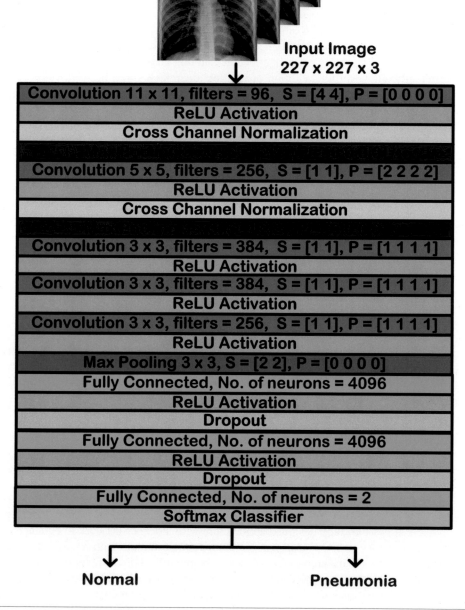

FIG. 4.4

Architecture of AlexNet CNN model.

extraction from the input image, whereas the source of nonlinearity in this series network is the ReLU activation function. It has been extensively used in the classification of medical images of various types [20–25].

4.4.2 Directed acyclic graph end-to-end pre-trained CNN model: ResNet18

The residual network has multiple variations, namely ResNet16, ResNet18, ResNet34, ResNet50, ResNet101, ResNet110, ResNet152, ResNet164, ResNet1202, and so forth. The ResNet stands for residual networks and was named by He et al. 2015 [26]. ResNet18 is a 72-layer architecture with 18 deep layers. The architecture of this network aimed at enabling large amounts of convolutional layers to function efficiently. However, the addition of multiple deep layers to a network often results in a degradation of the output. This is known as the problem of vanishing gradient where neural networks, while getting trained through back propagation, rely on the gradient descent, descending the loss function to find the minimizing weights. Due to the presence of multiple layers, the repeated multiplication results in the gradient becoming smaller and smaller thereby "vanishing" leading to a saturation in the network performance or even degrading the performance.

The primary idea of ResNet is the use of jumping connections that are mostly referred to as shortcut connections or identity connections. These connections primarily function by hopping over one or multiple layers forming shortcuts between these layers. The aim of introducing these shortcut connections was to resolve the predominant issue of vanishing gradient faced by deep networks. These shortcut connections remove the vanishing gradient issue by again using the activations of the previous layer. These identity mappings initially do not do anything much except skip the connections, resulting in the use of previous layer activations. This process of skipping the connection compresses the network; hence, the network learns faster. This compression of the connections is followed by expansion of the layers so that the residual part of the network could also train and explore more feature space. The input size to the network is $224 \times 224 \times 3$, which is predefined. The network is considered to be a DAG network due to its complex layered architecture and because the layers have input from multiple layers and give output to multiple layers. Residual networks and their variants have broadly been implemented for the analysis of medical images [22, 27–29]. Fig. 4.5 shows the layer architecture of ResNet18 CNN model.

The introduction of residual blocks overcomes the problem of vanishing gradient by implementation of skip connections and identity mapping. Identity mapping has no parameters and maps the input to the output, thereby allowing the compression of the network, at first, and then exploring multiple features of the input. Fig. 4.6 shows a typical residual block used in ResNet18 CNN model.

4.4.3 DAG end-to-end pre-trained CNN model: GoogLeNet

The GoogLeNet architecture was the 2014 winner of the ILSVRC and has a 144-layer architecture comprising of 22 deep layers and other pooling layers, ReLU activation layers, and dropouts, given by Szegedy et al. [30]. It is a carefully designed architecture with a deeper network to enhance the overall computational efficiency. It introduced an efficient inception module with an aim of reducing the computational complexity and the amount of parameters being utilized in the network. The GoogLeNet architecture includes the concept of bottleneck layers that are the 1×1 convolutions. These convolutions aim at reducing the dimensions, thereby contributing in the overall reduction of the computational bottlenecks. Another concept that enhances the performance of GoogLeNet is the replacement of fully

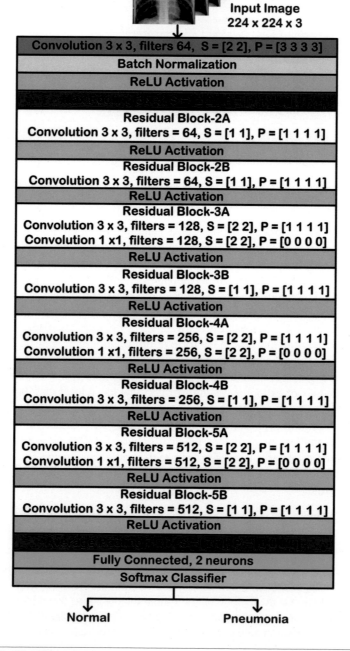

Input Image
224 x 224 x 3

Convolution 3 x 3, filters 64, S = [2 2], P = [3 3 3 3]
Batch Normalization
ReLU Activation
Residual Block-2A **Convolution 3 x 3, filters = 64, S = [1 1], P = [1 1 1 1]**
ReLU Activation
Residual Block-2B **Convolution 3 x 3, filters = 64, S = [1 1], P = [1 1 1 1]**
ReLU Activation
Residual Block-3A **Convolution 3 x 3, filters = 128, S = [2 2], P = [1 1 1 1]** **Convolution 1 x1, filters = 128, S = [2 2], P = [0 0 0 0]**
ReLU Activation
Residual Block-3B **Convolution 3 x 3, filters = 128, S = [1 1], P = [1 1 1 1]**
ReLU Activation
Residual Block-4A **Convolution 3 x 3, filters = 256, S = [2 2], P = [1 1 1 1]** **Convolution 1 x1, filters = 256, S = [2 2], P = [0 0 0 0]**
ReLU Activation
Residual Block-4B **Convolution 3 x 3, filters = 256, S = [1 1], P = [1 1 1 1]**
ReLU Activation
Residual Block-5A **Convolution 3 x 3, filters = 512, S = [2 2], P = [1 1 1 1]** **Convolution 1 x1, filters = 512, S = [2 2], P = [0 0 0 0]**
ReLU Activation
Residual Block-5B **Convolution 3 x 3, filters = 512, S = [1 1], P = [1 1 1 1]**
ReLU Activation
Fully Connected, 2 neurons
Softmax Classifier

Normal   **Pneumonia**

FIG. 4.5

Architecture of ResNet18 CNN model.

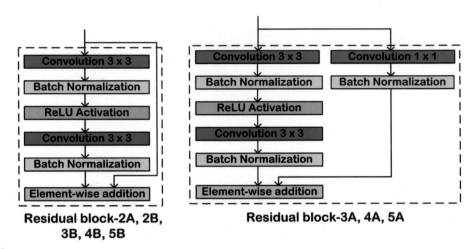

Residual block-2A, 2B, 3B, 4B, 5B

Residual block-3A, 4A, 5A

FIG. 4.6

Structure of residual block.

connected layers by the global average pooling (GAP) and the inception module. The GAP layers reduce the computation cost of the network due to the absence of the trainable weights in this layer. There are nine inception modules being applied in the middle of the network. The general layer architecture of GoogLeNet and the basic configuration of an inception module are shown in Fig. 4.7.

The inception network contains the grouping of all the convolutions (1×1, 3×3, 5×5). The final result of this combination of convolutions is the concatenation of the results of each convolution (1×1, 3×3, 5×5). These modules were introduced with an aim to reduce the disparity in evidence of an entity associated with the entity location in the form of information in an image. Extracting this location information often requires the selection of the appropriate kernel size since larger kernels mostly associate with extracting the information, which is distributed globally, whereas a smaller sized kernel is well-matched for the task of extracting the information that has a local distribution. The network is considered to be a DAG network due to its complex layered architecture and because the layers have input from multiple layers and give output to multiple layers. The GoogLeNet architecture has been applied broadly in the analysis of numerous medical images [31–33]. A general inception module consists of 1×1 convolution layers often referred to as the bottleneck layers. These 1×1 convolutions are introduced for dimensionality reduction in GoogLeNet. Fig. 4.8 shows an inception module used in GoogLeNet architecture.

4.5 Decision fusion

As the name suggests, decision fusion aims at combining the decisions taken by different classifiers to achieve a common consensus that is better than the individual decisions of the classifiers [34, 35]. In simple words, decision fusion is the method of combining the decisions taken by multiple classifiers to reach a common final decision. Here the decision of the classifier is the classification performed on the test dataset, which is the prediction on the test dataset. The process includes coalescing the information

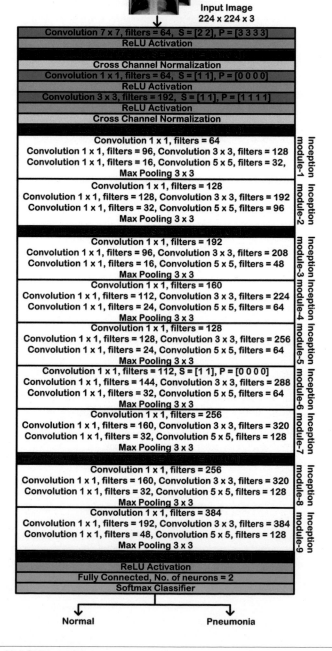

FIG. 4.7

Architecture of GoogLeNet CNN model.

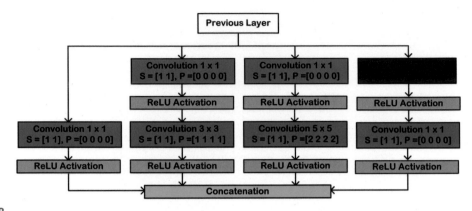

FIG. 4.8

Structure of inception module.

from different datasets or different classifiers after each data has been subjected to preliminary classification. Decision fusion is performed with an aim to enhance the performance of the classification task. Classifiers often have different classification performances depending on the type of data they are working with as well as their architecture. However, many times different classifiers have varied performance for the same classification problem. The decisions taken by a classifier are broadly of three types: (a) measurement level: this type of decision involves the classifier returning a real valued vector; (b) rank level: this type of decision involves the classifiers to return an ordered sequence of classes; and (c) abstract level: this is the most widely applied type of decision where the classifiers return a single class label as the decision. Fig. 4.9 shows the different types of decisions that can be taken by a classifier.

Fig. 4.10 shows the broad categorization of the decision fusion techniques.

On the other hand, the decision fusion techniques are broadly classified on the basis of the fusion architecture used; these include the following:

(a) Serial decision fusion: In this architecture, the classifiers are arranged in series; the output of one classifier acts as an input to the next. Fig. 4.11 shows the series decision fusion.

(b) Parallel decision fusion: In this, the classifiers are arranged in parallel and the classifiers perform classification simultaneously **and** then the decision fusion is performed. Fig. 4.12 shows the parallel decision fusion.

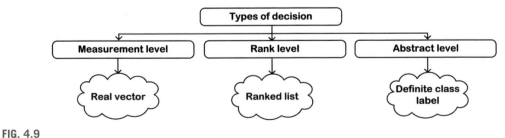

FIG. 4.9

Types of decisions.

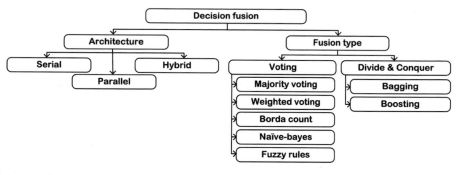

FIG. 4.10

Types of decision fusion.

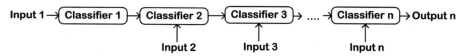

FIG. 4.11

Series decision fusion.

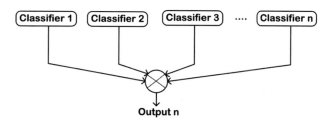

FIG. 4.12

Parallel decision fusion.

(c) Hybrid decision fusion: This is a hierarchical structure of classifiers. Fig. 4.13 shows the hybrid decision fusion.

On the basis of the fusion type, these techniques are of two types:

(a) Voting-based: In the voting-based decision fusion techniques, majority voting is the most popular and is widely used. Some of the other techniques include weighted voting in which a weight to each classifier is attached and then decision fusion is performed. Borda count is another technique in which the sums of reverse ranks are calculated to perform decision fusion [36]. Other voting techniques are probability-based, such as fuzzy rules, Naïve-Bayes, Dempster-Shafer theory, and so forth [35, 37, 38].

(b) Divide and conquer: In this decision fusion technique, the dataset is divided into subsets of equal sizes, and then the classification is performed followed by decision fusion on the results of those smaller dataset classifications. These divide and conquer methods include the concepts of bagging and boosting.

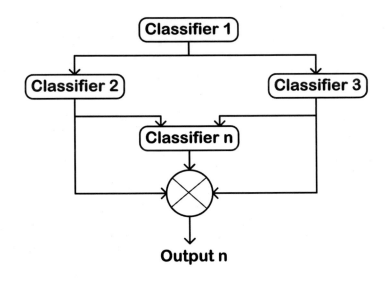

FIG. 4.13

Hybrid decision fusion.

The present work implements the majority voting of the different CNN-based pre-trained models with a parallel architecture of the decision fusion technique.

4.6 Experiments and results

Experiment 1: Designing end-to-end pre-trained CNN-based CAC system for chest radiographs using AlexNet

In Experiment 1, the CAC system for binary class classification of chest radiograph images is designed using AlexNet CNN model. The network has been trained using the augmented chest radiograph image dataset for classification of chest radiograph images. The results of performance evaluation of the CAC system designed using AlexNet CNN for chest radiographs are shown in Table 4.1.

From the results of Experiment 1, as shown in Table 4.1, it can be seen that the CAC system designed using end-to-end pre-trained AlexNet CNN model achieves 89.00% accuracy for the clas-

Table 4.1 Performance evaluation of CAC system designed using AlexNet CNN for chest radiographs.

Network/ classifier	Confusion matrix			Accuracy (%)	ICA_ Normal (%)	ICA_ Pneumonia (%)
		Normal	**Pneumonia**			
AlexNet/ softmax	Normal	49	1	89.00	98.00	80.00
	Pneumonia	10	40			

ICA_Normal, *individual class accuracy for Normal class;* ICA_Pneumonia, *individual class accuracy for Pneumonia class.*

sification of chest radiograph images into two classes: Normal and Pneumonia. The individual class accuracy of the Normal class is 98.00%, and for the Pneumonia class, the individual class accuracy obtained is 80.00%. From the total 100 images in the testing set, 11 images have been misclassified from which only one instance belongs to the Normal class and the remaining 10 misclassified images are of the Pneumonia class.

Code Snippet 4.1 shows the syntax of loading the training dataset. The chest X-ray images are divided and kept in three folders, namely training, validation, and testing. The training data is loaded from the path "H:\DataChestxray\Training\," which further contains two folders named as per the class labels of Normal and Pneumonia.

Code Snippet 4.2 shows the syntax of loading the validation dataset. The validation data is loaded from the path "H:\DataChestxray\Validation\," which further contains two folders named as per the class labels Normal and Pneumonia, just as those of the training dataset.

Code Snippet 4.3 shows the syntax of loading the testing dataset. The testing data is loaded from the path "H:\DataChestxray\Testing\," which further contains two folders named as per the class labels Normal and Pneumonia, just as those of the training and validation datasets.

After the dataset has been loaded, the target CNN model is loaded as shown in Code Snippet 4.4. For Experiment 1, the AlexNet CNN model is used; hence, it is loaded to further proceed with the training process.

Code Snippet 4.1 Loading the training dataset

```
%%Loading the training dataset%%
imds_train=imageDatastore('H:\DataChestxray\Training\','IncludeSubfolders',true,
'LabelSource','foldernames');
```

Code Snippet 4.2 Loading the validation dataset

```
%%Loading the validation dataset%%
imds_val=imageDatastore('H:\DataChestxray\Validation\','IncludeSubfolders',true,
'LabelSource','foldernames');
```

Code Snippet 4.3 Loading the testing dataset

```
%%Loading the testing dataset%%
imds_test=imageDatastore('H:\DataChestxray\Testing\','IncludeSubfolders',true,
'LabelSource','foldernames');
```

Code Snippet 4.4 Loading the AlexNet pre-trained CNN model

```
%%loading the AlexNet pre-trained CNN model%%
net = alexnet;
```

As the target network is also loaded into the MATLAB workspace, one needs to specify the training options so as to facilitate training of the CNN model. Code Snippet 4.5 shows the training options set for Experiment 1.

Code Snippet 4.6 shows the syntax of training the network using the training data and the CNN model loaded into the workspace on the previously defined training options.

Code Snippet 4.7 shows the syntax of projecting the test data onto the trained network. The predictions of the trained CNN model are in the form of a confusion matrix.

Once the network is trained, it is beneficial to save the network for future reference. This can be done using the save() function as shown in Code Snippet 4.8. The results of Experiment 1 are saved in a "mat" file named 'Exp1_alexnet.mat'.

Experiment 2: Designing end-to-end pre-trained CNN-based CAC system for chest radiographs using ResNet18

In Experiment 2, the CAC system for binary class classification of chest radiograph images is designed using ResNet18 CNN model. The network has been trained using the augmented chest

Code Snippet 4.5 Assigning the training options

```
%%specifying the training options %%
Training_options = trainingOptions('rmsprop', 'InitialLearnRate', 0.0001, 'Plots',
'training-progress', 'ValidationData', imds_val, 'ValidationFrequency',10,'Shuffle',
'every-epoch','MaxEpochs',10, 'MiniBatchSize',45);
```

Code Snippet 4.6 Training the AlexNet pre-trained CNN model

```
%%training the CNN model%%
Exp1_alexnet= trainNetwork(imds_train,lgraph_1, Training_options);
```

Code Snippet 4.7 Classifying the images and printing the confusion matrix

```
%%using trained network to classify images%%
[predictions,prediction_score] = classify(Exp1_alexnet,imds_test);
true_testing = imds_test.Labels;
nnz(predictions == true_testing)/numel(predictions);
[confusion_matrix, matrix_order] =confusionmat(true_testing,predictions);
heatmap(matrix_order, matrix_order, confusion_matrix);
accuracy = mean(predictions==true_testing)
```

Code Snippet 4.8 Saving the results

```
%%saving the trained AlexNet CNN model%%
save('Exp1_alexnet')
```

radiograph image dataset for classification of chest radiograph images. The results of performance evaluation of the CAC system designed using ResNet18 CNN for chest radiographs are shown in Table 4.2.

From the results of Experiment 2, as shown in Table 4.3, it can be seen that the CAC system using ResNet18 CNN model gives 88.00% accuracy for the classification of chest radiograph images into two classes: Normal and Pneumonia. The individual class accuracy of the Normal class is 100.00%, and for the Pneumonia class, the individual class accuracy value obtained is 76.00%. From the total 100 images in the testing set, 12 images have been misclassified, which all belong to the Pneumonia class.

Code Snippet 4.9 shows the syntax of loading the training dataset. The chest X-ray images are divided and kept in three folders namely training, validation, and testing. The training data is loaded from the path "H:\DataChestxray\Training\," which further contains two folders named as per the class labels of Normal and Pneumonia.

Code Snippet 4.10 shows the syntax of loading the validation dataset. The validation data is loaded from the path "H:\DataChestxray\Validation\," which further contains two folders named as per the class labels Normal and Pneumonia, just as those of the training dataset.

Table 4.2 **Performance evaluation of CAC system designed using ResNet18 CNN for chest radiographs.**

Network/ classifier	Confusion matrix			Accuracy (%)	ICA_ Normal (%)	ICA_ Pneumonia (%)
		Normal	Pneumonia			
ResNet18/ softmax	Normal	50	0	88.00	100.00	76.00
	Pneumonia	12	38			

ICA_Normal, *individual class accuracy for Normal class;* ICA_Pneumonia, *individual class accuracy for Pneumonia class.*

Table 4.3 **Performance evaluation of CAC system designed using GoogLeNet CNN for chest radiographs.**

Network/ classifier	Confusion matrix			Accuracy (%)	ICA_ Normal (%)	ICA_ Pneumonia (%)
		Normal	Pneumonia			
GoogLeNet/ softmax	Normal	48	2	90.00	96.00	84.00
	Pneumonia	8	42			

ICA_Normal, *individual class accuracy for Normal class;* ICA_Pneumonia, *individual class accuracy for Pneumonia class.*

Code Snippet 4.9 Loading the training dataset

```
%%Loading the training dataset%%
imds_train=imageDatastore('H:\DataChestxray\Training\','IncludeSubfolders',true,
'LabelSource','foldernames');
```

Code Snippet 4.10 Loading the validation dataset

```
%%Loading the validation dataset%%
imds_val=imageDatastore('H:\DataChestxray\Validation\','IncludeSubfolders',true,
'LabelSource','foldernames');
```

Code Snippet 4.11 Loading the testing dataset

```
%%Loading the testing dataset%%
imds_test=imageDatastore('H:\DataChestxray\Testing\','IncludeSubfolders',true,
'LabelSource','foldernames');
```

Code Snippet 4.11 shows the syntax of loading the testing dataset. The testing data is loaded from the path "H:\DataChestxray\Testing\," which further contains two folders named as per the class labels Normal and Pneumonia, just as those of the training and validation datasets.

After the dataset has been loaded, the target CNN model is loaded as shown in Code Snippet 4.12. For Experiment 2, ResNet18 CNN model is used; hence, it is loaded to further proceed with the training process.

As the target network is also loaded into the MATLAB workspace, now one needs to specify the training options so as to facilitate training of the CNN model. Code Snippet 4.13 shows the training options set for Experiment 2.

Code Snippet 4.14 shows the syntax of training the network using the training data and the CNN model loaded into the workspace on the previously defined training options.

Code Snippet 4.12 Loading the CNN model

```
%%loading the resnet18 pre-trained CNN model%%
net = resnet18;
```

Code Snippet 4.13 Assigning the training options

```
%%specifying the training options %%
Training_options = trainingOptions('rmsprop', 'InitialLearnRate',
0.0001,'Plots','training-progress','ValidationData',imds_val, 'ValidationFrequency',
10,'Shuffle','every-epoch','MaxEpochs',10, 'MiniBatchSize',45);
```

Code Snippet 4.14 Training the ResNet18 pre-trained CNN model

```
%%training the CNN model%%
Exp2_resnet18= trainNetwork(imds_train,lgraph_1, Training_options);
```

Code Snippet 4.15 Classifying the images and printing the confusion matrix

```
%%using trained network to classify images%%
[predictions,prediction_score] = classify(Exp2_resnet18,imds_test);
true_testing = imds_test.Labels;
nnz(predictions == true_testing)/numel(predictions);
[confusion_matrix, matrix_order] =confusionmat(true_testing,predictions);
heatmap(matrix_order, matrix_order, confusion_matrix);
accuracy = mean(predictions==true_testing)
```

Code Snippet 4.15 shows the syntax of projecting the test data onto the trained network. The predictions of the trained CNN model are in the form of a confusion matrix.

Once the network is trained, it is beneficial to save the network for future reference. This is done using the save() function as shown in Code Snippet 4.16. The results of Experiment 2 are saved in a "mat" file named 'Exp2_resnet18.mat'.

Experiment 3: Designing end-to-end pre-trained CNN-based CAC system for chest radiographs using GoogLeNet

In Experiment 3, the CAC system for binary class classification of chest radiograph images is designed using GoogLeNet CNN model. The network has been trained using the augmented chest radiograph image dataset for classification of chest radiograph images. The results of performance evaluation of CAC system designed using GoogLeNet CNN for chest radiographs are shown in Table 4.3.

From the results of Experiment 3, as shown in Table 4.3, it can be seen that the CAC system designed using GoogLeNet CNN model achieves 90% accuracy for the classification of chest radiograph images into two classes: Normal and Pneumonia. The individual class accuracy of the Normal class is 96%, and for the Pneumonia class, the individual class accuracy obtained is 84%. From the total 100 images in the testing set, 10 images have been misclassified, out of which 2 belong to the Normal class and 8 belong to the Pneumonia class.

Code Snippet 4.17 shows the syntax of loading the training dataset. The chest X-ray images are divided and kept in three folders, namely training, validation, and testing. The training data is loaded

---

Code Snippet 4.16 Saving the results

```
%%saving the trained AlexNet CNN model%%
save('Exp2_resnet18')
```

Code Snippet 4.17 Loading the training dataset

```
%%Loading the training dataset%%
imds_train=imageDatastore('H:\DataChestxray\Training\','IncludeSubfolders',true,
'LabelSource','foldernames');
```

from the path "H:\DataChestxray\Training\," which further contains two folders named as per the class labels of Normal and Pneumonia.

Code Snippet 4.18 shows the syntax of loading the validation dataset. The validation data is loaded from the path "H:\DataChestxray\Validation\," which further contains two folders named as per the class labels Normal and Pneumonia, just as those of the training dataset.

Code Snippet 4.19 shows the syntax of loading the testing dataset. The testing data is loaded from the path "H:\DataChestxray\Testing\," which further contains two folders named as per the class labels Normal and Pneumonia, just as those of the training and validation datasets.

After the dataset has been loaded, the target CNN model is loaded as shown in Code Snippet 4.20. For Experiment 3, GoogLeNet CNN model is used; hence, it is loaded to further proceed with the training process.

As the target network is also loaded into the MATLAB workspace, now one needs to specify the training options so as to facilitate training of the CNN model. Code Snippet 4.21 shows the training options set for Experiment 3.

Code Snippet 4.22 shows the syntax of training the network using the training data, and the CNN model is loaded into the workspace on the previously defined training options.

Code Snippet 4.18 Loading the validation dataset

```
%%Loading the validation dataset%%
imds_val=imageDatastore('H:\DataChestxray\Validation\','IncludeSubfolders',true,
'LabelSource','foldernames');
```

Code Snippet 4.19 Loading the testing dataset

```
%%Loading the testing dataset%%
imds_test=imageDatastore('H:\DataChestxray\Testing\','IncludeSubfolders',true,
'LabelSource','foldernames');
```

Code Snippet 4.20 Loading the GoogLeNet pre-trained CNN model

```
%%loading the GoogLeNet pre-trained CNN model%%
net = googlenet;
```

Code Snippet 4.21 Assigning the training options

```
%%specifying the training options %%
Training_options = trainingOptions('sgdm', 'InitialLearnRate', 0.0001, 'Plots',
'training-progress', 'ValidationData', imds_val, 'ValidationFrequency',10,'Shuffle',
'every-epoch','MaxEpochs',10, 'MiniBatchSize',45);
```

Code Snippet 4.22 Training the GoogLeNet pre-trained CNN model

```
%%training the CNN model%%
Exp3_GoogLeNet= trainNetwork(imds_train,lgraph_1,Training_options);
```

Code Snippet 4.23 Classifying the images and printing the confusion matrix

```
%%using trained network to classify images%%
[predictions,prediction_score] = classify(Exp3_GoogLeNet,imds_test);
true_testing = imds_test.Labels;
nnz(predictions == true_testing)/numel(predictions);
[confusion_matrix, matrix_order] = confusionmat(true_testing,predictions);
heatmap(matrix_order, matrix_order, confusion_matrix);
accuracy = mean(predictions==true_testing)
```

Code Snippet 4.24 Saving the results

```
%%saving the trained GoogLeNet CNN model%%
save('Exp3_GoogLeNet')
```

Code Snippet 4.23 shows the syntax of projecting the test data onto the trained network. The predictions of the trained CNN model are in the form of a confusion matrix.

Once the network is trained, it is beneficial to save the network for future reference. This is done using the save() function as shown in Code Snippet 4.24. The results of Experiment 3 are saved in a "mat" file named 'Exp3_GoogLeNet.mat'.

Experiment 4: Designing end-to-end pre-trained CNN-based CAC system for chest radiographs using decision fusion

In Experiment 4, the CAC system for binary class classification of chest radiograph images is designed using decision fusion of the pre-trained CNN models that have been trained using the augmented chest radiograph image dataset for classification of chest radiograph images in Experiments 1–3. The results of performance evaluation of the CAC system designed using decision fusion for binary classification of chest radiographs are shown in Table 4.4.

From the results of Experiment 4, as shown in Table 4.4, it can be seen that the CAC system designed using the decision fusion of the CNN models in Experiments 1–3 achieves 91.00% accuracy for the classification of chest radiograph images into two classes of Normal and Pneumonia. The individual class accuracy of the Normal class is 100.00%, and for the Pneumonia class, the individual class accuracy obtained is 82.00%. From the total 100 images in the testing set, 9 images have been misclassified, which all belong to the Pneumonia class. The ROC curve with its corresponding AUC values for the CAC system designed using the different CNN models is shown in Fig. 4.14.

Table 4.4 Performance evaluation of CAC system designed using decision fusion technique for chest radiograph images.

Network/classifier	Confusion matrix			Accuracy (%)	ICA_ Normal (%)	ICA_ Pneumonia (%)
		Normal	Pneumonia			
AlexNet+GoogLeNet+ ResNet18/softmax	Normal	50	0	91.00	100.00	82.00
	Pneumonia	9	41			

ICA_Normal, *individual class accuracy for Normal class;* ICA_Pneumonia, *individual class accuracy for Pneumonia class.*

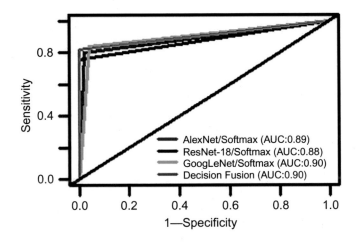

FIG. 4.14

The ROC curve with its corresponding AUC values for the CAC system designed using the different CNN models.

4.7 Concluding remarks

From the assessment of the experiments carried out in this chapter to evaluate the performance of the popularly used CNN networks AlexNet, ResNet-18, and GoogLeNet and on the basis of the results obtained from the experiments carried out in the present work, it is observed that GoogLeNet CNN model performs best for the classification of chest radiographs.

A comparative analysis of the obtained results from the experiments carried with different CNN models for the classification of chest radiographs is given in Table 4.5.

Therefore, for further analysis of the performance of machine learning-based classifiers, the GoogLeNet CNN model is used for deep feature extraction. The subsequent chapters deal with the design of a CAC system for chest radiographs using deep feature extraction, GoogLeNet, ANFC-LH classifier, and PCA-SVM classifier.

Table 4.5 **Comparative analysis of the obtained results for the classification of chest radiographs.**

Network/classifier	Accuracy (%)	ICA_Normal (%)	ICA_Pneumonia (%)
Experiment 1: Designing end-to-end pre-trained CNN-based CAC system for chest radiographs using AlexNet	89.00	98.00	80.00
Experiment 2: Designing end-to-end pre-trained CNN-based CAC system for chest radiographs using ResNet18	88.00	100.00	76.00
Experiment 3: Designing end-to-end pre-trained CNN-based CAC system for chest radiographs using GoogLeNet	90.00	96.00	84.00
Experiment 4: Designing end-to-end pre-trained CNN-based CAC system for chest radiographs using decision fusion	91.00	100.00	82.00

ICA_Normal, *individual class accuracy for Normal class;* ICA_Pneumonia, *individual class accuracy for Pneumonia class.*

References

[1] H. Kutlu, E. Avcı, A novel method for classifying liver and brain tumors using convolutional neural networks, discrete wavelet transform and long short-term memory networks, Sensors 19 (9) (2019) 1992.

[2] D. Jirak, M. Dezortová, P. Taimr, M. Hájek, Texture analysis of human liver, J. Magn. Reson. Imaging 15 (1) (2002) 68–74.

[3] A.E. Fetit, J. Novak, A.C. Peet, T.N. Arvanitis, Three-dimensional textural features of conventional MRI improve diagnostic classification of childhood brain tumours, NMR Biomed. 28 (9) (2015) 1174–1184.

[4] L. Ballerini, R.B. Fisher, B. Aldridge, J. Rees, A color and texture based hierarchical K-NN approach to the classification of non-melanoma skin lesions, in: Color Medical Image Analysis, Springer, Dordrecht, 2013, pp. 63–86.

[5] M. Nasir, M. Attique Khan, M. Sharif, I.U. Lali, T. Saba, T. Iqbal, An improved strategy for skin lesion detection and classification using uniform segmentation and feature selection based approach, Microsc. Res. Tech. 81 (6) (2018) 528–543.

[6] J. Shijie, W. Ping, J. Peiyi, H. Siping, Research on data augmentation for image classification based on convolution neural networks, in: 2017 Chinese Automation Congress (CAC), IEEE, 2017, pp. 4165–4170.

[7] Y. Zhu, Y. Chen, Z. Lu, S.J. Pan, G.R. Xue, Y. Yu, Q. Yang, Heterogeneous transfer learning for image classification, in: Twenty-Fifth AAAI Conference on Artificial Intelligence, 2011.

[8] M. Gadermayr, A.K. Dombrowski, B.M. Klinkhammer, P. Boor, D. Merhof, CNN cascades for segmenting whole slide images of the kidney, arXiv preprint arXiv: 1708.00251, 2017.

[9] V. Makde, J. Bhavsar, S. Jain, P. Sharma, Deep neural network based classification of tumourous and non-tumorous medical images, in: International Conference on Information and Communication Technology for Intelligent Systems, Springer, Cham, 2017, pp. 199–206.

[10] V.B. Kolachalama, P. Singh, C.Q. Lin, D. Mun, M.E. Belghasem, J.M. Henderson, J.M. Francis, D.J. Salant, V.C. Chitalia, Association of pathological fibrosis with renal survival using deep neural networks, Kidney Int. Rep. 3 (2) (2018) 464–475.

[11] J.W. Choi, Y. Ku, B.W. Yoo, J.A. Kim, D.S. Lee, Y.J. Chai, H.J. Kong, H.C. Kim, White blood cell differential count of maturation stages in bone marrow smear using dual-stage convolutional neural networks, PLoS One 12 (12) (2017) e0189259.

[12] J. Islam, Y. Zhang, Brain MRI analysis for Alzheimer's disease diagnosis using an ensemble system of deep convolutional neural networks, Brain Inform. 5 (2) (2018) 2.

[13] N. Gessert, M. Heyder, S. Latus, M. Lutz, A. Schlaefer, Plaque classification in coronary arteries from ivoct images using convolutional neural networks and transfer learning. arXiv preprint arXiv:1804.03904, 2018.

[14] S. Albawi, T.A. Mohammed, S. Al-Zawi, Understanding of a convolutional neural network, in: 2017 International Conference on Engineering and Technology (ICET), IEEE, 2017, pp. 1–6.

[15] S. Khan, H. Rahmani, S.A.A. Shah, M. Bennamoun, A Guide to Convolutional Neural Networks for Computer Vision, Synthesis Lectures on Computer Vision 8 (1) (2018) 1–207.

[16] S.S. Yadav, S.M. Jadhav, Deep convolutional neural network based medical image classification for disease diagnosis, J. Big Data 6 (1) (2019) 1–18.

[17] Q. Yang, An introduction to transfer learning, in: ADMA, October, 2008, p. 1.

[18] M. Raghu, C. Zhang, J. Kleinberg, S. Bengio, Transfusion: understanding transfer learning for medical imaging, 2019. arXiv preprint arXiv:1902.07208.

[19] K. Weiss, T.M. Khoshgoftaar, D. Wang, A survey of transfer learning, J. Big Data 3 (1) (2016) 1–40.

[20] A. Krizhevsky, I. Sutskever, G.E. Hinton, 2012 AlexNet. Adv. Neural Inf. Process. Syst, 2012, pp. 1–9.

[21] M. Toğaçar, B. Ergen, Z. Cömert, F. Özyurt, A deep feature learning model for pneumonia detection applying a combination of mRMR feature selection and machine learning models, IRBM 41 (4) (2020) 212–222.

[22] T. Rahman, M.E. Chowdhury, A. Khandakar, K.R. Islam, K.F. Islam, Z.B. Mahbub, M.A. Kadir, S. Kashem, Transfer learning with deep convolutional neural network (CNN) for pneumonia detection using chest X-ray, Appl. Sci. 10 (9) (2020) 3233.

[23] A. Abd Almisreb, M.A. Saleh, N.M. Tahir, Anomalous behaviour detection using transfer learning algorithm of series and DAG network, in: 2019 IEEE 9th International Conference on System Engineering and Technology (ICSET), IEEE, 2019, pp. 505–509.

[24] A. Bhandary, G.A. Prabhu, V. Rajinikanth, K.P. Thanaraj, S.C. Satapathy, D.E. Robbins, C. Shasky, Y.D. Zhang, J.M.R. Tavares, N.S.M. Raja, Deep-learning framework to detect lung abnormality—a study with chest X-ray and lung CT scan images, Pattern Recogn. Lett. 129 (2020) 271–278.

[25] W. Nawaz, S. Ahmed, A. Tahir, H.A. Khan, Classification of breast cancer histology images using alexnet, in: International Conference Image Analysis and Recognition, Springer, Cham, 2018, pp. 869–876.

[26] K. He, X. Zhang, S. Ren, J. Sun, Deep residual learning for image recognition, in: Proceedings of the IEEE Conference on Computer Vision and Pattern Recognition, 2016, pp. 770–778.

[27] A.F. Al Mubarok, J.A. Dominique, A.H. Thias, Pneumonia detection with deep convolutional architecture, in: 2019 International Conference of Artificial Intelligence and Information Technology (ICAIIT), IEEE, 2019, pp. 486–489.

[28] M.F. Hashmi, S. Katiyar, A.G. Keskar, N.D. Bokde, Z.W. Geem, Efficient pneumonia detection in chest xray images using deep transfer learning, Diagnostics 10 (6) (2020) 417.

[29] S. Ayyachamy, V. Alex, M. Khened, G. Krishnamurthi, Medical image retrieval using Resnet-18, in: Medical Imaging 2019: Imaging Informatics for Healthcare, Research, and Applications, vol. 10954, International Society for Optics and Photonics, 2019, p. 1095410.

[30] C. Szegedy, W. Liu, Y. Jia, P. Sermanet, S. Reed, D. Anguelov, D. Erhan, V. Vanhoucke, A. Rabinovich, Going deeper with convolutions, in: Proceedings of the IEEE Conference on Computer Vision and Pattern Recognition, 2015, pp. 1–9.

[31] C. Szegedy, S. Ioffe, V. Vanhoucke, A. Alemi, Inception-v4, inception-resnet and the impact of residual connections on learning, arXiv 2016, arXiv preprint arXiv:1602.07261, 2016.

[32] B. Khagi, B. Lee, J.Y. Pyun, G.R. Kwon, CNN models performance analysis on MRI images of OASIS dataset for distinction between healthy and Alzheimer's patient, in: 2019 International Conference on Electronics, Information, and Communication (ICEIC), IEEE, 2019, pp. 1–4.

[33] S. Serte, A. Serener, F. Al-Turjman, Deep learning in medical imaging: a brief review, Trans. Emerging Telecommun. Technol. (2020) e4080.

[34] S. Tulyakov, S. Jaeger, V. Govindaraju, D. Doermann, Review of classifier combination methods, in: Machine Learning in Document Analysis and Recognition, Springer, Berlin, Heidelberg, 2008, pp. 361–386.

[35] T.K. Ho, J.J. Hull, S.N. Srihari, Decision combination in multiple classifier systems, IEEE Trans. Pattern Anal. Mach. Intell. 16 (1) (1994) 66–75.

[36] A. Lumini, L. Nanni, Detector of image orientation based on Borda Count, Pattern Recogn. Lett. 27 (3) (2006) 180–186.

[37] N.M. Wanas, M.S. Kamel, Decision fusion in neural network ensembles, in: IJCNN'01. International Joint Conference on Neural Networks. Proceedings, vol. 4, IEEE, 2001, pp. 2952–2957 (Cat. No. 01CH37222).

[38] A.F.R. Rahman, M.C. Fairhurst, Multiple classifier decision combination strategies for character recognition: a review, Int. J. Document Anal. Recogn. 5 (4) (2003) 166–194.

Further reading

X. Gu, L. Pan, H. Liang, R. Yang, Classification of bacterial and viral childhood pneumonia using deep learning in chest radiography, in: Proceedings of the 3rd International Conference on Multimedia and Image Processing, 2018, pp. 88–93.

J.R. Zech, M.A. Badgeley, M. Liu, A.B. Costa, J.J. Titano, E.K. Oermann, Variable generalization performance of a deep learning model to detect pneumonia in chest radiographs: a cross-sectional study, PLoS Med. 15 (11) (2018) e1002683.

M.E. Chowdhury, T. Rahman, A. Khandakar, R. Mazhar, M.A. Kadir, Z.B. Mahbub, K.R. Islam, M.S. Khan, A. Iqbal, N. Al-Emadi, M.B.I. Reaz, Can AI help in screening viral and COVID-19 pneumonia? arXiv preprint arXiv:2003.13145, 2020.

Z. Li, J. Yu, X. Li, Y. Li, W. Dai, L. Shen, L. Mou, Z. Pu, PNet: an efficient network for pneumonia detection, in: 2019 12th International Congress on Image and Signal Processing, BioMedical Engineering and Informatics (CISP-BMEI), IEEE, 2019, pp. 1–5.

H. Sharma, J.S. Jain, P. Bansal, S. Gupta, Feature extraction and classification of chest X-ray images using CNN to detect pneumonia, in: 2020 10th International Conference on Cloud Computing, Data Science & Engineering (Confluence), IEEE, 2020, pp. 227–231.

K. El Asnaoui, Y. Chawki, Using X-ray images and deep learning for automated detection of coronavirus disease, J. Biomol. Struct. Dyn. (2020) 1–22 (just-accepted).

A.A. Saraiva, N.M.F. Ferreira, L.L. de Sousa, N.J.C. Costa, J.V.M. Sousa, D.B.S. Santos, A. Valente, S. Soares, Classification of images of childhood pneumonia using convolutional neural networks, in: BIOIMAGING, February, 2019, pp. 112–119.

D.S. Kermany, M. Goldbaum, W. Cai, C.C. Valentim, H. Liang, S.L. Baxter, A. McKeown, G. Yang, X. Wu, F. Yan, J. Dong, Identifying medical diagnoses and treatable diseases by image-based deep learning, Cell 172 (5) (2018) 1122–1131.

K. Jakhar, N. Hooda, Big data deep learning framework using Keras: a case study of pneumonia prediction, in: 2018 4th International Conference on Computing Communication and Automation (ICCCA), IEEE, 2018, pp. 1–5.

S. Rajaraman, S. Candemir, I. Kim, G. Thoma, S. Antani, Visualization and interpretation of convolutional neural network predictions in detecting pneumonia in pediatric chest radiographs, Appl. Sci. 8 (10) (2018) 1715.

E. Ayan, H.M. Ünver, Diagnosis of pneumonia from chest X-ray images using deep learning, in: 2019 Scientific Meeting on Electrical-Electronics & Biomedical Engineering and Computer Science (EBBT), IEEE, 2019, pp. 1–5.

K.E. El Asnaoui, Y. Chawki, A. Idri, Automated methods for detection and classification pneumonia based on x-ray images using deep learning. arXiv preprint arXiv:2003.14363, 2020.

G. Jain, D. Mittal, D. Thakur, M.K. Mittal, A deep learning approach to detect Covid-19 coronavirus with X-ray images, Biocybern. Biomed. Eng. 40 (4) (2020) 1391–1405.

I.D. Apostolopoulos, T.A. Mpesiana, Covid-19: automatic detection from x-ray images utilizing transfer learning with convolutional neural networks, Phys. Eng. Sci. Med. 43 (2) (2020) 635–640.

T. Ozturk, M. Talo, E.A. Yildirim, U.B. Baloglu, O. Yildirim, U.R. Acharya, Automated detection of COVID-19 cases using deep neural networks with X-ray images, Comput. Biol. Med. 121 (2020) 103792.

P.K. Sethy, S.K. Behera, Detection of coronavirus disease (covid-19) based on deep features, Preprints 2020030300 (2020) 2020.

G. Liang, L. Zheng, A transfer learning method with deep residual network for pediatric pneumonia diagnosis, Comput. Methods Prog. Biomed. 187 (2020) 104964.

D. Varshni, K. Thakral, L. Agarwal, R. Nijhawan, A. Mittal, Pneumonia detection using CNN based feature extraction, in: 2019 IEEE International Conference on Electrical, Computer and Communication Technologies (ICECCT), IEEE, 2019, pp. 1–7.

J. Civit-Masot, F. Luna-Perejón, M. Domínguez Morales, A. Civit, Deep learning system for COVID-19 diagnosis aid using X-ray pulmonary images, Appl. Sci. 10 (13) (2020) 4640.

M. Nixon, A. Aguado, Feature Extraction and Image Processing for Computer Vision, Academic Press, 2019.

Hybrid computer-aided classification system design using end-to-end CNN-based deep feature extraction and ANFC-LH classifier for chest radiographs

5.1 Introduction

This chapter covers the description of the experiment carried out for the design of hybrid CAC system using end-to-end Pre-trained CNN-based deep feature extraction and adaptive neuro-fuzzy classifier (ANFC) with linguistic hedges (LHs) classifier for chest radiographs. It explains in detail the concept of deep feature extraction using the Pre-trained end-to-end CNN model, feature selection, and architecture of ANFC classifier used for carrying out the experiment. The code snippets of the experiment aim at giving a better understanding to the programmatic implementation of designing this CAC system.

5.2 Experimental workflow

The experimental workflow followed for analyzing the performance of the Pre-trained GoogLeNet CNN model for deep feature extraction and classification of chest X-ray images into Normal class and Pneumonia class using ANFC-LH is shown in Fig. 5.1.

5.3 Deep feature extraction

Features are patterns of an object in an image that enable the identification of that object. They are the information about the contents of the image. In medical images these features may be the shape of the tumor, the opacity of the lung, or the color of the skin lesion. This includes the region of interest (ROI) and the patterns present in the ROI that enable the identification of the objects or that help in classification of the ROI. Features play an important role in influencing the predictions of the trained models. The task of feature extraction is the key step of converting the image input data into numerical data that can be easily understood by the machine and that contributes to the process of classification

Copyright © 2021 Elsevier Inc. All rights reserved.

141

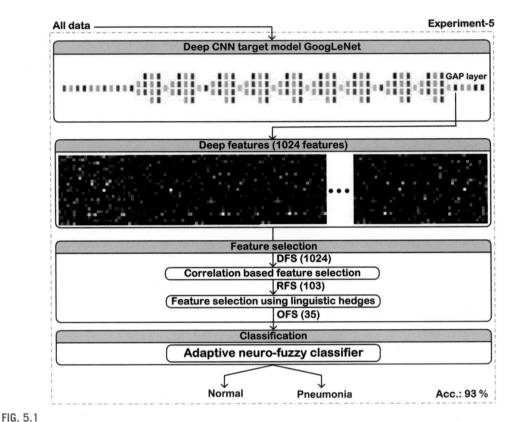

FIG. 5.1

Experimental workflow of CAC system designed using deep feature extraction by GoogLeNet and ANFC-LH classifier.

of the data. Feature extraction is similar to the dimensionality reduction process where an initial set of the raw data is divided and reduced to more manageable groups. In simpler terms, feature extraction is a method of mining an initial set of raw data from the input image dataset. A typical characteristic of feature extraction is that large datasets require a large number of variables to represent the extracted features efficiently. This often costs an immense amount of computing resources and processing time. The features can be extracted manually or through learning-based methods. Some of the types of feature extraction methods are shown in Fig. 5.2.

(a) Manual feature extraction: This is often referred to as handcrafted feature extraction. This type of feature extraction requires experts to perform the feature extraction as it requires domain knowledge to appropriately identify the key features and the ability to define those features correctly. This type of feature extraction is extremely brittle. Some of the problems associated with manual feature extraction are viewpoint variations, occlusions, illumination conditions, background clutter, and deformations. Some of the methods of feature extraction are gradient-based methods, local binary patterns, local intensity comparisons, and local intensity order statistics [1–6].

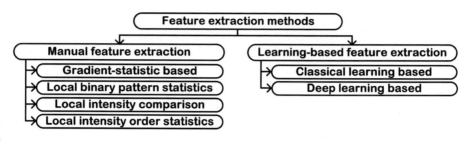

FIG. 5.2

Types of feature extraction methods.

(b) Learning-based feature extraction: This type of feature extraction aims at extracting hierarchy of features from the input data thereby sidestepping the concept of manual feature extraction. Deep learning-based feature extraction enables the users to extract ever deeper and higher dimensional features that are not possible to extract otherwise. The features extracted from the upper layers of the CNN are local features often known as lower dimensional data. As the network grows deeper, the features extracted are of higher dimensionality and more relevant. These features are often referred to as deep features that aim at bringing relevance to the classification task and removing unnecessary variation in the training process [7–10].

Deep feature extraction is the extraction of more complex features from the deeper layers of a CNN. The characteristic of a CNN is feature extraction and classification. The feature extraction is performed by the convolution layers stacked upon each other along with pooling layers and activation functions. These layers collectively perform the task of feature extraction on the input image datasets by alternatively performing the convolution, pooling, and nonlinear activations. The initial layers of the CNN extract higher and more basic features, but as the depth of the CNN increases, the ability of the network to extract features becomes stronger, and more complex features are extracted that even include those features that are missed by the human eye. For the extraction of deep features from an image, the input data is given to the Pre-trained CNN, and the activation values of the last fully connected layer or pooling layer are obtained and used as features. These features obtained can be further fed to the conventional machine learning classifiers for the classification of chest X-ray images into binary classes: Normal and Pneumonia [11–23].

5.3.1 GoogLeNet as a deep feature extractor

In the present work, the deep features are extracted from the best fine-tuned model decided on the basis of the classification results of Experiments 1–3 discussed in Chapter 4, resulting in the formation of a deep feature set (DFS). The GoogLeNet CNN model has a 144-layer architecture comprising of 22 deep layers and other pooling layers, rectified linear unit (ReLU) activation layers, and dropouts [24]. These layers comprise of five pooling layers that include four maximum pooling layers and one average pooling layer. This average pooling layer is referred to as the global average pool (GAP) layer. The detailed architecture of GoogLeNet CNN model has been discussed in Chapter 4. The present work uses the trained GoogLeNet model in Experiment 3 as a deep feature extractor. The features are extracted from the GAP layer of the network, which is the last pooling layer of the network. Fig. 5.3 shows the Pre-trained GoogLeNet used to carry out Experiment 3 in Chapter 4 as a deep feature extractor.

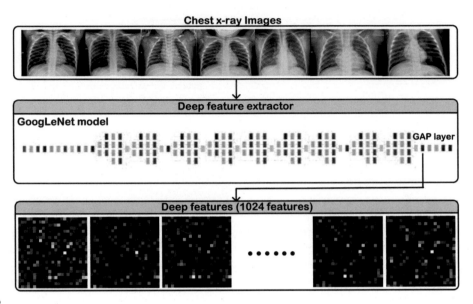

FIG. 5.3

GoogLeNet CNN model as deep feature extractor.

Code Snippet 5.1 shows the syntax to load the GoogLeNet CNN model trained in Experiment 3 in Chapter 4 to extract the features from its pooling layer.

Code Snippet 5.2 shows the extraction of training and testing features from the pooling layer of the GoogLeNet CNN model after it has been loaded into the MATLAB workspace.

Code Snippet 5.3 shows the syntax of writing the features extracted from the pooling layer to Microsoft Excel sheets. These .xlsx files or .csv files are then used as input to the feature selection methods and the machine learning-based classifiers.

Fig. 5.4 shows the visualization of deep feature maps of images extracted from the GAP layer of the GoogLeNet CNN model.

Code Snippet 5.1 Loading the saved GoogLeNet Pre-trained CNN model

```
%%Loading the saved GoogLeNet Pre-trained CNN model from experiment-3%%
load('Exp3_GoogLeNet');
```

Code Snippet 5.2 Feature extraction from the GoogLeNet Pre-trained CNN model

```
%%feature extraction%%
layer = 'pool5';
featuresTrain=activations(Exp3_GoogLeNet,imds_train,layer,'OutputAs','rows');
featuresTest=activations(Exp3_GoogLeNet,imds_test,layer,'OutputAs','rows');
```

Code Snippet 5.3 Saving the feature extracted from the GoogLeNet Pre-trained CNN model

```
%%saving the features in a excel sheet%%
xlswrite('H:\DataChestX-ray\FeatureExtraction\Exp5_Train.xlsx',featuresTrain);
xlswrite('H:\DataChestX-ray\FeatureExtraction\Exp5_Test.xlsx',featuresTest);
```

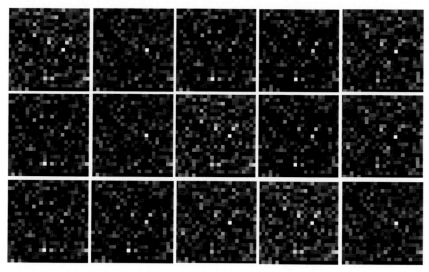

FIG. 5.4

Deep feature visualization.

Code Snippet 5.4 shows the syntax to load the image whose feature are to be visualized. Here a Normal chest radiograph is loaded from the path "H:\DataChestX-ray\Training\Normal\." Once the image is loaded into the workspace, the predefined activation function is used to generate the feature map.

Code Snippet 5.5 shows the syntax for visualizing the activation of the loaded chest radiograph from the GAP layer name pool5 of the GoogLeNet model.

Code Snippets 5.6 and 5.7 show the further steps followed, which include determining the size of the activation map and reshaping it using the predefined functions size() and reshape(), respectively.

Code Snippet 5.8 shows the final visualization of the features maps. The output of this is one of the feature maps shown in Fig. 5.3.

Code Snippet 5.4 Reading image from folder for feature visualization

```
%%Reading the image from the folder%%
CXR=imread('H:\DataChestX-ray\Training\Normal\CXR_1.jpg');
```

Code Snippet 5.5 Feature visualization

```
%%Extracting the feature map from the GAP layer of GoogLeNet%%
feature_map=activations(net,CXR,'pool5');
```

Code Snippet 5.6 Determining the size of feature map for feature visualization

```
%%Determining the size of the feature map from the GAP layer of GoogLeNet%%
size_CXR=size(feature_map);
```

Code Snippet 5.7 Reshaping the feature map for feature visualization

```
%%Reshaping the size of the feature map at the GAP layer of GoogLeNet%%
feature_map=reshape(feature_map,[size_CXR(1) size_CXR(2) 1 size_CXR(3)]);
```

Code Snippet 5.8 Feature visualization

```
%%feature visualization%%
figure(1),montage(mat2gray(feature_map)),title('GoogLeNet GAP layer features')
```

5.4 Feature selection

The task of feature selection involves the reduction of the initial set of raw data to a meaningful and manageable set of data. These sets of data are the features of the image that are often huge in number. A large number of variables are required to process these larger sets of features; hence, feature selection comes to the rescue by effectively reducing the size of the set of features, thereby reducing the requirement of the number of variables. This process of either selecting the features from the original feature set or combining features to form new features is known as feature selection and feature dimensionality reduction, respectively. Feature selection is performed in such a way that the new set generated describes the original dataset accurately. The feature selection methods are either filter-based methods or wrapper-based methods. The filter-based methods are more generic and widely used for feature selection. They include methods such as correlation-based feature selection, box plots, and chi-squared methods. The wrapper-based methods are computationally expensive as compared to the filter-based methods. These include genetic algorithm-based methods such as GA-SVM and GA-kNN [25–32]. The feature dimensionality methods aims at generating a new feature set from the existing one. The most popularly used method is principal component analysis (PCA) [33–36]. Fig. 5.5 shows different feature selection methods where the methods shaded in gray have been used in the present work.

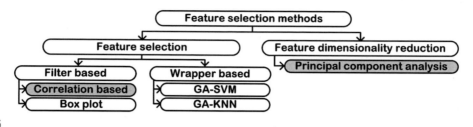

FIG. 5.5

Types of feature selection methods.

5.4.1 Correlation-based feature selection

The correlation-based feature selection (CFS) aims at extracting the best and most optimal set of features, which are nothing but a subset of the original set of features based on their correlation values. This technique is widely used as an attempt to select the optimal features from the original feature sets [37–39]. The CFS follows the basic idea that the features are uncorrelated to each other but have higher correlations to the class they belong to; here the reduced feature set (RFS) consists of the features that are uncorrelated to each other but have high correlation to their respective classes, either Normal or Pneumonia. The formula used to calculate the score, which is used as a threshold to select the optimal features that form the RFS, is given as:

$$S = \frac{k \times \overline{r_{cf}}}{\sqrt{k + k(k-1)\overline{r_{ff}}}}$$

where S: threshold score, k: number of features, $\overline{r_{cf}}$: mean correlation between feature and the class, and $\overline{r_{ff}}$: mean intercorrelation between features.

The CFS is programmatically implemented using Waikato Environment for Knowledge Analysis (WEKA) available at [40]. WEKA is an open source software that provides various data visualization tools and multiple algorithms to facilitate data analysis [41].

Here the DFS contains 1024 features extracted from the GAP layer of the GoogLeNet CNN model, which results in a RFS of 103 features when subjected to the CFS.

5.4.2 Feature selection using ANFC-LH

The feature set computed from the Pre-trained CNN contains a large number of features that may be redundant and negatively affect the classification performance of the CAC systems. Thus, the selection of relevant features is a prerequisite for the design of efficient CAC systems [12, 13, 16, 19, 42–46]. The advantages of feature selection are: faster training time, reduced complexity of classification model, and reduced overfitting.

In this module the extracted deep features from the pooling layer of the GoogLeNet CNN forms the DFS from which the features are selected on the basis of LHs.

The proposed work implements this feature selection method, which is fuzzy in nature and is based on LHs for the classification of chest radiographs into Normal and Pneumonia. The main aim is to achieve a faster, forthright, and productive CAC system. The LH functions by being applied to a set of fuzzy rules and then is custom-made by the conjugate gradient algorithm [43, 45, 46]. This results in the detection of some prominent features and the rejection of nonessential features on the basis of these power values [47–53].

The extracted feature space for classification of chest X-ray images that form the DFS (1024 features), when subjected to CFS, gives a RFS (103 features). Among these reduced features, in order to identify the features that are actually required for classification, feature selection using ANFC with LH is applied. All the features are not essential and relevant for the classification; hence, in order to increase the efficiency of the CAC system feature selection a wrapper-based method along with LH is applied so that only the essential features are selected [50–65].

The number of features in the present work after the deep feature extraction, which forms the DFS, is 1024. This DFS is subjected to a CFS process that reduces the 1024 features to 103 features (RFS) mainly on the values of the correlation coefficients. This RFS is further subjected to LH-based feature selection that generates an optimal feature set (OFS) of 35 features. Fig. 5.6 shows the relationship between input features and their LH value.

5.5 Adaptive neuro-fuzzy classifier

Image classification in machine learning is used to predict the class membership of the unknown data instance based on the class membership of the training data, which is known [43, 44, 66]. In the present work, ANFC is used, which is a multiple layered neural network with feed forward network

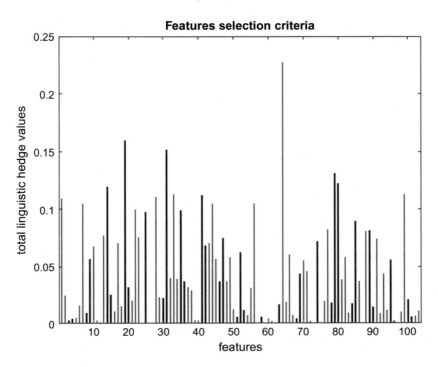

FIG. 5.6

Input features with their LH value.

capabilities. Its architecture consists of the following layers: (i) input layer, (ii) membership layer, (iii) power layer, (iv) fuzzification layer, (v) defuzzification layer, (vi) normalization layer, and (vii) output layer [42, 45, 46, 67–71]. The functionality of ANFC or the neuro-fuzzy classifier (NFC) is dependent on: a tool called the adaptive neuro-fuzzy inference system (ANFIS), whose main task is to unite the input datasets or the input feature vectors (IFVs); input membership functions (inputmf); rule-base, which has the rules that have been defined; and the output class [42–45, 48–51, 56, 70, 72–74]. The basic architecture of ANFC representing the various layers is depicted in Fig. 5.7. It shows the classification by ANFC for two classes {C1, C2} defined by two features {$\alpha 1$, $\alpha 2$} defined by three linguistic variable; in total, nine fuzzy rules are used. Fig. 5.8 shows the Sugeno rule-base viewer utilized by the ANFC in the present work.

5.6 Experiment and result

Experiment 5: Designing a hybrid CAC system for chest radiographs using deep feature extraction, GoogLeNet and ANFC-LH classifier

From the results of Experiments 1–3, as seen in Chapter 4, it can be noted that GoogLeNet CNN model achieves the highest accuracy (90.00%); therefore, for this experiment to evaluate the performance of the CNN as a feature extractor, the features from the GAP layer of GoogLeNet have been extracted. The deep feature set of 1024 features (DFS) extracted is reduced to 103 uncorrelated RFS by CFS. On application of LH on this RFS results on an OFS of 35 features. These are further fed to an ANFC-LH classifier for classification of chest X-ray images. The result of the performance evaluation of the Pre-trained GoogLeNet CNN model as feature extractor is shown in Table 5.1.

From the results obtained from Experiment 5, as shown in Table 5.1, it can be noted that the CAC system designed using the deep features extracted from the GoogLeNet CNN model fed to ANFC-LH classifier achieves an accuracy of 93.00% for the classification of chest X-ray images into two classes: Normal and Pneumonia. The individual class accuracy (ICA) value of the Normal class is 96.00%, and for the Pneumonia class, the ICA value obtained is 90.00%. Out of the total 100 instances in the testing set, seven instances have been incorrectly classified. Out of which two instances are of the Normal class, and the remaining five instances are of the Pneumonia class. The ROC curve with its corresponding AUC values for the hybrid CAC system designed using the GoogLeNet CNN model as deep feature extractor and ANFC-LH classifier is shown in Fig. 5.9.

5.7 Concluding remarks

This chapter discusses the concept of deep feature extraction from the trained CNN model, the process of feature selection, and a detailed view on the architecture of the NFC popularly known as the ANFC-LH classifier. From the experiment carried out in this chapter, it is observed that the CAC system design using deep feature extraction by GoogLeNet and ANFC-LH achieves an accuracy of 93.00% for the classification of chest radiographs. The next experiment in the subsequent chapter is carried out to evaluate the performance of same CAC system design using deep feature extraction with PCA-SVM classifier.

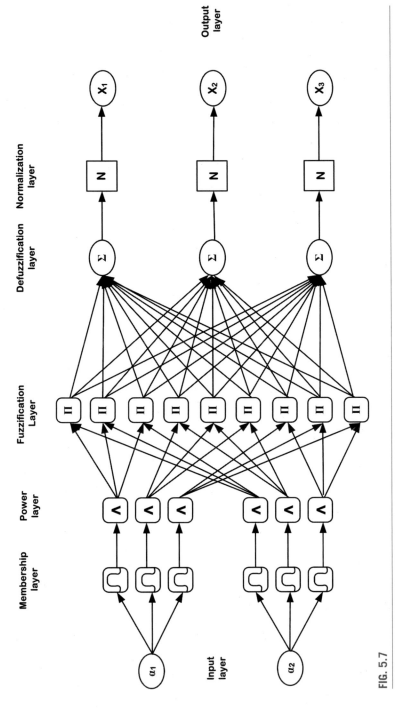

FIG. 5.7

Architecture of adaptive neuro-fuzzy classifier (ANFC).

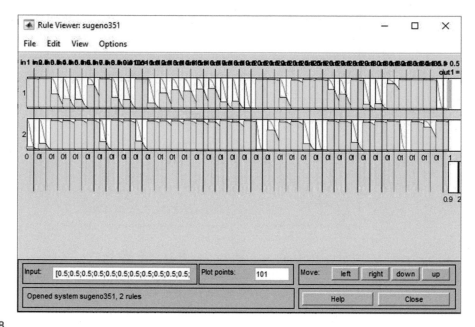

FIG. 5.8

Sugeno rule-base viewer for chest X-ray classification.

Table 5.1 Performance evaluation of Pre-trained GoogLeNet CNN model as feature extractor for deep feature extraction and classification of chest X-ray images.

Network/ classifier	Confusion matrix			Accuracy (%)	ICA_ Normal (%)	ICA_ Pneumonia (%)
		Normal	**Pneumonia**			
GoogLeNet/ ANFC-LH	Normal	48	2	93.00	96.00	90.00
	Pneumonia	5	45			

ICA_Normal, *individual class accuracy for Normal class;* ICA_Pneumonia, *individual class accuracy for Pneumonia class.*

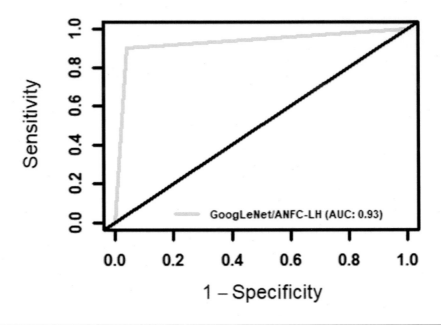

FIG. 5.9

The ROC curve with its corresponding AUC values for the hybrid CAC system designed using the GoogLeNet CNN model as deep feature extractor and ANFC-LH classifier.

References

[1] L.L.G. Oliveira, S.A. e Silva, L.H.V. Ribeiro, R.M. de Oliveira, C.J. Coelho, A.L.S. Andrade, Computer-aided diagnosis in chest radiography for detection of childhood pneumonia, Int. J. Med. Inform. 77 (8) (2008) 555–564.

[2] R.T. Sousa, O. Marques, F.A.A. Soares, I.I. Sene Jr., L.L. de Oliveira, E.S. Spoto, Comparative performance analysis of machine learning classifiers in detection of childhood pneumonia using chest radiographs, Procedia Comput. Sci. 18 (2013) 2579–2582.

[3] E. Naydenova, A. Tsanas, C. Casals-Pascual, M. De Vos, Smart diagnostic algorithms for automated detection of childhood pneumonia in resource-constrained settings, in: 2015 IEEE Global Humanitarian Technology Conference (GHTC), IEEE, 2015, pp. 377–384.

[4] P. Banerjee, A.K. Bhunia, A. Bhattacharyya, P.P. Roy, S. Murala, Local neighborhood intensity pattern—a new texture feature descriptor for image retrieval, Expert Syst. Appl. 113 (2018) 100–115.

[5] T.J. Alhindi, S. Kalra, K.H. Ng, A. Afrin, H.R. Tizhoosh, Comparing LBP, HOG and deep features for classification of histopathology images, in: 2018 International Joint Conference on Neural Networks (IJCNN), IEEE, 2018, pp. 1–7.

[6] T. Kobayashi, N. Otsu, Image feature extraction using gradient local auto-correlations, in: European Conference on Computer Vision, Springer, Berlin, Heidelberg, 2008, pp. 346–358.

[7] P. Simon, V. Uma, Deep learning based feature extraction for texture classification, Procedia Comput. Sci. 171 (2020) 1680–1687.

[8] A. Boyd, A. Czajka, K. Bowyer, Deep learning-based feature extraction in iris recognition: use existing models, fine-tune or train from scratch? in: 2019 IEEE 10th International Conference on Biometrics Theory, Applications and Systems (BTAS), IEEE, 2019, pp. 1–9.

[9] N. O'Mahony, S. Campbell, A. Carvalho, S. Harapanahalli, G.V. Hernandez, L. Krpalkova, D. Riordan, J. Walsh, Deep learning vs. traditional computer vision, in: Science and Information Conference, Springer, Cham, 2019, pp. 128–144.

[10] S. Dara, P. Tumma, Feature extraction by using deep learning: a survey, in: 2018 Second International Conference on Electronics, Communication and Aerospace Technology (ICECA), IEEE, 2018, pp. 1795–1801.

[11] M. Nixon, A. Aguado, Feature Extraction and Image Processing for Computer Vision, Academic Press, 2019.

[12] A. Yang, X. Yang, W. Wu, H. Liu, Y. Zhuansun, Research on feature extraction of tumor image based on convolutional neural network, IEEE Access 7 (2019) 24204–24213.

[13] M. Srinivas, D. Roy, C.K. Mohan, Discriminative feature extraction from X-ray images using deep convolutional neural networks, in: 2016 IEEE International Conference on Acoustics, Speech and Signal Processing (ICASSP), IEEE, 2016, pp. 917–921.

[14] V. Chouhan, S.K. Singh, A. Khamparia, D. Gupta, P. Tiwari, C. Moreira, R. Damaševičius, V.H.C. De Albuquerque, A novel transfer learning based approach for pneumonia detection in chest X-ray images, Appl. Sci. 10 (2) (2020) 559.

[15] H. Ravishankar, P. Sudhakar, R. Venkataramani, S. Thiruvenkadam, P. Annangi, N. Babu, V. Vaidya, Understanding the mechanisms of deep transfer learning for medical images, in: Deep Learning and Data Labeling for Medical Applications, Springer, Cham, 2016, pp. 188–196.

[16] H. Wu, P. Xie, H. Zhang, D. Li, M. Cheng, Predict pneumonia with chest X-ray images based on convolutional deep neural learning networks, J. Intell. Fuzzy Syst. (2020) 1–15 (Preprint).

[17] K. Suzuki, Overview of deep learning in medical imaging, Radiol. Phys. Technol. 10 (3) (2017) 257–273.

[18] A. Wibisono, J. Adibah, F.S. Priatmadji, N.Z. Viderisa, A. Husna, P. Mursanto, Segmentation-based knowledge extraction from chest X-ray images, in: 2019 4th Asia-Pacific Conference on Intelligent Robot Systems (ACIRS), IEEE, 2019, pp. 225–230.

[19] S.M. Anwar, M. Majid, A. Qayyum, M. Awais, M. Alnowami, M.K. Khan, Medical image analysis using convolutional neural networks: a review, J. Med. Syst. 42 (11) (2018) 226.

[20] N. Dey, Y.D. Zhang, V. Rajinikanth, R. Pugalenthi, N.S.M. Raja, Customized VGG19 architecture for pneumonia detection in chest X-rays, Pattern Recogn. Lett. 143 (2021) 67–74.

[21] D. Varshni, K. Thakral, L. Agarwal, R. Nijhawan, A. Mittal, Pneumonia detection using CNN based feature extraction, in: 2019 IEEE International Conference on Electrical, Computer and Communication Technologies (ICECCT), IEEE, 2019, pp. 1–7.

[22] M.F. Hashmi, S. Katiyar, A.G. Keskar, N.D. Bokde, Z.W. Geem, Efficient pneumonia detection in chest xray images using deep transfer learning, Diagnostics 10 (6) (2020) 417.

[23] M. Toğaçar, B. Ergen, Z. Cömert, F. Özyurt, A deep feature learning model for pneumonia detection applying a combination of mRMR feature selection and machine learning models, IRBM 41 (4) (2020) 212–222.

[24] C. Szegedy, W. Liu, Y. Jia, P. Sermanet, S. Reed, D. Anguelov, D. Erhan, V. Vanhoucke, A. Rabinovich, Going deeper with convolutions, in: Proceedings of the IEEE Conference on Computer Vision and Pattern Recognition, 2015, pp. 1–9.

[25] Q. Liu, Q. Gu, Z. Wu, Feature selection method based on support vector machine and shape analysis for high-throughput medical data, Comput. Biol. Med. 91 (2017) 103–111.

[26] H.H. Hsu, C.W. Hsieh, Feature selection via correlation coefficient clustering, JSW 5 (12) (2010) 1371–1377.

[27] G. Chandrashekar, F. Sahin, A survey on feature selection methods, Comput. Electr. Eng. 40 (1) (2014) 16–28.

[28] A. Jović, K. Brkić, N. Bogunović, A review of feature selection methods with applications, in: 2015 38th International Convention on Information and Communication Technology, Electronics and Microelectronics (MIPRO), IEEE, 2015, pp. 1200–1205.

[29] J. Hua, W.D. Tembe, E.R. Dougherty, Performance of feature-selection methods in the classification of high-dimension data, Pattern Recogn. 42 (3) (2009) 409–424.

[30] B. Remeseiro, V. Bolon-Canedo, A review of feature selection methods in medical applications, Comput. Biol. Med. 112 (2019) 103375.

[31] M. Allam, M. Nandhini, A study on optimization techniques in feature selection for medical image analysis, Int. J. Comput. Sci. Eng. 9 (3) (2017) 75–82.

[32] J. Tang, S. Alelyani, H. Liu, Feature selection for classification: a review, in: Data Classification: Algorithms and Applications, 2014, p. 37.

[33] I.T. Jolliffe, J. Cadima, Principal component analysis: a review and recent developments, Philos. Trans. Royal Soc. A Math. Phys. Eng. Sci. 374 (2065) (2016) 20150202.

[34] M. Brems, A one-stop shop for principal component analysis, Medium Towards Data Science 17 (2017).

[35] V. Powell, L. Lehe, Principal Component Analysis Explained Visually, 2015, DISQUS, Available: http://setosa.io/ev/principal-componentanalysis/. (Accessed 11 July 2016).

[36] J. Rasheed, A.A. Hameed, C. Djeddi, A. Jamil, F. Al-Turjman, A machine learning-based framework for diagnosis of COVID-19 from chest X-ray images, Interdiscip. Sci. Computat. Life Sci. (2021) 1–15.

[37] I. Jain, V.K. Jain, R. Jain, Correlation feature selection based improved-binary particle swarm optimization for gene selection and cancer classification, Appl. Soft Comput. 62 (2018) 203–215.

[38] K. Michalak, H. Kwaśnicka, Correlation-based feature selection strategy in classification problems, Int. J. Appl. Math. Comput. Sci. 16 (2006) 503–511.

[39] M.A. Hall, Correlation-based feature selection for discrete and numeric class machine learning, in: Proceedings of the Seventeenth International Conference on Machine Learning, Morgan Kaufmann Publishers Inc., 2000, pp. 359–366.

[40] Weka. https://www.cs.waikato.ac.nz/ml/weka/.

[41] I.H. Witten, E. Frank, Data Mining Practical Machine Learning Tools and Techniques With Java Implementations, Morgan Kaufman, San Francisco, 2005.

[42] J. Rawat, A. Singh, H.S. Bhadauria, J. Virmani, J.S. Devgun, Leukocyte classification using adaptive neuro-fuzzy inference system in microscopic blood images, Arab. J. Sci. Eng. 43 (12) (2018) 7041–7058.

[43] N. Dey, A.S. Ashour, F. Shi, V.E. Balas, Soft Computing Based Medical Image Analysis, Academic Press, 2018.

[44] I. Kumar, J. Virmani, H.S. Bhadauria, M.K. Panda, Classification of breast density patterns using PNN, NFC, and SVM classifiers, in: soft Computing Based Medical Image Analysis, Academic Press, 2018, pp. 223–243.

[45] B. Cetisli, Development of an adaptive neuro-fuzzy classifier using linguistic hedges: part 1, Expert Syst. Appl. 37 (8) (2010) 6093–6101.

[46] B. Cetisli, The effect of linguistic hedges on feature selection: part 2, Expert Syst. Appl. 37 (8) (2010) 6102–6108.

[47] N.B. Khameneh, H. Arabalibeik, P. Salehian, S. Setayeshi, Abnormal red blood cells detection using adaptive neuro-fuzzy system, in: Mmvr, 2012, pp. 30–34.

[48] E.D. Übeyli, Adaptive neuro-fuzzy inference systems for automatic detection of breast cancer, J. Med. Syst. 33 (5) (2009) 353.

[49] T. Uçar, A. Karahoca, D. Karahoca, Tuberculosis disease diagnosis by using adaptive neuro fuzzy inference system and rough sets, Neural Comput. Applic. 23 (2) (2013) 471–483.

[50] S. Roy, S. Sadhu, S.K. Bandyopadhyay, D. Bhattacharyya, T.H. Kim, Brain tumor classification using adaptive neuro-fuzzy inference system from MRI, Int. J. Bio-Sci. Bio-Technol. 8 (3) (2016) 203–218.

[51] M.I. Obayya, N.F. Areed, A.O. Abdulhadi, Liver cancer identification using adaptive neuro-fuzzy inference system, Int. J. Comput. Applic. 140 (8) (2016) 1–7.

[52] S. Kar, D.D. Majumder, An investigative study on early diagnosis of prostate cancer using neuro-fuzzy classification system for pattern recognition, Int. J. Fuzzy Syst. 19 (2) (2017) 423–439.

[53] S. Kar, D.D. Majumder, A novel approach of mathematical theory of shape and neuro-fuzzy based diagnostic analysis of cervical cancer, Pathol. Oncol. Res. 25 (2) (2019) 777–790.

[54] P. Melin, G. Prado-Arechiga, Design of a neuro-fuzzy system for diagnosis of arterial hypertension, in: New Hybrid Intelligent Systems for Diagnosis and Risk Evaluation of Arterial Hypertension, Springer, Cham, 2018, pp. 15–22.

[55] S. Kar, D.D. Majumder, A novel approach of diffusion tensor visualization based neuro fuzzy classification system for early detection of Alzheimer's disease, J. Alzheimer's Dis. Rep. 3 (1) (2019) 1–18.

[56] E.K. Roy, S.K. Aditya, Prediction of acute myeloid leukemia subtypes based on artificial neural network and adaptive neuro-fuzzy inference system approaches, in: Innovations in Electronics and Communication Engineering, Springer, Singapore, 2019, pp. 427–439.

[57] A. Badnjevic, L. Gurbeta, E. Custovic, An expert diagnostic system to automatically identify asthma and chronic obstructive pulmonary disease in clinical settings, Sci. Rep. 8 (1) (2018) 1–9.

[58] V.P. Kolosov, N.S. Bezrukov, D.Y. Naumov, Y.M. Perelman, A.G. Prikhodko, Prediction of osmotic airway hyperresponsiveness in patients with bronchial asthma using adaptive neuro-fuzzy network, in: 2015 International Conference on Biomedical Engineering and Computational Technologies (SIBIRCON), IEEE, 2015, pp. 130–133.

[59] M. Imran, S.A. Alsuhaibani, A neuro-fuzzy inference model for diabetic retinopathy classification, in: Intelligent Data Analysis for Biomedical Applications, Academic Press, 2019, pp. 147–172.

[60] V.I. Osubor, A.O. Egwali, A neuro fuzzy approach for the diagnosis of postpartum depression disorder, Iran J. Comput. Sci. 1 (4) (2018) 217–225.

[61] A. Karahoca, D. Karahoca, A. Kara, Diagnosis of diabetes by using adaptive neuro fuzzy inference systems, in: 2009 Fifth International Conference on Soft Computing, Computing with Words and Perceptions in System Analysis, Decision and Control, IEEE, 2009, pp. 1–4.

[62] S. Kavitha, K. Duraiswamy, Adaptive neuro-fuzzy inference system approach for the automatic screening of diabetic retinopathy in fundus images, J. Comput. Sci. 7 (7) (2011) 1020–1026. https://doi.org/10.3844/jcssp.2011.1020.1026.

[63] S. Alby, B.L. Shivakumar, A prediction model for type 2 diabetes using adaptive neuro-fuzzy interface system, Biomed. Res. 0970-938X, (2018).

[64] S. Banerjee, S. Mitra, B.U. Shankar, Synergetic neuro-fuzzy feature selection and classification of brain tumors, in: 2017 IEEE International Conference on Fuzzy Systems (FUZZ-IEEE), IEEE, 2017, pp. 1–6.

[65] X.D. Wang, J. Feng, Y.L. Li, Z. Li, Q.P. Wang, Computer aided detection for breast calcification clusters based on improved instance selection and an adaptive neuro-fuzzy network, in: 2013 10th International Conference on Fuzzy Systems and Knowledge Discovery (FSKD), IEEE, 2013, July, pp. 184–189.

[66] A. García-Floriano, Á. Ferreira-Santiago, O. Camacho-Nieto, C. Yáñez-Márquez, A machine learning approach to medical image classification: detecting age-related macular degeneration in fundus images, Comput. Electr. Eng. 75 (2019) 218–229.

[67] R. Kher, T. Pawar, V. Thakar, H. Shah, Physical activities recognition from ambulatory ECG signals using neuro-fuzzy classifiers and support vector machines, J. Med. Eng. Technol. 39 (2) (2015) 138–152.

[68] Q.H. Do, J.F. Chen, A neuro-fuzzy approach in the classification of students' academic performance, Computat. Intell. Neurosci. 2013 (2013) 49–55.

[69] M.M. Khan, S.K. Chalup, A. Mendes, Parkinson's disease data classification using evolvable wavelet neural networks, in: Australasian Conference on Artificial Life and Computational Intelligence, Springer, Cham, 2016, pp. 113–124.

[70] S. Devi, S. Kumar, G.S. Kushwaha, An adaptive neuro fuzzy inference system for prediction of anxiety of students, in: 8th International Conference on Advanced Computational Intelligence, 14–16 February 2016, Chiang Mai, Thailand, 2016.

[71] M.A. Chikh, M. Ammar, R. Marouf, A neuro-fuzzy identification of ECG beats, J. Med. Syst. 36 (2) (2012) 903–914.

[72] E.D. Übeyli, Adaptive neuro-fuzzy inference system for classification of ECG signals using Lyapunov exponents, Comput. Methods Prog. Biomed. 93 (3) (2009) 313–321.

[73] E.D. Übeyli, Automatic detection of electroencephalographic changes using adaptive neuro-fuzzy inference system employing Lyapunov exponents, Expert Syst. Appl. 36 (5) (2009) 9031–9038.

[74] E.D. Übeyli, Automatic diagnosis of diabetes using adaptive neuro-fuzzy inference systems, Expert. Syst. 27 (4) (2010) 259–266.

Hybrid computer-aided classification system design using end-to-end Pre-trained CNN-based deep feature extraction and PCA-SVM classifier for chest radiographs

6.1 Introduction

This chapter covers the exhaustive description of the experiments carried out for the design of a hybrid computer-aided classification (CAC) system using an end-to-end Pre-trained GoogLeNet convolution neural network (CNN) model as deep feature extractor and principal component analysis support vector machine (PCA-SVM) classifier for chest radiographs. It explains in detail the concepts of feature dimensionality reduction and the steps involved in implementing PCA and SVM classifier. The code snippets of the experiment aim at giving a better understanding to the programmatic implementation of designing this CAC system.

6.2 Experimental workflow

The experimental workflow followed for analyzing the performance of a CAC system designed for binary classification of chest radiographs using deep feature extraction, GoogLeNet CNN model, and PCA-SVM is shown in Fig. 6.1.

6.3 Deep feature extraction

The process of extracting the features of an image from the deep layers of a CNN is referred to as deep feature extraction, and the features extracted are called deep features. This process involves the steps of providing the input data to the Pre-trained CNN, and then the respective activation values from the fully connected layer usually present at the end of the network or pooling layer are obtained. The process of deep feature extraction has been discussed in detail in Chapter 5. In the present work, the deep features are extracted from the best fine-tuned model decided on the basis of the classification results

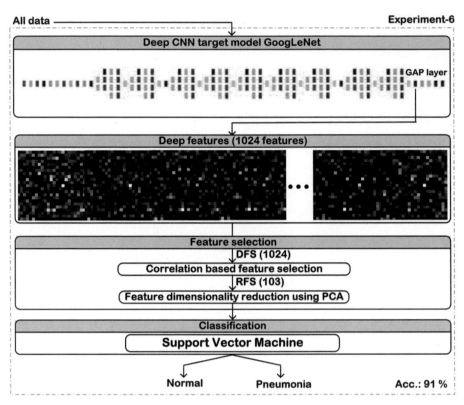

FIG. 6.1

Experimental workflow of CAC system designed using deep feature extraction, GoogLeNet CNN model, and PCA-SVM classifier.

of Experiments 1–3, discussed in Chapter 4, consequentially forming a set of deep features that are extracted from the best performing CNN model. This feature set is referred to as a deep feature set (DFS).

The following code snippets show the process of feature extraction and feature map visualization of the extracted features. Code Snippet 6.1 shows the syntax to load the GoogLeNet CNN model trained in Experiment 3, discussed in Chapter 4, to extract the features from its pooling layer.

Code Snippet 6.2 shows the extraction of training and testing features from the pooling layer of the GoogLeNet CNN model after it has been loaded into the MATLAB workspace.

Code Snippet 6.3 shows the syntax of writing the features extracted from the pooling layer to Microsoft Excel sheets. These .xlsx files or .csv files are then used as input to the feature selection methods and machine learning-based classifiers.

Code Snippet 6.1 Loading the saved GoogLeNet Pre-trained CNN model

```
%%loading the saved GoogLeNet Pre-trained CNN model%%
load('Exp3_GoogLeNet');
```

Code Snippet 6.2 Feature extraction from the GoogLeNet Pre-trained CNN model

```
%%feature extraction%%
layer = 'pool5';
featuresTrain=activations(Exp3_GoogLeNet,imds_train,layer,'OutputAs','rows');
featuresTest=activations(Exp3_GoogLeNet,imds_test,layer,'OutputAs','rows');
```

Code Snippet 6.3 Saving the feature extracted from the GoogLeNet Pre-trained CNN model

```
%%saving the features in a excel sheet%%
xlswrite('H:\DataChestX-ray\FeatureExtraction\Exp6_Train.xlsx',featuresTrain);
xlswrite('H:\DataChestX-ray\FeatureExtraction\Exp6_Test.xlsx',featuresTest);
```

6.4 Feature selection and dimensionality reduction

The process of feature selection and different methods of feature selection have been discussed in the previous chapter along with the details of GoogLeNet as a deep feature extractor and the feature visualization.

6.4.1 Correlation-based feature selection

Correlation-based feature selection (CFS) is a filter-based feature selection technique that aims at extracting the best and most optimal set of features, which are nothing but a subset of the original set of features, on the basis of their correlation values. This technique is widely used as an attempt to select the optimal features from the original feature sets [1–12]. The CFS follows the basic idea that the features are not correlated to each other but have higher correlations to the class to which they belong; here, the reduced feature set (RFS) consists of the features that are uncorrelated to each other but have high correlation to their respective classes, either Normal or Pneumonia. A detailed explanation of CFS is given in Chapter 5.

The DFS contains the features extracted from the pooling layer of the GoogLeNet CNN, that is, the global average pool (GAP) layer, which when subjected to the CFS, results in an RFS. The DFS consists of 1024 features extracted from the GAP layer, and after CFS, the RFS consists of 103 features.

6.4.2 PCA-based feature dimensionality reduction

In the present work, PCA is used as a dimensionality reduction technique for the deep feature space, which is extracted from the Pre-trained GoogLeNet CNN model in the form of a DFS. This DFS, after further application of CFS, forms an RFS. The PCA helps in finding optimal principal components (PCs) that are highly useful in the classification task [13–16]. The steps involved for the implementation of PCA are given in Fig. 6.2.

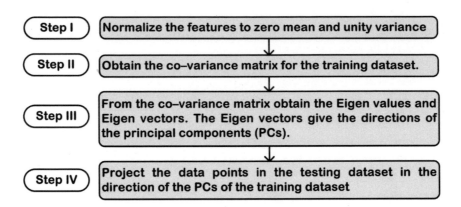

FIG. 6.2

Steps in principal component analysis. *PC,* principal component.

The total resultant optimal PCs that need to be taken into consideration for the job of classification are obtained by repetition of the experiments in an iterative manner. In this way, the PCs are calculated empirically mainly by stepping through the few initial PCs that primarily lie in the range of 2–15 in an attempt to build a model.

6.5 SVM classifier

The SVM classifier is a member of the supervised machine learning algorithms class. The basic concept that the SVM works on is decision boundaries. The SVM applies functions called kernels that perform the mapping of the training data to a feature space of a higher dimensionality [17–21]. The training data, which is mainly nonlinear in nature, is taken from the input space. Some of the most common kernels used in SVM are: (a) polynomial kernel, (b) radial basis function or Gaussian radial basis function, and (c) sigmoid kernel. The present work implements the SVM classifier using the LibSVM library [22], and the kernel used is the Gaussian radial basis function kernel. Among the multiple steps involved in implementing SVM, the most crucial step is attaining a good, generalized performance. The parameters represented by C and γ play a major role in achieving a good and well-generalized performance of the SVM classifier. Here the parameter C is responsible for the regularization of the result; hence, it is called the regularization parameter. Similarly, the parameter γ is associated with the kernel performance; hence it is called the kernel parameter. The main aim of regularization parameter C is to maximize the margin, which is the distance between the support vectors, while keeping the error of training as low as possible. In the present work, a k-fold cross validation is carried out, where $k = 10$ on the training dataset. Here each combination of (C, γ) is chosen, such that:

$$C \in \left\{2^{-4}, 2^{-3} \ldots 2^{15}\right\}$$

$$\gamma = \left\{2^{-12}, 2^{-11} \ldots 2^{4}\right\}$$

The grid search procedure followed in the parameter space aims at giving the optimum values of the regularization parameter C and the kernel parameter γ, such that the training accuracy is maximum at the optimum value of (C, γ) [23–27]. The extracted feature values are normalized in the range [0,1] by using the min-max normalization algorithm. This normalization is performed in order to dodge any bias that could be caused by the presence of unbalanced feature values. The SVM has been widely used in classification of medical images [28–39]. The steps followed in SVM are given in Fig. 6.3.

6.6 Experiment and result

Experiment 6: Designing a hybrid CAC system for chest radiographs using deep feature extraction, GoogLeNet, and PCA-SVM classifier

From the results of Experiments 1–3, as described in Chapter 4, it can be seen that the GoogLeNet CNN model attains the highest accuracy (90.00%). Hence, for this experiment to evaluate the performance of designing a hybrid CAC system for chest radiographs using GoogLeNet, deep feature extraction, and PCA-SVM classifier, the GoogLeNet CNN is used as the deep feature extractor. The features from the GAP layer of GoogLeNet CNN are extracted forming a DFS of 1024 features. This DFS is reduced to 103 uncorrelated features resulting in the formation of an RFS by CFS. This RFS acts as an input to the PCA-SVM classifier for the classification of chest radiographic images. The result of the performance evaluation of the hybrid CAC system designed using deep feature extraction, GoogLeNet CNN model, and PCA-SVM classifier is shown in Table 6.1.

From the results of Experiment 6, as shown in Table 6.1, it can be seen that the hybrid CAC system designed using the deep features extracted from the GoogLeNet CNN model fed to PCA-SVM classifier achieves 91.00% accuracy for the classification of chest radiograph images into binary classes: Normal and Pneumonia. The individual class accuracy value of Normal class is 96.00%, and for the Pneumonia class, the individual class accuracy value obtained is 86.00%. From the total 100 images in the testing set, 9 images have been incorrectly classified, from which 2 images belong to the Normal class and 7 images belong to the Pneumonia class. The ROC curve with its corresponding AUC values for the hybrid CAC system designed using the GoogLeNet CNN model as deep feature extractor and PCA-SVM classifier is shown in Fig. 6.4.

6.7 Concluding remarks

This chapter gives a detailed overview of the PCA feature dimensionality technique and explains in detail the steps involved for classification of the images using the SVM classifier. From the experiment carried out in this chapter, it is observed that designing the hybrid CAC system through deep feature extraction by GoogLeNet and PCA-SVM achieves 91.00% accuracy for the classification of chest radiographs. The next chapter aims at understanding the lightweight CNN model, its architecture, and experiments conducted to evaluate the performance of designing lightweight CNN-based CAC systems for classification of chest radiographs.

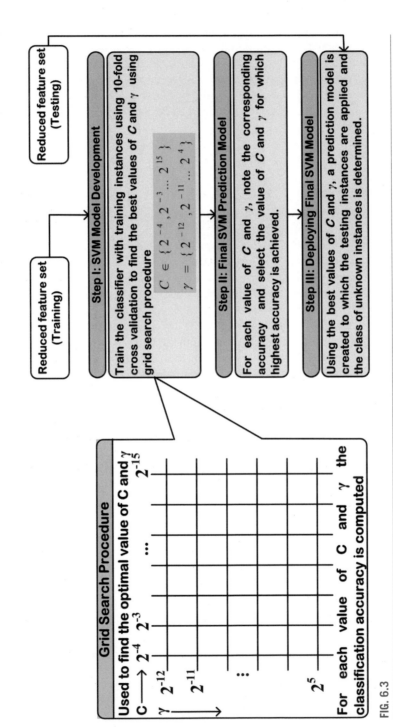

FIG. 6.3

Support vector machine classifier.

Table 6.1 Performance evaluation of CAC system designed for chest radiographs using deep feature extraction, GoogLeNet CNN, and PCA-SVM classifier.

Network/ classifier	Confusion matrix			Accuracy (%)	ICA_ Normal (%)	ICA_ Pneumonia (%)
		Normal	Pneumonia			
GoogLeNet/ PCA-SVM	Normal	48	2	91.00	96.00	86.00
	Pneumonia	7	43			

ICA_Normal, *individual class accuracy for Normal class;* ICA_Pneumonia, *individual class accuracy for Pneumonia class.*

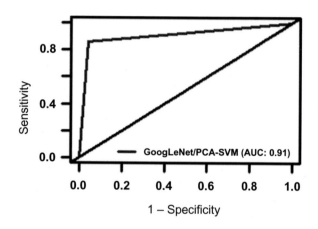

FIG. 6.4

The ROC curve with its corresponding AUC values for the hybrid CAC system designed using the GoogLeNet CNN model as deep feature extractor and PCA-SVM classifier.

References

[1] I. Jain, V.K. Jain, R. Jain, Correlation feature selection based improved-binary particle swarm optimization for gene selection and cancer classification, Appl. Soft Comput. 62 (2018) 203–215.

[2] K. Michalak, H. Kwaśnicka, Correlation-based feature selection strategy in classification problems, Int. J. Appl. Math. Comput. Sci. 16 (2006) 503–511.

[3] M.A. Hall, Correlation-based feature selection for discrete and numeric class machine learning, in: Proceedings of the Seventeenth International Conference on Machine Learning, Morgan Kaufmann Publishers Inc., 2000, pp. 359–366.

[4] M. Toğaçar, B. Ergen, Z. Cömert, F. Özyurt, A deep feature learning model for pneumonia detection applying a combination of mRMR feature selection and machine learning models, IRBM 41 (4) (2020) 212–222.

[5] Q. Liu, Q. Gu, Z. Wu, Feature selection method based on support vector machine and shape analysis for high-throughput medical data, Comput. Biol. Med. 91 (2017) 103–111.

[6] H.H. Hsu, C.W. Hsieh, Feature selection via correlation coefficient clustering, JSW 5 (12) (2010) 1371–1377.

[7] G. Chandrashekar, F. Sahin, A survey on feature selection methods, Comput. Electr. Eng. 40 (1) (2014) 16–28.

[8] A. Jović, K. Brkić, N. Bogunović, A review of feature selection methods with applications, in: 2015 38th International Convention on Information and Communication Technology, Electronics and Microelectronics (MIPRO), IEEE, 2015, pp. 1200–1205.

[9] J. Hua, W.D. Tembe, E.R. Dougherty, Performance of feature-selection methods in the classification of high-dimension data, Pattern Recogn. 42 (3) (2009) 409–424.

[10] B. Remeseiro, V. Bolon-Canedo, A review of feature selection methods in medical applications, Comput. Biol. Med. 112 (2019) 103375.

[11] M. Allam, M. Nandhini, A study on optimization techniques in feature selection for medical image analysis, Int. J. Comput. Sci. Eng. 9 (3) (2017) 75–82.

[12] J. Tang, S. Alelyani, H. Liu, Feature selection for classification: a review, in: Data Classification: Algorithms and Applications, CRC Press, 2014, pp. 37–64. https://doi.org/10.1201/b17320.

[13] I.T. Jolliffe, J. Cadima, Principal component analysis: a review and recent developments, Philos. Trans. Royal Soc. A Math. Phys. Eng. Sci. 374 (2065) (2016) 20150202.

[14] M. Brems, A one-stop shop for principal component analysis, Medium Towards Data Science 17 (2017).

[15] V. Powell, L. Lehe, Principal Component Analysis Explained Visually, 2015, DISQUS, Available: http://setosa.io/ev/principal-componentanalysis/. (Accessed 11 July 2016).

[16] J. Rasheed, A.A. Hameed, C. Djeddi, et al., A machine learning-based framework for diagnosis of COVID-19 from chest X-ray images, Interdiscip. Sci. Comput. Life Sci. 13 (2021) 103–117, https://doi.org/10.1007/s12539-020-00403-6.

[17] L. Wang (Ed.), Support Vector Machines: Theory and Applications, vol. 177, Springer Science & Business Media, 2005.

[18] A. Pradhan, Support vector machine—a survey, Int. J. Emerging Technol. Adv. Eng. 2 (8) (2012) 82–85.

[19] S. Suthaharan, Support vector machine, in: Machine Learning Models and Algorithms for Big Data Classification, Springer, Boston, MA, 2016, pp. 207–235.

[20] J. Zhou, K.L. Chan, V.F.H. Chong, S.M. Krishnan, Extraction of brain tumor from MR images using one-class support vector machine, in: 2005 IEEE Engineering in Medicine and Biology 27th Annual Conference, IEEE, 2006, pp. 6411–6414.

[21] Y. Jiang, Z. Li, L. Zhang, P. Sun, An improved svm classifier for medical image classification, in: International Conference on Rough Sets and Intelligent Systems Paradigms, Springer, Berlin, Heidelberg, 2007, pp. 764–773.

[22] C.C. Chang, C.J. Lin, LIBSVM: A Library of Support Vector Machines, 2012, Software available at http://www. csie. ntu. edu. tw/~ cjlin/libsvm.

[23] A.V.D. Sánchez, Advanced support vector machines and kernel methods, Neurocomputing 55 (1–2) (2003) 5–20.

[24] A. Karatzoglou, D. Meyer, K. Hornik, Support vector machines in R, J. Stat. Softw. 15 (9) (2006) 1–28.

[25] K. Pelckmans, J.A. Suykens, T. Van Gestel, J. De Brabanter, L. Lukas, B. Hamers, B. De Moor, J. Vandewalle, LS-SVMlab: a matlab/c toolbox for least squares support vector machines, 2002. Tutorial. KULeuven-ESAT. Leuven, Belgium, 142 (1–2).

[26] D. Meyer, F.T. Wien, Support vector machines. The Interface to libsvm in package e 1071, 28, 2015.

[27] T.A. Gomes, R.B. Prudêncio, C. Soares, A.L. Rossi, A. Carvalho, Combining meta-learning and search techniques to select parameters for support vector machines, Neurocomputing 75 (1) (2012) 3–13.

[28] J. Virmani, V. Kumar, N. Kalra, N. Khandelwal, SVM-based characterization of liver ultrasound images using wavelet packet texture descriptors, J. Digit. Imaging 26 (3) (2013) 530–543.

[29] J. Virmani, N. Dey, V. Kumar, PCA-PNN and PCA-SVM based CAD systems for breast density classification, in: Applications of Intelligent Optimization in Biology and Medicine, Springer, Cham, 2016, pp. 159–180.

[30] J. Virmani, V. Kumar, N. Kalra, N. Khandelwa, PCA-SVM based CAD system for focal liver lesions using B-mode ultrasound images, Def. Sci. J. 63 (5) (2013) 478–486.

[31] J. Virmani, V. Kumar, N. Kalra, N. Khandelwal, SVM-based characterisation of liver cirrhosis by singular value decomposition of GLCM matrix, Int. J. Artif. Intell. Soft Comput. 3 (3) (2013) 276–296.

[32] S. Rana, S. Jain, J. Virmani, SVM-based characterization of focal Kidney lesions from B-mode ultrasound images, JUIT (0975-8585) (2016). http://ir.juit.ac.in/123456789/6908.

[33] A.E. Hassanein, T.H. Kim, Breast cancer MRI diagnosis approach using support vector machine and pulse coupled neural networks, J. Appl. Logic 10 (4) (2012) 274–284.

[34] Y.H. Chan, Y.Z. Zeng, H.C. Wu, M.C. Wu, H.M. Sun, Effective pneumothorax detection for chest X-ray images using local binary pattern and support vector machine, J. Healthc. Eng. 2018 (2018) 2908517.

[35] A.E. Hassanien, L.N. Mahdy, K.A. Ezzat, H.H. Elmousalami, H.A. Ella, Automatic x-ray covid-19 lung image classification system based on multi-level thresholding and support vector machine, med Rxiv (2020).

[36] R.T. Sousa, O. Marques, F.A.A. Soares, I.I. Sene Jr., L.L. de Oliveira, E.S. Spoto, Comparative performance analysis of machine learning classifiers in detection of childhood pneumonia using chest radiographs, Procedia Comput. Sci. 18 (2013) 2579–2582.

[37] A. Depeursinge, J. Iavindrasana, A. Hidki, G. Cohen, A. Geissbuhler, A. Platon, P.A. Poletti, H. Müller, Comparative performance analysis of state-of-the-art classification algorithms applied to lung tissue categorization, J. Digit. Imaging 23 (1) (2010) 18–30.

[38] J. Yao, A. Dwyer, R.M. Summers, D.J. Mollura, Computer-aided diagnosis of pulmonary infections using texture analysis and support vector machine classification, Acad. Radiol. 18 (3) (2011) 306–314.

[39] E. Naydenova, A. Tsanas, C. Casals-Pascual, M. De Vos, Smart diagnostic algorithms for automated detection of childhood pneumonia in resource-constrained settings, in: 2015 IEEE Global Humanitarian Technology Conference (GHTC), IEEE, 2015, pp. 377–384.

Further reading

M. Nixon, A. Aguado, Feature Extraction and Image Processing for Computer Vision, Academic Press, 2019.

A. Yang, X. Yang, W. Wu, H. Liu, Y. Zhuansun, Research on feature extraction of tumor image based on convolutional neural network, IEEE Access 7 (2019) 24204–24213.

M. Srinivas, D. Roy, C.K. Mohan, Discriminative feature extraction from X-ray images using deep convolutional neural networks, in: 2016 IEEE International Conference on Acoustics, Speech and Signal Processing (ICASSP), IEEE, 2016, pp. 917–921.

V. Chouhan, S.K. Singh, A. Khamparia, D. Gupta, P. Tiwari, C. Moreira, R. Damaševičius, V.H.C. De Albuquerque, A novel transfer learning based approach for pneumonia detection in chest X-ray images, Appl. Sci. 10 (2) (2020) 559.

H. Ravishankar, P. Sudhakar, R. Venkataramani, S. Thiruvenkadam, P. Annangi, N. Babu, V. Vaidya, Understanding the mechanisms of deep transfer learning for medical images, in: Deep Learning and Data Labeling for Medical Applications, Springer, Cham, 2016, pp. 188–196.

H. Wu, P. Xie, H. Zhang, D. Li, M. Cheng, Predict pneumonia with chest X-ray images based on convolutional deep neural learning networks, J. Intell. Fuzzy Syst. (2020) 1–15 (Preprint).

K. Suzuki, Overview of deep learning in medical imaging, Radiol. Phys. Technol. 10 (3) (2017) 257–273.

A. Wibisono, J. Adibah, F.S. Priatmadji, N.Z. Viderisa, A. Husna, P. Mursanto, Segmentation-based knowledge extraction from chest X-ray images, in: 2019 4th Asia-Pacific Conference on Intelligent Robot Systems (ACIRS), IEEE, 2019, pp. 225–230.

S.M. Anwar, M. Majid, A. Qayyum, M. Awais, M. Alnowami, M.K. Khan, Medical image analysis using convolutional neural networks: a review, J. Med. Syst. 42 (11) (2018) 226.

N. Dey, A.S. Ashour, F. Shi, V.E. Balas, Soft Computing Based Medical Image Analysis, Academic Press, 2018.

I. Kumar, J. Virmani, H.S. Bhadauria, M.K. Panda, Classification of breast density patterns using PNN, NFC, and SVM classifiers, in: Soft Computing Based Medical Image Analysis, Academic Press, 2018, pp. 223–243.

A. Badnjevic, L. Gurbeta, E. Custovic, An expert diagnostic system to automatically identify asthma and chronic obstructive pulmonary disease in clinical settings, Sci. Rep. 8 (1) (2018) 1–9.

A. García-Floriano, Á. Ferreira-Santiago, O. Camacho-Nieto, C. Yáñez-Márquez, A machine learning approach to medical image classification: detecting age-related macular degeneration in fundus images, Comput. Electr. Eng. 75 (2019) 218–229.

L.L.G. Oliveira, S.A. e Silva, L.H.V. Ribeiro, R.M. de Oliveira, C.J. Coelho, A.L.S. Andrade, Computer-aided diagnosis in chest radiography for detection of childhood pneumonia, Int. J. Med. Inform. 77 (8) (2008) 555–564.

P. Simon, V. Uma, Deep learning based feature extraction for texture classification, Procedia Comput. Sci. 171 (2020) 1680–1687.

A. Boyd, A. Czajka, K. Bowyer, Deep learning-based feature extraction in iris recognition: use existing models, fine-tune or train from scratch? in: 2019 IEEE 10th International Conference on Biometrics Theory, Applications and Systems (BTAS), IEEE, 2019, pp. 1–9.

N. O'Mahony, S. Campbell, A. Carvalho, S. Harapanahalli, G.V. Hernandez, L. Krpalkova, D. Riordan, J. Walsh, Deep learning vs. traditional computer vision, in: Science and Information Conference, Springer, Cham, 2019, pp. 128–144.

S. Dara, P. Tumma, Feature extraction by using deep learning: a survey, in: 2018 Second International Conference on Electronics, Communication and Aerospace Technology (ICECA), IEEE, 2018, pp. 1795–1801.

N. Dey, Y.D. Zhang, V. Rajinikanth, R. Pugalenthi, N.S.M. Raja, Customized VGG19 architecture for pneumonia detection in chest X-rays, Pattern Recogn. Lett. 143 (2021) 67–74.

D. Varshni, K. Thakral, L. Agarwal, R. Nijhawan, A. Mittal, Pneumonia detection using CNN based feature extraction, in: In 2019 IEEE International Conference on Electrical, Computer and Communication Technologies (ICECCT), IEEE, 2019, pp. 1–7.

M.F. Hashmi, S. Katiyar, A.G. Keskar, N.D. Bokde, Z.W. Geem, Efficient pneumonia detection in chest xray images using deep transfer learning, Diagnostics 10 (6) (2020) 417.

Lightweight end-to-end Pre-trained CNN-based computer-aided classification system design for chest radiographs

7.1 Introduction

In this chapter, there is an exhaustive description of the experiments carried out for the design of lightweight end-to-end Pre-trained convolution neural network-based (CNN-based) computer-aided classification (CAC) systems for chest radiographs. It explains in detail the architectural composition of the lightweight Pre-trained CNN models SqueezeNet, ShuffleNet, and MobileNetV2 used for carrying out the experiments. The code snippets of the different experiments aim at giving a better understanding to the programmatic implementation of designing these CAC systems.

7.2 Experimental workflow

The experimental workflow followed for analyzing the performance of CAC systems designed for binary classification of chest radiographs using Pre-trained lightweight CNN models is shown in Fig. 7.1.

7.3 Lightweight CNN model

For efficient lightweight network architecture, certain properties are highly desirable that: (a) include the maximized use of balanced convolutions, preferably equivalent to the channel width; (b) analyze the cost of convolutions and their combinations being used; (c) aim at the reduction of degree of fragmentation; and (d) decrease the number of element-wise operations. All these properties combined result in the overall reduction of memory use and an immense increase in processing time [1–3]. Some of the lightweight CNN models include ShuffleNet that depend on group convolutions; MobileNetV2 uses inverted bottleneck layers of 1×1 convolutions as well as depth-wise convolutions with rectified linear unit (ReLU) activations on deep feature maps. However, these auto-generated structures are highly fragmented but are an even tradeoff for the efficiency of the network. Similarly, a lightweight SqueezeNet CNN model uses the bottleneck layers to reduce the number of convolutions and a concept of fire modules consisting of squeeze and expand layers.

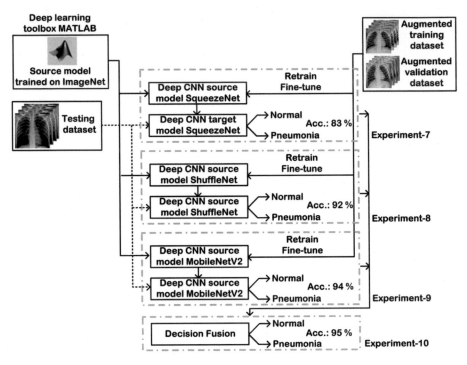

FIG. 7.1

Experimental workflow of designing lightweight CNN-based CAC systems for binary classification of chest radiographs.

7.4 Architecture of lightweight Pre-trained CNN networks used in the present work

The basic architecture of CNN models are either series networks that are stacked layers in a contiguous manner or DAG networks where the output of one layer is an input to multiple layers at different levels. The types of series and DAG networks have been discussed in Chapter 4.

7.4.1 DAG lightweight end-to-end Pre-trained CNN model: SqueezeNet

SqueezeNet Lightweight CNN model was introduced by the researchers at DeepScale, University of California, Berkeley, and Stanford in 2016 [4]. It is a 68-layer architecture having 18 deep layers, and comprising of eight fire modules majorly contributing in compactness and robustness of the lightweight networks. The main aim of its design was to create networks with fewer parameters, thus resulting in lower requirement of storage space and transmission bandwidth. This reduction in the number of parameters was done by replacing the 3×3 convolution filters with 1×1 convolution filters; this contributed to a reduction of parameters to one-ninth. Additionally, the number of the input channels was also reduced by using a new concept of squeeze layers and delayed downsampling also aimed at enhanced accuracy of the CNN model for classification tasks. The network has an input size of $227 \times 227 \times 3$, and it also has been widely used in the analysis of medical images [5–15]. The general layer architecture of SqueezeNet and the configuration of a fire module are shown in Fig. 7.2.

The basic building block of SqueezeNet is the fire module. These fire modules are comprised of two layers: (a) squeeze layer: contains convolution of size 1×1; and (b) expand layer: contains a combination of convolutions of two different sizes, that is, 1×1 and 3×3. Basic SqueezeNet architecture totals eight fire modules. The structure of fire module is shown in Fig. 7.3.

7.4.2 DAG lightweight end-to-end Pre-trained CNN model: ShuffleNet

The ShuffleNet lightweight CNN model was given by Zhang et al. [16] in 2017. It is a 50-layer deep lightweight CNN model with fewer parameters and an input size of $224 \times 224 \times 3$. They proposed a CNN model suitable and especially designed for mobile devices, which is highly efficient in terms of computation and power consumption. As other CNN models such as ResNet and Xception networks turned out to be inefficient in smaller networks, the researchers proposed: (a) the use of point-wise group convolution with an aim to reduce the computation complexity, and (b) the use of channel shuffle operations with an aim to increase the efficacy of flow of information through the feature channels. The building blocks of the ShuffleNet lightweight CNN model are the bottleneck layers, the ShuffleNet block with stride=1, and the ShuffleNet block with stride=2. These building blocks are shown in Fig. 7.4. Along with the addition of these blocks, a batch Normalization layer is added to enhance the end-to-end training after each convolution. The network begins with a 3×3 convolution and maximum pooling layers continued by a series of stages that involve the combination and repetition of the building blocks and finally terminates with a global average pooling (GAP) and fully connected layer. The ShuffleNet units consist of group convolutions, depth-wise convolutions, and channel shuffle layers that act as the novelty added by the researchers to make the lightweight network more efficient. The lightweight ShuffleNet CNN model has been widely used in medical image analysis [17–23].

7.4.3 DAG lightweight end-to-end Pre-trained CNN model: MobileNetV2

This lightweight MobileNetV2 CNN model was proposed by Sandler et al. [24] in 2019. It is based on the MobileNetV1 architecture given by Howard et al. [25] in 2017. MobileNetV2 is a 53-layer deep lightweight CNN model with fewer parameters and an input size of 224×224. The MobileNetV1 architecture used the concept of depth-wise separable convolutions that applies a single filter to each input channel, and the point-wise convolutions ($1 \times 11 \times 1$) aim at combining the output of the depth-wise convolutions. The MobileNetV2 lightweight CNN model is made up of mainly two blocks: (a) block with stride=[1 1], often called the residual block with S=[1 1]; and (b) block with stride=[2 2], which mainly aims at downsizing. The depth-wise convolution performs filtering, which is lightweight in nature. This is achieved simply by applying one convolution filter per input channel and forms the first layer of the MobileNetV2 blocks. The 1×1 convolution forms the second layer of the MobileNetV2 blocks and is known as the point-wise convolution. These 1×1 convolutions are responsible for structuring new features through the linear combination of input channels. Fig. 7.5 shows the structure of the building blocks of the MobileNetV2 CNN model with stride=[1 1] and stride=[2 2]. The MobileNetV2 CNN model has been widely used in medical image analysis [20, 26–34].

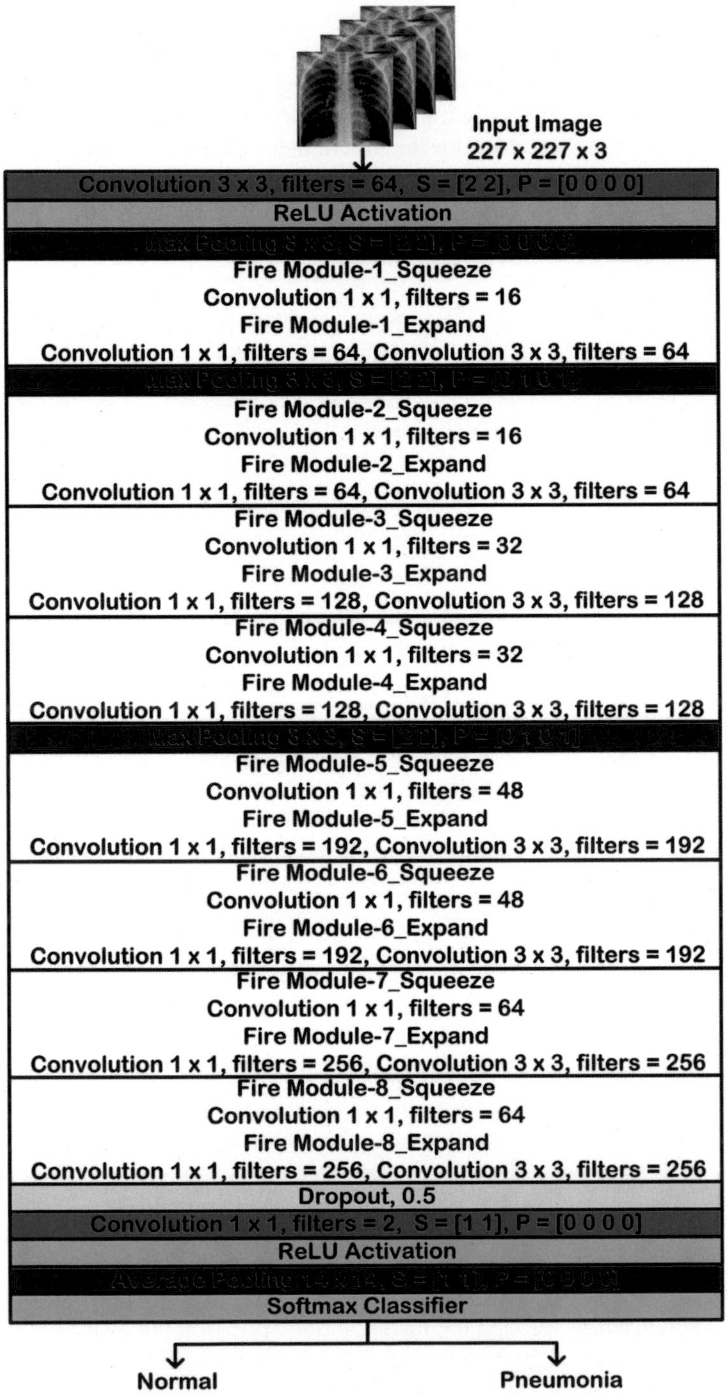

Input Image
227 x 227 x 3

Convolution 3 x 3, filters = 64, S = [2 2], P = [0 0 0 0]
ReLU Activation
Max Pooling 3 x 3, S = [2 2], P = [0 0 0 0]
Fire Module-1_Squeeze **Convolution 1 x 1, filters = 16** **Fire Module-1_Expand** **Convolution 1 x 1, filters = 64, Convolution 3 x 3, filters = 64**
Max Pooling 3 x 3, S = [2 2], P = [0 1 0 1]
Fire Module-2_Squeeze **Convolution 1 x 1, filters = 16** **Fire Module-2_Expand** **Convolution 1 x 1, filters = 64, Convolution 3 x 3, filters = 64**
Fire Module-3_Squeeze **Convolution 1 x 1, filters = 32** **Fire Module-3_Expand** **Convolution 1 x 1, filters = 128, Convolution 3 x 3, filters = 128**
Fire Module-4_Squeeze **Convolution 1 x 1, filters = 32** **Fire Module-4_Expand** **Convolution 1 x 1, filters = 128, Convolution 3 x 3, filters = 128**
Max Pooling 3 x 3, S = [2 2], P = [0 1 0 1]
Fire Module-5_Squeeze **Convolution 1 x 1, filters = 48** **Fire Module-5_Expand** **Convolution 1 x 1, filters = 192, Convolution 3 x 3, filters = 192**
Fire Module-6_Squeeze **Convolution 1 x 1, filters = 48** **Fire Module-6_Expand** **Convolution 1 x 1, filters = 192, Convolution 3 x 3, filters = 192**
Fire Module-7_Squeeze **Convolution 1 x 1, filters = 64** **Fire Module-7_Expand** **Convolution 1 x 1, filters = 256, Convolution 3 x 3, filters = 256**
Fire Module-8_Squeeze **Convolution 1 x 1, filters = 64** **Fire Module-8_Expand** **Convolution 1 x 1, filters = 256, Convolution 3 x 3, filters = 256**
Dropout, 0.5
Convolution 1 x 1, filters = 2, S = [1 1], P = [0 0 0 0]
ReLU Activation
Average Pooling 14 x 14, S = [1 1], P = [0 0 0 0]
Softmax Classifier

Normal   **Pneumonia**

FIG. 7.2

Architecture of SqueezeNet CNN model.

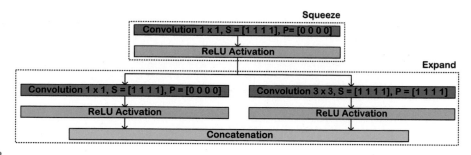

FIG. 7.3

Structure of fire module.

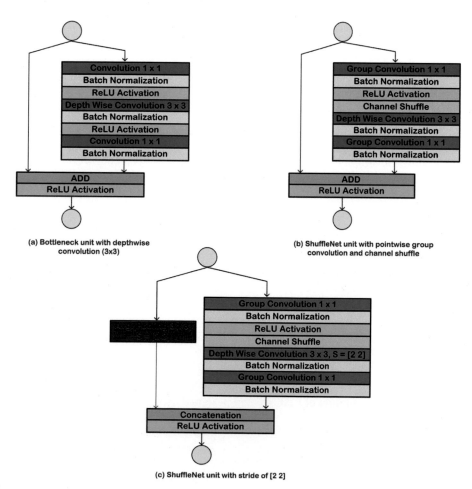

FIG. 7.4

Structure of the building blocks of lightweight ShuffleNet CNN model.

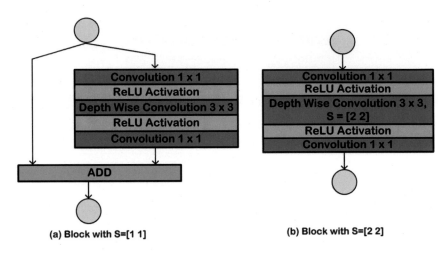

(a) Block with S=[1 1]   (b) Block with S=[2 2]

FIG. 7.5

Structure of the building blocks of lightweight MobileNetV2 CNN model.

7.5 Decision fusion

In simple words, decision fusion is the method of combining the decision taken by multiple classifiers to reach a common final decision. Here the decision of the classifier is the classification performed on the test dataset, which is the prediction on the test dataset. The process includes combining the information from different datasets or different classifiers after the data has been subjected to preliminary classification. This is discussed in detail in Chapter 4.

7.6 Experiments and results

Experiment 7: Designing lightweight end-to-end Pre-trained CNN-based CAC system for chest radiographs using SqueezeNet

In this experiment, the CAC system for binary class classification of chest radiograph images is designed using SqueezeNet CNN model, which has been trained using the augmented chest radiograph image dataset for classification of chest radiograph images. The results of the performance evaluation of Pre-trained SqueezeNet model are shown in Table 7.1.

Table 7.1 Performance evaluation of CAC system designed using lightweight SqueezeNet CNN for chest radiographs.

Network/ classifier	Confusion matrix			Accuracy (%)	ICA_Normal (%)	ICA_Pneumonia (%)
		Normal	Pneumonia			
SqueezeNet/ softmax	Normal	49	1	83.00	98.00	68.00
	Pneumonia	16	34			

ICA_Normal, individual class accuracy for Normal class; ICA_Pneumonia, individual class accuracy for Pneumonia class.

From the results of Experiment 7, as shown in Table 7.1, it can be seen that the CAC system designed using SqueezeNet CNN model achieves 83.00% accuracy for the classification of chest radiographic images into two classes: Normal and Pneumonia. The individual class accuracy value of the Normal class is 98.00%, and for the Pneumonia class, the individual class accuracy value obtained is 68.00%. From the total 100 images in the testing set, 17 images have been incorrectly classified, from which only one belongs to the Normal class and the remaining 16 belong to the Pneumonia class.

Code Snippet 7.1 shows the syntax of loading the training dataset. The chest X-ray images are divided and kept in three folders, namely training, validation, and testing. The training data is loaded from the path "H:\DataChestX-ray\Training\," which further contains two folders named as per the class labels of Normal and Pneumonia.

Code Snippet 7.1 Loading the training dataset

```
%%Loading the training dataset%%
imds_train=imageDatastore('H:\DataChestX-ray\Training\','IncludeSubfolders',true,
'LabelSource','foldernames');
```

Code Snippet 7.2 shows the syntax of loading the validation dataset. The validation data is loaded from the path "H:\DataChestX-ray\Validation\," which further contains two folders named as per the class labels, Normal and Pneumonia, just as those of the training dataset.

Code Snippet 7.2 Loading the validation dataset

```
%%Loading the validation dataset%%
imds_val=imageDatastore('H:\DataChestX-ray\Validation\','IncludeSubfolders',true,
'LabelSource','foldernames');
```

Code Snippet 7.3 shows the syntax of loading the testing dataset. The testing data is loaded from the path "H:\DataChestX-ray\Testing\," which further contains two folders named as per the class labels, Normal and Pneumonia, just as those of the training and validation datasets.

Code Snippet 7.3 Loading the testing dataset

```
%%Loading the testing dataset%%
imds_test=imageDatastore('H:\DataChestX-ray\Testing\','IncludeSubfolders',true,
'LabelSource','foldernames');
```

After the dataset has been loaded, the target CNN model is loaded as shown in Code Snippet 7.4. For Experiment 7, SqueezeNet CNN model is used; hence, it is loaded to further proceed with the training process.

Code Snippet 7.4 Loading the SqueezeNet Pre-trained CNN model

```
%%loading the SqueezeNet Pre-trained CNN model%%
net = squeezenet;
```

As the target network is also loaded into the MATLAB workspace, now one needs to specify the training options so as to facilitate training of the CNN model. Code Snippet 7.5 shows the training options set for Experiment 7.

Code Snippet 7.5 Assigning the training options

```
%%specifying the training options %%
Training_options= trainingOptions('rmsprop','InitialLearnRate',0.0001, 'Plots',
'training-progress', 'ValidationData', imds_val, 'ValidationFrequency', 10,
'Shuffle', 'every-epoch', 'MaxEpochs', 10, 'MiniBatchSize',45);
```

Code Snippet 7.6 shows the syntax of training the network using the training data and the CNN model is loaded into the workspace on the previously defined training options.

Code Snippet 7.6 Training the SqueezeNet Pre-trained CNN model

```
%%training the CNN model%%
Exp7_squeezenet = trainNetwork(imds_train,lgraph,Training_options );
```

Code Snippet 7.7 shows the syntax of projecting the test data onto the trained network. The predictions of the trained CNN model are in the form of a confusion matrix.

Code Snippet 7.7 Classifying the images and printing the confusion matrix

```
%%using trained network to classify images%%
[predictions,prediction_score] = classify(Exp7_squeezenet,imds_test);
true_testing = imds_test.Labels;
nnz(predictions == true_testing)/numel(predictions);
[confusion_matrix, matrix_order] =confusionmat(true_testing,predictions);
heatmap(matrix_order, matrix_order, confusion_matrix);
accuracy = mean(predictions==true_testing)
```

Once the network is trained, it is beneficial to save the network for future reference. This can be done using the save() function as shown in Code Snippet 7.8. The results of Experiment 7 are saved in a "mat" file named 'Exp7_squeezenet.mat'.

Code Snippet 7.8 Saving the results

```
%%saving the trained SqueezeNet CNN model%%
save('Exp7_squeezenet')
```

Experiment 8: Designing lightweight end-to-end Pre-trained CNN-based CAC system for chest radiographs using ShuffleNet

Table 7.2 Performance evaluation of CAC system designed using lightweight ShuffleNet CNN for chest radiographs.

Network/ classifier	Confusion matrix			Accuracy (%)	ICA_ Normal (%)	ICA_Pneumonia (%)
		Normal	**Pneumonia**			
ShuffleNet/ softmax	Normal	50	0	92.00	100.00	84.00
	Pneumonia	8	42			

ICA_Normal, individual class accuracy for Normal class; ICA_Pneumonia, individual class accuracy for Pneumonia class.

In this experiment, the CAC system for binary class classification of chest radiograph images is designed using ShuffleNet CNN model, which has been trained using the augmented chest radiograph image dataset for classification of chest radiograph images. The results of the performance evaluation of the CAC system designed for binary classification of chest radiographs using ShuffleNet is shown in Table 7.2.

From the results of Experiment 8, as shown in Table 7.2, it can be seen that the CAC system designed using ShuffleNet CNN model achieves 92.00% accuracy for the classification of chest radiographic images into two classes: Normal and Pneumonia. The individual class accuracy value of the Normal class is 100.00%, and for the Pneumonia class, the individual class accuracy value obtained is 84.00%. From the total 100 images in the testing set, eight images have been incorrectly classified, all of which belong to the Pneumonia class.

Code Snippet 7.9 shows the syntax of loading the training dataset. The chest X-ray images are divided and kept in three folders, namely training, validation, and testing. The training data is loaded from the path "H:\DataChestX-ray\Training\," which further contains two folders named as per the class labels of Normal and Pneumonia.

Code Snippet 7.9 Loading the training dataset

```
%%Loading the training dataset%%
imds_train=imageDatastore('H:\DataChestX-ray\Training\','IncludeSubfolders',true,
'LabelSource','foldernames');
```

Code Snippet 7.10 shows the syntax of loading the validation dataset. The validation data is loaded from the path "H:\DataChestX-ray\Validation\," which further contains two folders named as per the class labels, Normal and Pneumonia, just as those of the training dataset.

Code Snippet 7.10 Loading the validation dataset

```
%%Loading the validation dataset%%
imds_val=imageDatastore('H:\DataChestX-ray\Validation\','IncludeSubfolders',true,
'LabelSource','foldernames');
```

Code Snippet 7.11 shows the syntax of loading the testing dataset. The testing data is loaded from the path "H:\DataChestX-ray\Testing\," which further contains two folders named as per the class labels, Normal and Pneumonia, just as those of the training and validation datasets.

Code Snippet 7.11 Loading the testing dataset

```
%%Loading the testing dataset%%
imds_test=imageDatastore('H:\DataChestX-ray\Testing\','IncludeSubfolders',true,
'LabelSource','foldernames');
```

After the dataset has been loaded, the target CNN model is loaded as shown in Code Snippet 7.12. For Experiment 8, ShuffleNet CNN model is used and hence it is loaded to further proceed with the training process.

Code Snippet 7.12 Loading the ShuffleNet Pre-trained CNN model

```
%%loading the ShuffleNet Pre-trained CNN model%%
net = shufflenet;
```

As the target network is also loaded into the MATLAB workspace, now one needs to specify the training options so as to facilitate training of the CNN model. Code Snippet 7.13 shows the training options set for Experiment 8.

Code Snippet 7.13 Assigning the training options

```
%%specifying the training options %%
Training_options= trainingOptions('rmsprop','InitialLearnRate',0.0001,'Plots',
'training-progress', 'ValidationData', imds_val, 'ValidationFrequency',
10,'Shuffle','every-epoch','MaxEpochs',10, 'MiniBatchSize',45);
```

Code Snippet 7.14 shows the syntax of training the network using the training data, and the CNN model is loaded into the workspace on the previously defined training options.

Code Snippet 7.14 Training the ShuffleNet Pre-trained CNN model

```
%%training the CNN model%%
Exp8_shufflenet = trainNetwork(imds_train,lgraph,Training_options );
```

Code Snippet 7.15 shows the syntax of projecting the test data onto the trained network. The predictions of the trained CNN model are in the form of a confusion matrix.

Code Snippet 7.15 Classifying the images and print the confusion matrix

```
%%using trained network to classify images%%
[predictions,prediction_score] = classify(Exp8_shufflenet,imds_test);
true_testing = imds_test.Labels;
nnz(predictions == true_testing)/numel(predictions);
[confusion_matrix, matrix_order] =confusionmat(true_testing,predictions);
heatmap(matrix_order, matrix_order, confusion_matrix);
accuracy = mean(predictions==true_testing)
```

Once the network is trained, it is beneficial to save the network for future reference. This can be done using the save() function as shown in Code Snippet 7.16. The results of Experiment 8 are saved in a "mat" file named 'Exp8_shufflenet.mat'.

Code Snippet 7.16 Saving the results

```
%%saving the trained ShuffleNet CNN model%%
save('Exp8_shufflenet')
```

Experiment 9: Designing lightweight end-to-end Pre-trained CNN-based CAC system for chest radiographs using mobileNetV2

In this experiment, the CAC system for binary class classification of chest radiographic images is designed using MobileNetV2 CNN model, which has been trained using the augmented chest radiograph image dataset for classification of chest radiograph images. The results of the performance evaluation of Pre-trained MobileNetV2 model are shown in Table 7.3.

From the results of Experiment 9, as shown in Table 7.3, it can be seen that the CAC system designed using lightweight MobileNetV2 CNN model achieves 94.00% accuracy for the classification of chest radiograph images into two classes: Normal and Pneumonia. The individual class accuracy value of the Normal class is 98.00%, and for the Pneumonia class, the individual class accuracy value obtained is 90.00%. From the total 100 images in the testing set, six images have been incorrectly classified, from which only one belongs to the Normal class and the remaining five belongs to the Pneumonia class.

Code Snippet 7.17 shows the syntax of loading the training dataset. The chest X-ray images are divided and kept in three folders, namely training, validation, and testing. The training data is loaded from the path "H:\DataChestX-ray\Training\," which further contains two folders named as per the class labels of Normal and Pneumonia.

Code Snippet 7.17 Loading the training dataset

```
%%Loading the training dataset%%
imds_train=imageDatastore('H:\DataChestX-ray\Training\','IncludeSubfolders',true,
'LabelSource','foldernames');
```

Table 7.3 Performance evaluation of CAC system designed using lightweight MobileNetV2 CNN for chest radiographs.

Network/ classifier	Confusion matrix			Accuracy (%)	ICA_Normal (%)	ICA_Pneumonia (%)
		Normal	Pneumonia			
MobileNetV2/ softmax	Normal	49	1	94.00	98.00	90.00
	Pneumonia	5	45			

ICA_Normal, individual class accuracy for Normal class; ICA_Pneumonia, individual class accuracy for Pneumonia class.

Code Snippet 7.18 shows the syntax of loading the validation dataset. The validation data is loaded from the path "H:\DataChestX-ray\Validation\," which further contains two folders named as per the class labels, Normal and Pneumonia, just as those of the training dataset.

Code Snippet 7.18 Loading the validation dataset

```
%%Loading the validation dataset%%
imds_val=imageDatastore('H:\DataChestX-ray\Validation\','IncludeSubfolders',true,
'LabelSource','foldernames');
```

Code Snippet 7.19 shows the syntax of loading the testing dataset. The testing data is loaded from the path "H:\DataChestX-ray\Testing\," which further contains two folders named as per the class labels, Normal and Pneumonia, just as those of training and validation datasets.

Code Snippet 7.19 Loading the testing dataset

```
%%Loading the testing dataset%%
imds_test=imageDatastore('H:\DataChestX-ray\Testing\','IncludeSubfolders',true,
'LabelSource','foldernames');
```

After the dataset has been loaded, the target CNN model is loaded as shown in Code Snippet 7.20. For Experiment 9, MobileNetV2 CNN model is used, and it is loaded to further proceed with the training process.

Code Snippet 7.20 Loading the MobileNetV2 Pre-trained CNN model

```
%%loading the MobileNetV2 Pre-trained CNN model%%
net = mobilenetv2;
```

As the target network is also loaded into the MATLAB workspace, now one needs to specify the training options so as to facilitate training of the CNN model. Code Snippet 7.21 shows the training options set for Experiment 9.

Code Snippet 7.21 Assigning the training options

```
%%specifying the training options %%
Training_options= trainingOptions('adam','InitialLearnRate',0.0001,'Plots',
'training-progress', 'ValidationData', imds_val, 'ValidationFrequency',
10,'Shuffle','every-epoch','MaxEpochs',10, 'MiniBatchSize',45);
```

Code Snippet 7.22 shows the syntax of training the network using the training data, and the CNN model is loaded into the workspace on the previously defined training options.

Code Snippet 7.22 Training the `MobileNetV2` **Pre-trained CNN model**

```
%%training the CNN model%%
Exp9_MobileNetV2 = trainNetwork(imds_train,lgraph,Training_options );
```

Code Snippet 7.23 shows the syntax of projecting the test data onto the trained network. The predictions of the trained CNN model are in the form of a confusion matrix.

Code Snippet 7.23 Classifying the images and print the confusion matrix

```
%%using trained network to classify images%%
[predictions,prediction_score] = classify(Exp9_MobileNetV2,imds_test);
true_testing = imds_test.Labels;
nnz(predictions == true_testing)/numel(predictions);
[confusion_matrix, matrix_order] =confusionmat(true_testing,predictions);
heatmap(matrix_order, matrix_order, confusion_matrix);
accuracy = mean(predictions==true_testing)
```

Once the network is trained, it is beneficial to save the network for future reference. This can be done using the save() function as shown in Code Snippet 7.24. The results of Experiment 9 are saved in a "mat" file named `'Exp9_MobileNetV2.mat'`.

Code Snippet 7.24 Saving the results

```
%%saving the trained MobileNetV2 CNN model%%
save('Exp9_MobileNetV2')
```

Experiment 10: Designing lightweight end-to-end Pre-trained CNN-based CAC system for chest radiographs using decision fusion

In this experiment, the CAC system for binary class classification of chest radiograph images is designed using decision fusion of the Pre-trained lightweight CNN model that has been trained using the augmented chest radiograph image dataset for classification of chest radiograph images in Experiments 7–9. The results of the performance evaluation of the CAC system designed using decision fusion of the Pre-trained lightweight CNN models are shown in Table 7.4.

Table 7.4 Performance evaluation of CAC system designed using decision fusion of the Pre-trained lightweight CNN models.

Network/classifier	Confusion matrix			Accuracy (%)	ICA_Normal (%)	ICA_Pneumonia (%)
		Normal	Pneumonia			
SqueezeNet + ShuffleNet + MobileNetV2/softmax	Normal	50	0	95.00	100.00	90.00
	Pneumonia	5	45			

ICA_Normal, individual class accuracy for Normal class; ICA_Pneumonia, individual class accuracy for Pneumonia class.

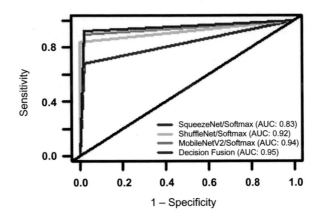

FIG. 7.6

The ROC curve with its corresponding AUC values for the CAC system designed using the lightweight CNN model.

From the result of Experiment 10, as shown in Table 7.4, it can be seen that the CAC system designed using the decision fusion of the Pre-trained lightweight CNN model in Experiments 7–9, achieves 95.00% accuracy for the classification of chest radiograph images into two classes: Normal and Pneumonia. The individual class accuracy value of the Normal class is 100.00%, and for the Pneumonia class, the individual class accuracy value obtained is 90.00%. From the total 100 images in the testing set, five images have been incorrectly classified, which all belong to the Pneumonia class.

The ROC curve with its corresponding AUC values for the CAC system designed using the lightweight CNN models is shown in Fig. 7.6.

7.7 Concluding remarks

This chapter discusses the architecture of SqueezeNet, ShuffleNet, and MobileNetV2 lightweight CNN models and the designing of CAC systems for the binary classification of chest radiographs. From the experiments carried out, it is observed that the CAC system designed for chest radiographs using the lightweight MobileNetV2 CNN model achieves 94.00% accuracy for the classification of chest radiographs. A comparative analysis of the obtained results from the experiments carried with different lightweight CNN models for the classification of chest radiographs is given in Table 7.5.

Further experiments in the subsequent chapters are carried out to evaluate the performance of the same designing lightweight CNN-based CAC system using deep feature extraction, MobileNetV2, ANFC-LH classifiers, and PCA-SVM classifier.

Table 7.5 Comparative analysis of the obtained results for the classification of chest radiographs.

Network/classifier	Accuracy (%)	ICA_Normal (%)	ICA_Pneumonia (%)
Experiment 7: Designing lightweight end-to-end Pre-trained CNN-based CAC system for chest radiographs using SqueezeNet	83.00	98.00	68.00
Experiment 8: Designing lightweight end-to-end Pre-trained CNN-based CAC system for chest radiographs using ShuffleNet	92.00	100.00	84.00
Experiment 9: Designing lightweight end-to-end Pre-trained CNN-based CAC system for chest radiographs using MobileNetV2	94.00	98.00	90.00
Experiment 10: Designing lightweight end-to-end Pre-trained CNN-based CAC system for chest radiographs using decision fusion	95.00	100.00	90.00

ICA_Normal, individual class accuracy for Normal class; ICA_Pneumonia, individual class accuracy for Pneumonia class.

References

[1] J. Gu, Z. Wang, J. Kuen, L. Ma, A. Shahroudy, B. Shuai, T. Liu, X. Wang, G. Wang, J. Cai, T. Chen, Recent advances in convolutional neural networks, Pattern Recognit. 77 (2018) 354–377.

[2] H. Vaseli, Z. Liao, A.H. Abdi, H. Girgis, D. Behnami, C. Luong, F.T. Dezaki, N. Dhungel, R. Rohling, K. Gin, P. Abolmaesumi, Designing lightweight deep learning models for echocardiography view classification, in: Medical Imaging 2019: Image-Guided Procedures, Robotic Interventions, and Modeling, vol. 10951, International Society for Optics and Photonics, 2019, p. 109510F.

[3] A. Singh, S. Sengupta, V. Lakshminarayanan, Explainable deep learning models in medical image analysis, J. Imaging 6 (6) (2020) 52.

[4] F.N. Iandola, S. Han, M.W. Moskewicz, K. Ashraf, W.J. Dally, K. Keutzer, SqueezeNet: AlexNet-level accuracy with 50x fewer parameters and <0.5 MB model size, arXiv preprint arXiv:1602.07360, 2016.

[5] T. Rahman, M.E. Chowdhury, A. Khandakar, K.R. Islam, K.F. Islam, Z.B. Mahbub, M.A. Kadir, S. Kashem, Transfer learning with deep convolutional neural network (CNN) for pneumonia detection using chest X-ray, Appl. Sci. 10 (9) (2020) 3233.

[6] A. Pal, S. Jaiswal, S. Ghosh, N. Das, M. Nasipuri, Segfast: a faster squeezenet based semantic image segmentation technique using depth-wise separable convolutions, in: Proceedings of the 11th Indian Conference on Computer Vision, Graphics and Image Processing, 2018, pp. 1–7.

[7] F. Ucar, D. Korkmaz, COVIDiagnosis-Net: deep Bayes-SqueezeNet based diagnosis of the coronavirus disease 2019 (COVID-19) from X-ray images, Med. Hypotheses 140 (2020) 109761.

[8] K. Nakamichi, H. Lu, H. Kim, K. Yoneda, F. Tanaka, Classification of circulating tumor cells in fluorescence microscopy images based on SqueezeNet, in: 2019 19th International Conference on Control, Automation and Systems (ICCAS), IEEE, 2019, pp. 1042–1045.

[9] X. Qian, E.W. Patton, J. Swaney, Q. Xing, T. Zeng, Machine learning on cataracts classification using SqueezeNet, in: 2018 4th International Conference on Universal Village (UV), IEEE, 2018, pp. 1–3.

[10] Kriti, J. Virmani, N. Dey, V. Kumar, PCA-PNN and PCA-SVM based CAD systems for breast density classification, in: Applications of Intelligent Optimization in Biology and Medicine, Springer, Cham, 2016, pp. 159–180.

[11] B.B. Ahn, The Compact 3D Convolutional Neural Network for Medical Images, Standford University, 2017.

[12] M. Polsinelli, L. Cinque, G. Placidi, A light cnn for detecting covid-19 from ct scans of the chest, Pattern Recogn. Lett. 140 (2020) 95–100.

[13] M. Polsinelli, L. Cinque, G. Placidi, A light CNN for detecting COVID-19 from CT scans of the chest, Pattern Recogn. Lett. 140 (2020) 95–100.

[14] A. Abbas, M.M. Abdelsamea, M.M. Gaber, Classification of COVID-19 in chest X-ray images using DeTraC deep convolutional neural network, Appl. Intell. (2020) 1–11.

[15] A.K. Mishra, S.K. Das, P. Roy, S. Bandyopadhyay, Identifying COVID19 from chest CT images: a deep convolutional neural networks based approach, J. Healthc. Eng. (2020), 8843664.

[16] X. Zhang, X. Zhou, M. Lin, J. Sun, Shufflenet: an extremely efficient convolutional neural network for mobile devices, in: Proceedings of the IEEE Conference on Computer Vision and Pattern Recognition, 2018, pp. 6848–6856.

[17] N.E.M. Khalifa, M.H.N. Taha, A.E. Hassanien, S.H.N. Taha, The detection of COVID-19 in CT medical images: a deep learning approach, in: Big Data Analytics and Artificial Intelligence Against COVID-19: Innovation Vision and Approach, Springer, Cham, 2020, pp. 73–90.

[18] A.G. Cococi, D.M. Armanda, I.I. Felea, R. Dogaru, Disease detection on medical images using light-weight Convolutional Neural Networks for resource constrained platforms, in: 2020 International Symposium on Electronics and Telecommunications (ISETC), IEEE, 2020, pp. 1–4.

[19] A. Panday, A Complete Survey on Automatically Diagnosing COVID-19 in the Field of Computer Vision and A Collection of Medical Images, 2020, August 16. https://doi.org/10.31224/osf.io/z9bfv.

[20] M. Hu, H. Lin, Z. Fan, W. Gao, L. Yang, C. Liu, Q. Song, Learning to recognize chest-Xray images faster and more efficiently based on multi-kernel depthwise convolution, IEEE Access 8 (2020) 37265–37274.

[21] A.M. Alqudah, S. Qazan, A. Alqudah, Automated systems for detection of COVID-19 using chest X-ray images and lightweight convolutional neural networks, Research Square (2020), https://doi:10.21203/rs.3.rs-24305/v1.2020.

[22] P.K. Sethy, S.K. Behera, P.K. Ratha, P. Biswas, Detection of coronavirus disease (COVID-19) based on deep features and support vector machine, Preprints (2020), 2020030300.

[23] B. Abraham, M.S. Nair, Computer-aided detection of COVID-19 from X-ray images using multi-CNN and Bayesnet classifier, Biocybern. Biomed. Eng. 40 (4) (2020) 1436–1445.

[24] M. Sandler, A. Howard, M. Zhu, A. Zhmoginov, L.C. Chen, Mobilenetv2: inverted residuals and linear bottlenecks, in: Proceedings of the IEEE Conference on Computer Vision and Pattern Recognition, 2018, pp. 4510–4520.

[25] A.G. Howard, M. Zhu, B. Chen, D. Kalenichenko, W. Wang, T. Weyand, M. Andreetto, H. Adam, Mobilenets: efficient convolutional neural networks for mobile vision applications, arXiv preprint arXiv:1704.04861, 2017.

[26] K.E. El Asnaoui, Y. Chawki, A. Idri, Automated methods for detection and classification pneumonia based on x-ray images using deep learning, arXiv preprint arXiv:2003.14363, 2020.

[27] K. El Asnaoui, Y. Chawki, Using X-ray images and deep learning for automated detection of coronavirus disease, J. Biomol. Struct. Dyn. (2020) 1–12.

[28] I.D. Apostolopoulos, T.A. Mpesiana, Covid-19: automatic detection from x-ray images utilizing transfer learning with convolutional neural networks, Phys. Eng. Sci. Med. 43 (2) (2020) 635–640.

[29] M.F. Hashmi, S. Katiyar, A.G. Keskar, N.D. Bokde, Z.W. Geem, Efficient pneumonia detection in chest xray images using deep transfer learning, Diagnostics 10 (6) (2020) 417.

[30] J. Sivasamy, T. Subashini, Classification and predictions of lung diseases from chest X-rays using MobileNet, Int. J. Anal. Exp. Modal Anal. 12 (3) (2020) 665–672.

[31] R. Sethi, M. Mehrotra, D. Sethi, Deep learning based diagnosis recommendation for COVID-19 using chest x-rays images, in: 2020 Second International Conference on Inventive Research in Computing Applications (ICIRCA), IEEE, 2020, pp. 1–4.

[32] R. Mohammadi, M. Salehi, H. Ghaffari, A.A. Rohani, R. Reiazi, Transfer learning-based automatic detection of coronavirus disease 2019 (COVID-19) from chest X-ray images, J. Biomed. Phys. Eng. 10 (5) (2020) 559.

[33] E.F. Ohata, G.M. Bezerra, J.V.S. das Chagas, A.V.L. Neto, A.B. Albuquerque, V.H.C. de Albuquerque, P.P. Reboucas Filho, Automatic detection of COVID-19 infection using chest X-ray images through transfer learning, IEEE/CAA J. Autom. Sinica 8 (1) (2020) 239–248.

[34] H. Mukherjee, S. Ghosh, A. Dhar, S.M. Obaidullah, K.C. Santosh, K. Roy, Deep neural network to detect COVID-19: one architecture for both CT scans and chest X-rays, Appl. Intell. (2020) 1–13.

Further reading

M. Robinson, A. Whelan, S. Burton, B. Bolon, H. Ellis, Deep Learning Course, 2020.

Hybrid computer-aided classification system design using lightweight end-to-end Pre-trained CNN-based deep feature extraction and ANFC-LH classifier for chest radiographs

8.1 Introduction

This chapter covers the exhaustive description of the experiments carried out for the design of a hybrid computer-aided classification (CAC) system using lightweight end-to-end Pre-trained MobileNetV2 CNN model as a deep feature extractor and adaptive neuro-fuzzy classifier with linguistic hedges ANFC-LH classifier for chest radiographs. The code snippets of the experiment aim at giving a better understanding to the programmatic implementation of designing this CAC system.

8.2 Experimental workflow

The experimental workflow followed for analyzing the performance of the CAC system designed for chest radiographs using deep feature extraction, MobileNetV2 CNN model, and ANFC-LH classifier is shown in Fig. 8.1.

8.3 Deep feature extraction

The process of extracting features of an image from the deep layers of a CNN is referred to as deep feature extraction, and the features extracted are called deep features. The deep feature extraction is discussed in Chapter 5. This process involves the steps of providing the input data to the Pre-trained CNN, and then the respective activation values from the fully connected layer that are usually present at the end of the network or pooling layer are obtained. The deep features extracted can further act as inputs to the conventional machine learning-based classifiers; hence, various machine learning algorithms can be implemented for the classification of chest radiograph images into two classes: Normal and Pneumonia [1–13].

Deep Learning for Chest Radiographs. https://doi.org/10.1016/B978-0-323-90184-0.00009-6
Copyright © 2021 Elsevier Inc. All rights reserved.

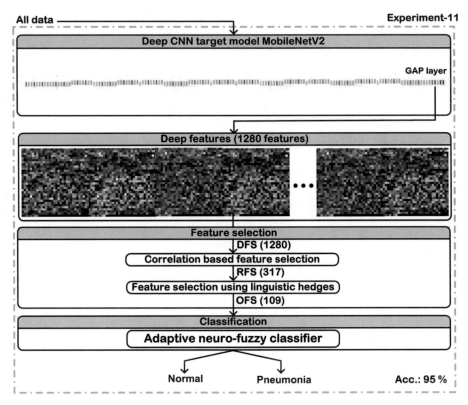

FIG. 8.1

Experimental workflow of hybrid CAC system designed using deep feature extraction, lightweight MobileNetV2 CNN model, and ANFC-LH classifier.

8.3.1 Lightweight MobileNetV2 CNN model as deep feature extractor

In the present work, the deep features are extracted from the best fine-tuned lightweight MobileNetV2 CNN model whose classification results of Experiment 9 are given in Chapter 7. A set of deep features are extracted from the best performing lightweight CNN model. This feature set is referred to as a deep feature set (DFS). The MobileNetV2 architecture is discussed in Chapter 7. The DFS is formed by extracting features from the global average pool (GAP) layer of the trained MobileNetV2 CNN model. Fig. 8.2 shows the lightweight MobileNetV2 CNN model as a deep feature extractor.

Code Snippet 8.1 shows the syntax to load the MobileNetV2 CNN model trained in Experiment 9 in Chapter 7 to extract the features from its pooling layer.

Code Snippet 8.1 Loading the saved MobileNetV2 Pre-trained CNN model

```
%%loading the saved MobileNetV2 Pre-trained CNN model%%
load('Exp9_MobileNetV2');
```

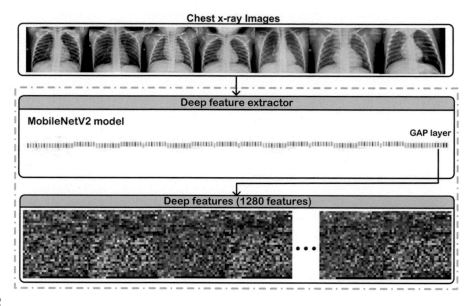

FIG. 8.2

MobileNetV2 CNN model as deep feature extractor.

Code Snippet 8.2 shows the extraction of training and testing features from the pooling layer of the MobileNetV2 CNN model after it has been loaded into the MATLAB workspace.

Code Snippet 8.2 Feature extraction from the MobileNetV2 Pre-trained CNN model

```
%%feature extraction%%
layer = 'pool5';
featuresTrain=activations(Exp9_MobileNetV2,imds_train,layer,'OutputAs','rows');
featuresTest=activations(Exp9_MobileNetV2,imds_test,layer,'OutputAs','rows');
```

Code Snippet 8.3 shows the syntax of writing the features extracted from the pooling layer to Microsoft Excel sheets. These .xlsx files or .csv files are then used as input to the machine learning-based classifiers.

Code Snippet 8.3 Saving the feature extracted from the MobileNetV2 Pre-trained CNN model

```
%%saving the features in a excel sheet%%
xlswrite('H:\DataChestX-ray\FeatureExtraction\Exp11_Train.xlsx',featuresTrain);
xlswrite('H:\DataChestX-ray\FeatureExtraction\Exp11_Test.xlsx',featuresTest);
```

Fig. 8.3 shows the visualization of deep feature maps of images extracted by the MobileNetV2 from the GAP layer.

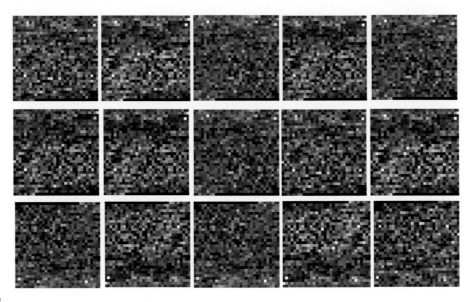

FIG. 8.3

Deep feature visualization.

Code Snippet 8.4 shows the syntax to load the image whose features are to be visualized. Here a Normal chest radiograph is loaded from the path "H:\DataChestX-ray\Training\Normal\." Once the image is loaded into the workspace, the predefined activation function is used to generate the feature map.

Code Snippet 8.4 Reading image from folder for feature visualization

```
%%Reading the image from the folder%%
CXR=imread('H:\DataChestX-ray\Training\Normal\CXR_1.jpg');
```

Code Snippet 8.5 shows the syntax for visualizing the activation of the loaded chest radiograph from the GAP layer named pool5 of the MobileNetV2 model.

Code Snippet 8.5 Feature visualization

```
%%Extracting the feature map at the GAP layer of MobileNetV2%%
feature_map=activations(net,CXR,'pool5');
```

Code Snippets 8.6 and 8.7 show the further steps followed, which include determining the size of the activation map, reshaping it, and using the predefined functions size() and reshape(), respectively.

Code Snippet 8.6 Determining the size of feature map for feature visualization

```
%%Determining the size of the feature map at the GAP layer of MobileNetV2%%
size_CXR=size(feature_map);
```

Code Snippet 8.7 Reshaping the feature map for feature visualization

```
%%Reshaping the size of the feature map at the GAP layer of MobileNetV2%%
feature_map=reshape(feature_map,[size_CXR(1) size_CXR(2) 1 size_CXR(3)]);
```

Code Snippet 8.8 shows the final visualization of the features maps. The output of this is one of the feature maps previously shown in Fig. 8.3.

Code Snippet 8.8 Feature visualization

```
%%feature visualization%%
figure(1),montage(mat2gray(feature_map)),title('GoogLeNet GAP layer features')
```

8.4 Feature selection

The process of feature selection and different methods of feature selection are discussed in Chapter 5.

8.4.1 Correlation-based feature selection

Correlation-based feature selection (CFS) is a filter-based feature selection technique that aims at extracting the best and most optimal set of features, which are nothing but a subset of the original set of features, on the basis of their correlation values. This technique is widely used as an attempt to select the optimal features from the original feature sets [14–27]. The CFS follows the basic idea that the features are not correlated to each other but have higher correlations to the class they belong to. Here the reduced feature set (RFS) consists of the features that are uncorrelated to each other but have high correlation to their respective classes, either Normal or Pneumonia. The CFS has been discussed earlier in detail in Chapter 5.

Here the DFS contains the features extracted from the pooling layer of the lightweight MobileNetV2 CNN, that is, the GAP layer, which when subjected to the CFS results in an RFS. Here the DFS consists of 1280 features extracted from the GAP layer, and after CFS, the RFS consists of 317 features.

8.4.2 Feature selection using ANFC-LH

This wrapper-based feature selection technique aims at further optimizing the number of features that are vital for performing the task of classification. The DFS extracted from the Pre-trained CNN model may contain huge numbers of redundant features, which may adversely affect the performance of the CAC systems designed for the task of classification. Therefore, the careful selection of features that are relevant and essential is an important prerequisite for designing highly efficient CAC systems. The major benefits of the task of feature selection are the enhanced performance in terms of results and faster training time of the networks. Other benefits include the reduction in the complex nature of the classification model. Additionally, feature selection also aims at reducing overfitting of the models being trained for the task of classification.

In this module, the extracted deep features from the pooling layer of the lightweight MobileNetV2 CNN forms the DFS from which the features are selected by CFS forming an RFS. From RFS, the features are selected on the basis of LH. The extracted feature space for classification of chest radiographs

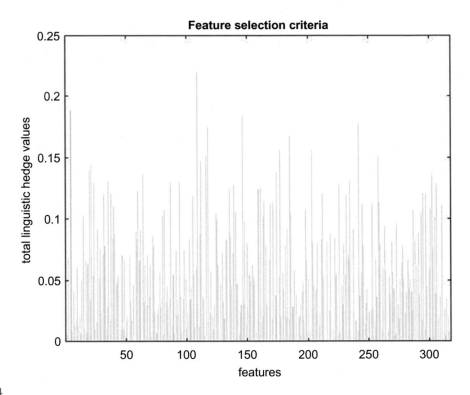

FIG. 8.4

Input features and their calculated power of LH value.

forms the DFS (1280 features), which when subjected to CFS, forms an RFS of 317 features. Among these features, in order to identify the features that are actually required for classification, feature selection using ANFC with LH is applied to this RFS. All the features are not essential and relevant for the classification, and in order to increase the efficiency of the CAC system, feature selection using a wrapper-based method along with LH is applied so that only essential features are selected. The detailed feature selection using ANFC-LH is discussed in Chapter 5.

This RFS (317 features) is subjected to an LH-based feature selection process, which reduces the features to an optimal feature set (OFS) of 109 features mainly because of their ability to distinguish among the numerous variety of Normal and Pneumonia chest radiographs. Fig. 8.4 shows the relationship between input features and their calculated power of LH value.

8.5 Adaptive neuro-fuzzy classifier

Image classification, in conventional machine learning, is defined as a technique of predicting the class membership of testing the data instances merely on the basis of the knowledge of the class memberships of the training data [28–41]. Here the training data is the known data that enables the machine learning algorithm to learn and then perform the task of classification, and the testing data is considered the

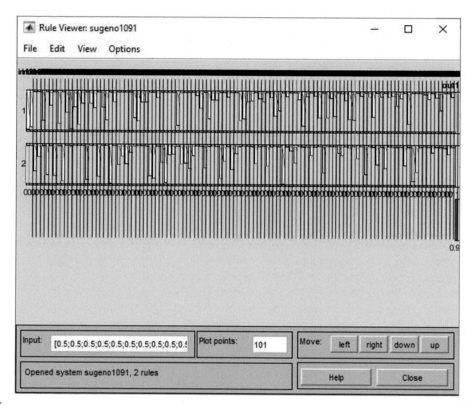

FIG. 8.5

Sugeno rule-base viewer for chest radiograph classification.

unknown data that the machine learning classifier or algorithm needs to correctly classify. The present work applies ANFC for chest radiographs. ANFC is a multilayered neural network with feed-forward network capabilities. Its architecture consists of the following layers: (i) input layer, (ii) membership layer, (iii) power layer, (iv) fuzzification layer, (v) defuzzification layer, (vi) normalization layer, and (vii) output layer [28, 31, 32, 42–46]. The functionality of ANFC or the neuro-fuzzy classifier (NFC) is dependent on a tool called the adaptive neuro-fuzzy inference system (ANFIS) tool. The NFC functions on the ANFIS and the sugeno rule-base viewer used in the present work is shown in Fig. 8.5. The detailed architecture of ANFC is discussed earlier in Chapter 5.

8.6 Experiment and results

Experiment 11: Designing hybrid CAC system for chest radiographs using deep feature extraction, lightweight MobileNetV2 and ANFC-LH classifier

From the results of Experiments 7–9, as seen in Chapter 7, it can be seen that lightweight MobileNetV2 CNN model achieves the highest accuracy (94.00%). Therefore, for this experiment to evaluate the performance of the lightweight CNN as feature extractor, the features from the GAP layer

Table 8.1 Performance evaluation of CAC system designed for chest radiographs using deep feature extraction, lightweight MobileNetV2 CNN model and ANFC-LH classifier.

Network/ classifier	Confusion matrix			Accuracy (%)	ICA_ Normal (%)	ICA_ Pneumonia (%)
		Normal	Pneumonia			
MobileNetV2/ ANFC-LH	Normal	49	1	95.00	98.00	92.00
	Pneumonia	4	46			

ICA_Normal, *individual class accuracy for Normal class;* ICA_Pneumonia, *individual class accuracy for Pneumonia class.*

of MobileNetV2 have been extracted forming a DFS (1280 features). On application of CFS, the DFS of 1280 features extracted is reduced to 317 uncorrelated features forming an RFS; this set is then subjected to the LH for further formation of an OFS of 109 features. This OFS is further fed to an ANFC-LH classifier for classification of chest radiograph images. The result of the performance evaluation of the hybrid CAC system designed for binary classification of chest radiographs using lightweight MobileNetV2 CNN model, deep feature extraction, and ANFC-LH classifier is shown in Table 8.1.

From the results of Experiment 11, as shown in Table 8.1, it can be seen that the CAC system designed using the deep features extracted from the MobileNetV2 CNN model fed to ANFC-LH classifier achieves 95.00% accuracy for the classification of chest radiograph images into two classes: Normal and Pneumonia. The individual class accuracy value of the Normal class is 98.00%, and for the Pneumonia class, the individual class accuracy value obtained is 92.00%. From the total 100 images in the testing set, five images have been incorrectly classified, out of which only one instance is of the Normal class and the remaining four images are of the Pneumonia class. The ROC curve with its corresponding AUC values for the hybrid CAC system designed using deep feature extraction, lightweight MobileNetV2 CNN model, and the ANFC-LH classifier is shown in Fig. 8.6.

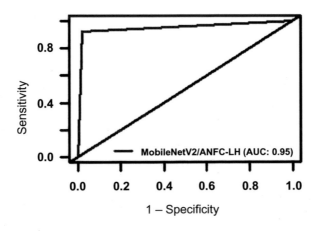

FIG. 8.6

The ROC curve with its corresponding AUC values for the CAC system designed using deep feature extraction, lightweight MobileNetV2 CNN model and ANFC-LH classifier.

8.7 Concluding remarks

This chapter discusses the concepts of deep feature extraction, feature selection, and the design of CAC system for the deep feature extraction using lightweight MobileNetV2 CNN model and ANFC-LH classifier. From the experiments carried out, it is observed that designing a CAC system for chest radiographs using deep feature extraction, lightweight MobileNetV2 CNN, and ANFC-LH classifier achieves 95.00% accuracy.

The experiments in the subsequent chapters are carried out to evaluate the performance of designing lightweight CNN-based hybrid CAC system using deep feature extraction, lightweight MobileNetV2, and PCA-SVM classifier.

References

[1] M. Nixon, A. Aguado, Feature Extraction and Image Processing for Computer Vision, Academic Press, 2019.

[2] A. Yang, X. Yang, W. Wu, H. Liu, Y. Zhuansun, Research on feature extraction of tumor image based on convolutional neural network, IEEE Access 7 (2019) 24204–24213.

[3] M. Srinivas, D. Roy, C.K. Mohan, Discriminative feature extraction from X-ray images using deep convolutional neural networks, in: 2016 IEEE International Conference on Acoustics, Speech and Signal Processing (ICASSP), IEEE, 2016, pp. 917–921.

[4] V. Chouhan, S.K. Singh, A. Khamparia, D. Gupta, P. Tiwari, C. Moreira, R. Damaševičius, V.H.C. De Albuquerque, A novel transfer learning based approach for pneumonia detection in chest X-ray images, Appl. Sci. 10 (2) (2020) 559.

[5] H. Ravishankar, P. Sudhakar, R. Venkataramani, S. Thiruvenkadam, P. Annangi, N. Babu, V. Vaidya, Understanding the mechanisms of deep transfer learning for medical images, in: Deep Learning and Data Labeling for Medical Applications, Springer, Cham, 2016, pp. 188–196.

[6] H. Wu, P. Xie, H. Zhang, D. Li, M. Cheng, Predict pneumonia with chest X-ray images based on convolutional deep neural learning networks, J. Intell. Fuzzy Syst. 39 (3) (2020) 2893–2907 (preprint).

[7] K. Suzuki, Overview of deep learning in medical imaging, Radiol. Phys. Technol. 10 (3) (2017) 257–273.

[8] A. Wibisono, J. Adibah, F.S. Priatmadji, N.Z. Viderisa, A. Husna, P. Mursanto, Segmentation-based knowledge extraction from chest X-ray images, in: 2019 4th Asia-Pacific Conference on Intelligent Robot Systems (ACIRS), IEEE, 2019, pp. 225–230.

[9] S.M. Anwar, M. Majid, A. Qayyum, M. Awais, M. Alnowami, M.K. Khan, Medical image analysis using convolutional neural networks: a review, J. Med. Syst. 42 (11) (2018) 226.

[10] N. Dey, Y.D. Zhang, V. Rajinikanth, R. Pugalenthi, N.S.M. Raja, Customized VGG19 architecture for pneumonia detection in chest X-rays, Pattern Recogn. Lett. 143 (2021) 67–74.

[11] D. Varshni, K. Thakral, L. Agarwal, R. Nijhawan, A. Mittal, Pneumonia detection using CNN based feature extraction, in: 2019 IEEE International Conference on Electrical, Computer and Communication Technologies (ICECCT), IEEE, 2019, pp. 1–7.

[12] M.F. Hashmi, S. Katiyar, A.G. Keskar, N.D. Bokde, Z.W. Geem, Efficient pneumonia detection in chest xray images using deep transfer learning, Diagnostics 10 (6) (2020) 417.

[13] M. Toğaçar, B. Ergen, Z. Cömert, F. Özyurt, A deep feature learning model for pneumonia detection applying a combination of mRMR feature selection and machine learning models, IRBM 41 (4) (2020) 212–222.

[14] I. Jain, V.K. Jain, R. Jain, Correlation feature selection based improved-binary particle swarm optimization for gene selection and cancer classification, Appl. Soft Comput. 62 (2018) 203–215.

[15] M. Hall, Correlation-based feature selection for discrete and numeric class machine learning, in: Proceedings of the Seventeenth International Conference on Machine Learning, Morgan Kaufmann Publishers Inc., 2000, pp. 359–366.

[16] Q. Liu, Q. Gu, Z. Wu, Feature selection method based on support vector machine and shape analysis for high-throughput medical data, Comput. Biol. Med. 91 (2017) 103–111.

[17] H.H. Hsu, C.W. Hsieh, Feature selection via correlation coefficient clustering, JSW 5 (12) (2010) 1371–1377.

[18] G. Chandrashekar, F. Sahin, A survey on feature selection methods, Comput. Electr. Eng. 40 (1) (2014) 16–28.

[19] A. Jović, K. Brkić, N. Bogunović, A review of feature selection methods with applications, in: 2015 38th International Convention on Information and Communication Technology, Electronics and Microelectronics (MIPRO), IEEE, 2015, pp. 1200–1205.

[20] J. Hua, W.D. Tembe, E.R. Dougherty, Performance of feature-selection methods in the classification of high-dimension data, Pattern Recogn. 42 (3) (2009) 409–424.

[21] B. Remeseiro, V. Bolon-Canedo, A review of feature selection methods in medical applications, Comput. Biol. Med. 112 (2019) 103375.

[22] M. Allam, M. Nandhini, A study on optimization techniques in feature selection for medical image analysis, Int. J. Comput. Sci. Eng. 9 (3) (2017) 75–82.

[23] J. Tang, S. Alelyani, H. Liu, Feature selection for classification: a review, in: Data Classification: Algorithms and Applications, 2014. p. 37.

[24] I.T. Jolliffe, J. Cadima, Principal component analysis: a review and recent developments, Philos. Trans. Royal Soc. A Math. Phys. Eng. Sci. 374 (2065) (2016) 20150202.

[25] M. Brems, A one-stop shop for principal component analysis, Medium Towards Data Science 17 (2017).

[26] V. Powell, L. Lehe, Principal Component Analysis Explained Visually, 2015, DISQUS, Available: http://setosa.io/ev/principal-componentanalysis/. (Accessed 11 July 2016).

[27] J. Rasheed, A.A. Hameed, C. Djeddi, et al., A machine learning-based framework for diagnosis of COVID-19 from chest X-ray images, Interdiscip. Sci. Comput. Life Sci. 13 (2021) 103–117, https://doi.org/10.1007/s12539-020-00403-6.

[28] J. Rawat, A. Singh, H.S. Bhadauria, J. Virmani, J.S. Devgun, Leukocyte classification using adaptive neuro-fuzzy inference system in microscopic blood images, Arab. J. Sci. Eng. 43 (12) (2018) 7041–7058.

[29] N. Dey, A.S. Ashour, F. Shi, V.E. Balas, Soft Computing Based Medical Image Analysis, Academic Press, 2018.

[30] I. Kumar, J. Virmani, H.S. Bhadauria, M.K. Panda, Classification of breast density patterns using PNN, NFC, and SVM classifiers, in: Soft Computing Based Medical Image Analysis, Academic Press, 2018, pp. 223–243.

[31] B. Cetisli, Development of an adaptive neuro-fuzzy classifier using linguistic hedges: part 1, Expert Syst. Appl. 37 (8) (2010) 6093–6101.

[32] S. Devi, S. Kumar, G.S. Kushwaha, An adaptive neuro fuzzy inference system for prediction of anxiety of students, in: 8th International Conference on Advanced Computational Intelligence, Chiang Mai, Thailand, 14–16 February 2016, 2016.

[33] E.D. Übeyli, Adaptive neuro-fuzzy inference systems for automatic detection of breast cancer, J. Med. Syst. 33 (5) (2009) 353.

[34] E.D. Übeyli, Adaptive neuro-fuzzy inference system for classification of ECG signals using Lyapunov exponents, Comput. Methods Prog. Biomed. 93 (3) (2009) 313–321.

[35] E.D. Übeyli, Automatic detection of electroencephalographic changes using adaptive neuro-fuzzy inference system employing Lyapunov exponents, Expert Syst. Appl. 36 (5) (2009) 9031–9038.

[36] E.D. Übeyli, Automatic diagnosis of diabetes using adaptive neuro-fuzzy inference systems, Expert. Syst. 27 (4) (2010) 259–266.

[37] T. Uçar, A. Karahoca, D. Karahoca, Tuberculosis disease diagnosis by using adaptive neuro fuzzy inference system and rough sets, Neural Comput. Applic. 23 (2) (2013) 471–483.

[38] S. Roy, S. Sadhu, S.K. Bandyopadhyay, D. Bhattacharyya, T.H. Kim, Brain tumor classification using adaptive neuro-fuzzy inference system from MRI, Int. J. Bio-Sci. Bio-Technol. 8 (3) (2016) 203–218.

[39] M.I. Obayya, N.F. Areed, A.O. Abdulhadi, Liver cancer identification using adaptive neuro-fuzzy inference system, Int. J. Comput. Applic. 140 (8) (2016) 1–7.

[40] E.K. Roy, S.K. Aditya, Prediction of acute myeloid leukemia subtypes based on artificial neural network and adaptive neuro-fuzzy inference system approaches, in: Innovations in Electronics and Communication Engineering, Springer, Singapore, 2019, pp. 427–439.

[41] A. García-Floriano, Á. Ferreira-Santiago, O. Camacho-Nieto, C. Yáñez-Márquez, A machine learning approach to medical image classification: detecting age-related macular degeneration in fundus images, Comput. Electr. Eng. 75 (2019) 218–229.

[42] B. Cetisli, The effect of linguistic hedges on feature selection: part 2, Expert Syst. Appl. 37 (8) (2010) 6102–6108.

[43] R. Kher, T. Pawar, V. Thakar, H. Shah, Physical activities recognition from ambulatory ECG signals using neuro-fuzzy classifiers and support vector machines, J. Med. Eng. Technol. 39 (2) (2015) 138–152.

[44] Q.H. Do, J.F. Chen, A neuro-fuzzy approach in the classification of students' academic performance, Comput. Intell. Neurosci. 2013 (2013) 49–55.

[45] M.M. Khan, S.K. Chalup, A. Mendes, Parkinson's disease data classification using evolvable wavelet neural networks, in: Australasian Conference on Artificial Life and Computational Intelligence, Springer, Cham, 2016, pp. 113–124.

[46] M.A. Chikh, M. Ammar, R. Marouf, A neuro-fuzzy identification of ECG beats, J. Med. Syst. 36 (2) (2012) 903–914.

Further reading

[47] K. Michalak, H. Kwaśnicka, Correlation-based feature selection strategy in classification problems, Int. J. Appl. Math. Comput. Sci. 16 (2006) 503–511.

[48] N.B. Khameneh, H. Arabalibeik, P. Salehian, S. Setayeshi, Abnormal red blood cells detection using adaptive neuro-fuzzy system, in: Mmvr, 2012, pp. 30–34.

[49] P. Melin, G. Prado-Arechiga, Design of a neuro-fuzzy system for diagnosis of arterial hypertension, in: New Hybrid Intelligent Systems for Diagnosis and Risk Evaluation of Arterial Hypertension, Springer, Cham, 2018, pp. 15–22.

[50] S. Kar, D.D. Majumder, An investigative study on early diagnosis of prostate cancer using neuro-fuzzy classification system for pattern recognition, Int. J. Fuzzy Syst. 19 (2) (2017) 423–439.

[51] S. Kar, D.D. Majumder, A novel approach of mathematical theory of shape and neuro-fuzzy based diagnostic analysis of cervical cancer, Pathol. Oncol. Res. 25 (2) (2019) 777–790.

[52] S. Kar, D.D. Majumder, A novel approach of diffusion tensor visualization based neuro fuzzy classification system for early detection of Alzheimer's disease, J. Alzheimer's Dis. Rep. 3 (1) (2019) 1–18.

[53] A. Badnjevic, L. Gurbeta, E. Custovic, An expert diagnostic system to automatically identify asthma and chronic obstructive pulmonary disease in clinical settings, Sci. Rep. 8 (1) (2018) 1–9.

[54] V.P. Kolosov, N.S. Bezrukov, D.Y. Naumov, Y.M. Perelman, A.G. Prikhodko, Prediction of osmotic airway hyperresponsiveness in patients with bronchial asthma using adaptive neuro-fuzzy network, in: 2015 International Conference on Biomedical Engineering and Computational Technologies (SIBIRCON), IEEE, 2015, pp. 130–133.

[55] M. Imran, S.A. Alsuhaibani, A neuro-fuzzy inference model for diabetic retinopathy classification, in: Intelligent Data Analysis for Biomedical Applications, Academic Press, 2019, pp. 147–172.

[56] V.I. Osubor, A.O. Egwali, A neuro fuzzy approach for the diagnosis of postpartum depression disorder, Iran J. Comput. Sci. 1 (4) (2018) 217–225.

[57] A. Karahoca, D. Karahoca, A. Kara, Diagnosis of diabetes by using adaptive neuro fuzzy inference systems, in: In 2009 Fifth International Conference on Soft Computing, Computing with Words and Perceptions in System Analysis, Decision and Control, IEEE, 2009, pp. 1–4.

[58] S. Kavitha, K. Duraiswamy, Adaptive neuro-fuzzy inference system approach for the automatic screening of diabetic retinopathy in fundus images, J. Comput. Sci. 7 (7) (2011) 1020–1026, https://doi.org/10.3844/jcssp.2011.1020.1026.

[59] S. Alby, B.L. Shivakumar, A prediction model for type 2 diabetes using adaptive neuro-fuzzy interface system, Biomed. Res. 29 (0) (2018).

[60] S. Banerjee, S. Mitra, B.U. Shankar, Synergetic neuro-fuzzy feature selection and classification of brain tumors, in: 2017 IEEE International Conference on Fuzzy Systems (FUZZ-IEEE), IEEE, 2017, pp. 1–6.

[61] X.D. Wang, J. Feng, Y.L. Li, Z. Li, Q.P. Wang, Computer aided detection for breast calcification clusters based on improved instance selection and an adaptive neuro-fuzzy network, in: 2013 10th International Conference on Fuzzy Systems and Knowledge Discovery (FSKD), IEEE, 2013, July, pp. 184–189.

[62] L.L.G. Oliveira, S.A. e Silva, L.H.V. Ribeiro, R.M. de Oliveira, C.J. Coelho, A.L.S. Andrade, Computer-aided diagnosis in chest radiography for detection of childhood pneumonia, Int. J. Med. Inform. 77 (8) (2008) 555–564.

[63] R.T. Sousa, O. Marques, F.A.A. Soares, I.I. Sene Jr., L.L. de Oliveira, E.S. Spoto, Comparative performance analysis of machine learning classifiers in detection of childhood pneumonia using chest radiographs, Procedia Comput. Sci. 18 (2013) 2579–2582.

[64] E. Naydenova, A. Tsanas, C. Casals-Pascual, M. De Vos, Smart diagnostic algorithms for automated detection of childhood pneumonia in resource-constrained settings, in: 2015 IEEE Global Humanitarian Technology Conference (GHTC), IEEE, 2015, pp. 377–384.

[65] Weka. https://www.cs.waikato.ac.nz/ml/weka/.

[66] I.H. Witten, E. Frank, Data Mining Practical Machine Learning Tools and Techniques With Java Implementations, Morgan Kaufman, San Francisco, 2005.

[67] P. Banerjee, A.K. Bhunia, A. Bhattacharyya, P.P. Roy, S. Murala, Local neighborhood intensity pattern—a new texture feature descriptor for image retrieval, Expert Syst. Appl. 113 (2018) 100–115.

[68] T.J. Alhindi, S. Kalra, K.H. Ng, A. Afrin, H.R. Tizhoosh, Comparing LBP, HOG and deep features for classification of histopathology images, in: 2018 International Joint Conference on Neural Networks (IJCNN), IEEE, 2018, pp. 1–7.

[69] T. Kobayashi, N. Otsu, Image feature extraction using gradient local auto-correlations, in: European Conference on Computer Vision, Springer, Berlin, Heidelberg, 2008, pp. 346–358.

[70] P. Simon, V. Uma, Deep learning based feature extraction for texture classification, Procedia Comput. Sci. 171 (2020) 1680–1687.

[71] A. Boyd, A. Czajka, K. Bowyer, Deep learning-based feature extraction in iris recognition: use existing models, fine-tune or train from scratch? in: 2019 IEEE 10th International Conference on Biometrics Theory, Applications and Systems (BTAS), IEEE, 2019, pp. 1–9.

[72] N. O'Mahony, S. Campbell, A. Carvalho, S. Harapanahalli, G.V. Hernandez, L. Krpalkova, D. Riordan, J. Walsh, Deep learning vs. traditional computer vision, in: Science and Information Conference, Springer, Cham, 2019, pp. 128–144.

[73] S. Dara, P. Tumma, Feature extraction by using deep learning: a survey, in: 2018 Second International Conference on Electronics, Communication and Aerospace Technology (ICECA), IEEE, 2018, pp. 1795–1801.

[74] C. Szegedy, W. Liu, Y. Jia, P. Sermanet, S. Reed, D. Anguelov, D. Erhan, V. Vanhoucke, A. Rabinovich, Going deeper with convolutions, in: Proceedings of the IEEE Conference on Computer Vision and Pattern Recognition, 2015, pp. 1–9.

Hybrid computer-aided classification system design using lightweight end-to-end Pre-trained CNN-based deep feature extraction and PCA-SVM classifier for chest radiographs

9.1 Introduction

This chapter covers the exhaustive description of the experiments carried out for the design of a hybrid computer-aided classification (CAC) system using lightweight end-to-end Pre-trained MobileNetV2 convolution neural network (CNN) model as deep feature extractor and principal component analysis and support vector machine (PCA-SVM) classifier for chest radiographs. The code snippets of the experiment aim at giving a better understanding to the programmatic implementation of designing this CAC system.

9.2 Experimental workflow

The experimental workflow followed for analyzing the performance of a hybrid CAC system designed for chest radiographs using deep feature extraction, lightweight MobileNetV2 CNN model, and PCA-SVM classifier is shown in Fig. 9.1.

9.3 Deep feature extraction

The process of extracting features of an image from the deep layers of a CNN is referred to as deep feature extraction, and the features extracted are called as deep features. This process involves the steps for providing the input data to the Pre-trained CNN, and then the respective activation values from the fully connected layer that is usually present at the end of the network or the various pooling layers present at different levels are obtained. This process of deep feature extraction is discussed in detail in Chapter 5, whereas deep feature extraction using lightweight MobileNetV2 CNN model is discussed

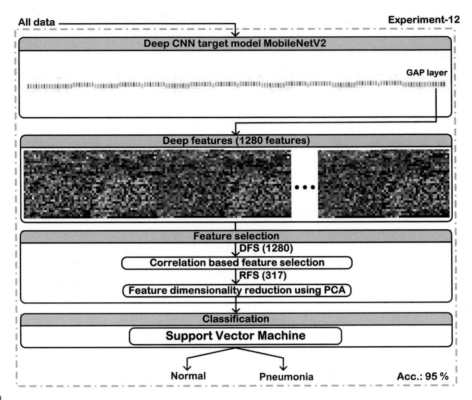

FIG. 9.1

Experimental workflow of hybrid CAC system designed for chest radiographs using deep feature extraction, lightweight MobileNetV2 CNN model and PCA-SVM classifier.

in Chapter 8. In the present work, the deep features are extracted from the best fine-tuned lightweight MobileNetV2 CNN model whose classification results of Experiment 9 are given in Chapter 7, consequentially forming a set of deep features that are extracted from the best performing lightweight CNN model. This feature set is referred to as a deep feature set (DFS).

The following code snippets show the process of feature extraction and feature map visualization of the extracted deep features. Code Snippet 9.1 shows the syntax to load the MobileNetV2 CNN model trained in Experiment 9 in Chapter 7 to extract the features from its pooling layer.

Code Snippet 9.2 shows the extraction of training and testing features from the pooling layer of the MobileNetV2 CNN model after it has been loaded into the MATLAB workspace.

Code Snippet 9.1 Loading the saved MobileNetV2 Pre-trained CNN model

```
%%loading the saved MobileNetV2 Pre-trained CNN model%%
load('Exp9_MobileNetV2');
```

Code Snippet 9.2 Feature extraction from the MobileNetV2 Pre-trained CNN model

---

```
%%feature extraction%%
layer = 'pool5';
featuresTrain=activations(Exp9_MobileNetV2,imds_train,layer,'OutputAs','rows');
featuresTest=activations(Exp9_MobileNetV2,imds_test,layer,'OutputAs','rows');
```

Code Snippet 9.3 Saving the features extracted from the MobileNetV2 Pre-trained CNN model

---

```
%%saving the features in a excel sheet%%
xlswrite('H:\DataChestX-ray\FeatureExtraction\Exp12_Train.xlsx',featuresTrain);
xlswrite('H:\DataChestX-ray\FeatureExtraction\Exp12_Test.xlsx',featuresTest);
```

Code Snippet 9.3 shows the syntax of writing the features extracted from the pooling layer to Microsoft Excel sheets. These .xlsx files or .csv files are then used as input to the machine learning-based classifiers.

9.4 Feature selection and dimensionality reduction

The process of feature selection and different methods of feature selection are discussed in Chapter 5.

9.4.1 Correlation-based feature selection

Correlation-based feature selection (CFS) aims at extracting the best and most optimal set of features, which are nothing but a subset of the original set of features, on the basis of their correlation values. This technique is widely used as an attempt to select the optimal features from the original feature sets [1–12]. The CFS follows the basic idea that the features are not correlated to each other but have higher correlations to the class they belong to. Here the reduced feature set (RFS) consists of the features that are uncorrelated to each other but have high correlation to their respective classes, either Normal or Pneumonia. The detailed CFS is discussed in Chapter 5.

Here the DFS contains the features extracted from the pooling layer of the lightweight MobileNetV2 CNN, that is, the global average pool (GAP) layer, which when subjected to the CFS results in an RFS. Here the DFS consists of 1280 features, and after CFS, the RFS consists of 317 features.

9.4.2 PCA-based feature dimensionality reduction

After the task of feature extraction and feature selection by CFS, the RFS may contain some features that may be correlated to each other. These correlated features are not of much use, as they do not provide any considerate amount of useful information that may help in the classification of chest radiograph images into Normal and Pneumonia classes. Hence these are highly redundant in nature. In the present work, PCA is used for dimensionality reduction of the deep feature space, which is extracted from the Pre-trained lightweight MobileNetV2 CNN model in the form of an RFS. The PCA helps in finding optimal principal components (PCs) that are highly useful in the classification task [13–16]. The detailed steps of PCA for feature dimensionality reduction are discussed in Chapter 6.

9.5 SVM classifier

The SVM classifier is a member of the supervised machine learning algorithms class. The basic concept that the SVM works on is decision boundaries [17–21]. Among the multiple steps involved in implementing SVM, the most crucial step is attaining a good, generalized performance. The parameters represented by C and γ play a major role in achieving a good and well-generalized performance of the SVM classifier. Here the parameter C is responsible for the regularization of the result; hence, it is called the regularization parameter. Similarly, the parameter γ is associated with the kernel performance; hence, it is called the kernel parameter. The main aim of regularization parameter C is to maximize the margin while keeping the error of training as low as possible. In the present work, a k-fold cross validation is carried out on the training dataset, where $k = 10$. Here each combination of (C, γ) is chosen, such that:

$$C \in \left\{2^{-4}, 2^{-3} \ldots 2^{15}\right\}$$

$$\gamma = \left\{2^{-12}, 2^{-11} \ldots 2^{4}\right\}$$

The grid search procedure followed in the parameter space aims at giving the optimum values of the regularization parameter C and the kernel parameter γ, such that the training accuracy is maximum at the optimum value of (C, γ) [22–26]. The detailed steps of SVM are discussed in Chapter 6.

9.6 Experiment and results

Experiment 12: Designing hybrid CAC system for chest radiographs using deep feature extraction by lightweight mobileNetV2 and PCA-SVM classifier

From the results of Experiments 7–9, as described in Chapter 7, it can be seen that lightweight MobileNetV2 CNN model achieves the highest accuracy (94.00%). Therefore, for this experiment to evaluate the performance of the lightweight CNN as feature extractor, the features from the GAP layer of MobileNetV2 have been extracted. It forms a DFS of 1280 features, which after CFS, result in an RFS of 317 features. This is further fed to a PCA-SVM classifier for deep feature extraction and classification of chest radiograph images. The result of the performance evaluation of a hybrid CAC system designed for chest radiographs using deep feature extraction, lightweight MobileNetV2 CNN model, and PCA-SVM classifier is shown in Table 9.1.

From the results of Experiment 12, as shown in Table 9.1, it can be seen that the hybrid CAC system designed using deep features extracted, lightweight MobileNetV2 CNN model, and PCA-SVM classifier achieves 95.00% accuracy for the classification of chest radiograph images into two classes: Normal and Pneumonia. The individual class accuracy value of the Normal class is 100.00%, and for the Pneumonia class, the individual class accuracy value obtained is 90.00%. From the total 100 images in the testing set, 5 images have been incorrectly classified, from which there are no instances of the Normal class, that is, all 5 images belong to the Pneumonia class. The ROC curve with its

Table 9.1 Performance evaluation of hybrid CAC system designed for chest radiographs using deep feature extraction, lightweight MobileNetV2 CNN model and PCA-SVM classifier.

Network/classifier	Confusion matrix			Accuracy (%)	ICA_ Normal (%)	ICA_ Pneumonia (%)
		Normal	Pneumonia			
MobileNetV2/ PCA-SVM	Normal	50	0	95.00	100.00	90.00
	Pneumonia	5	45			

ICA_Normal, *individual class accuracy for Normal class;* ICA_Pneumonia, *individual class accuracy for Pneumonia class.*

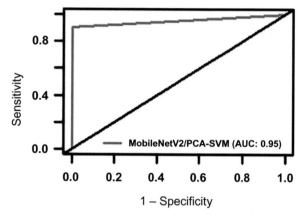

FIG. 9.2

The ROC curve with its corresponding AUC values for the CAC system designed using the lightweight MobileNetV2 CNN model as deep feature extractor and PCA-SVM classifier.

corresponding AUC values for the CAC system designed using the lightweight MobileNetV2 CNN model as deep feature extractor and PCA-SVM classifier is shown in the Fig. 9.2.

9.7 Concluding remarks

This chapter discusses the concepts of deep feature extraction, feature dimensionality reduction, and the design of a CAC system for deep feature extraction using lightweight MobileNetV2 CNN model and PCA-SVM classifier. From the experiment carried out, it is observed that the designing lightweight CNN-based CAC system for deep feature extraction and classification of chest radiographs using MobileNetV2 and PCA-SVM as the classifier achieves 95.00% accuracy.

References

[1] I. Jain, V.K. Jain, R. Jain, Correlation feature selection based improved-binary particle swarm optimization for gene selection and cancer classification, Appl. Soft Comput. 62 (2018) 203–215.
[2] K. Michalak, H. Kwaśnicka, Correlation-based feature selection strategy in classification problems, Int. J. Appl. Math. Comput. Sci. 16 (2006) 503–511.

[3] M.A. Hall, Correlation-based feature selection for discrete and numeric class machine learning, in: Proceedings of the Seventeenth International Conference on Machine Learning, Morgan Kaufmann Publishers Inc., 2000, pp. 359–366.

[4] M. Toğaçar, B. Ergen, Z. Cömert, F. Özyurt, A deep feature learning model for pneumonia detection applying a combination of mRMR feature selection and machine learning models, IRBM 41 (4) (2020) 212–222.

[5] Q. Liu, Q. Gu, Z. Wu, Feature selection method based on support vector machine and shape analysis for high-throughput medical data, Comput. Biol. Med. 91 (2017) 103–111.

[6] H.H. Hsu, C.W. Hsieh, Feature selection via correlation coefficient clustering, JSW 5 (12) (2010) 1371–1377.

[7] G. Chandrashekar, F. Sahin, A survey on feature selection methods, Comput. Electr. Eng. 40 (1) (2014) 16–28.

[8] A. Jović, K. Brkić, N. Bogunović, A review of feature selection methods with applications, in: 2015 38th International Convention on Information and Communication Technology, Electronics and Microelectronics (MIPRO), IEEE, 2015, pp. 1200–1205.

[9] J. Hua, W.D. Tembe, E.R. Dougherty, Performance of feature-selection methods in the classification of high-dimension data, Pattern Recogn. 42 (3) (2009) 409–424.

[10] B. Remeseiro, V. Bolon-Canedo, A review of feature selection methods in medical applications, Comput. Biol. Med. 112 (2019) 103375.

[11] M. Allam, M. Nandhini, A study on optimization techniques in feature selection for medical image analysis, Int. J. Comput. Sci. Eng. 9 (3) (2017) 75–82.

[12] J. Tang, S. Alelyani, H. Liu, Feature selection for classification: a review, in: Data Classification: Algorithms and Applications, CRC Press, 2014, p. 37.

[13] I.T. Jolliffe, J. Cadima, Principal component analysis: a review and recent developments, Philos. Trans. Royal Soc. A Math. Phys. Eng. Sci. 374 (2065) (2016) 20150202.

[14] M. Brems, A one-stop shop for principal component analysis, Medium Towards Data Science 17 (2017).

[15] V. Powell, L. Lehe, Principal Component Analysis Explained Visually, 2015, DISQUS, Available: http://setosa.io/ev/principal-componentanalysis/. Accessed 11 July 2016.

[16] J. Rasheed, A.A. Hameed, C. Djeddi, A. Jamil, F. Al-Turjman, A machine learning-based framework for diagnosis of COVID-19 from chest X-ray images, Interdiscip. Sci. Comput. Life Sci. 13 (1) (2021) 103–117.

[17] L. Wang (Ed.), Support Vector Machines: Theory and Applications, vol. 177, Springer Science & Business Media, 2005.

[18] A. Pradhan, Support vector machine-a survey, Int. J. Emerging Technol. Adv. Eng. 2 (8) (2012) 82–85.

[19] S. Suthaharan, Support vector machine, in: Machine Learning Models and Algorithms for Big Data Classification, Springer, Boston, MA, 2016, pp. 207–235.

[20] J. Zhou, K.L. Chan, V.F.H. Chong, S.M. Krishnan, Extraction of brain tumor from MR images using one-class support vector machine, in: 2005 IEEE Engineering in Medicine and Biology 27th Annual Conference, IEEE, 2006, pp. 6411–6414.

[21] Y. Jiang, Z. Li, L. Zhang, P. Sun, An improved svm classifier for medical image classification, in: International Conference on Rough Sets and Intelligent Systems Paradigms, Springer, Berlin, Heidelberg, 2007, pp. 764–773.

[22] A. Sánchez, V.D., Advanced support vector machines and kernel methods, Neurocomputing 55 (1–2) (2003) 5–20.

[23] A. Karatzoglou, D. Meyer, K. Hornik, Support vector machines in R, J. Stat. Softw. 15 (9) (2006) 1–28.

[24] K. Pelckmans, J.A. Suykens, T. Van Gestel, J. De Brabanter, L. Lukas, B. Hamers, B. De Moor, J. Vandewalle, LS-SVMlab: a matlab/c toolbox for least squares support vector machines. Tutorial. KULeuven-ESAT. Leuven, Belgium, 142 (1–2), 2002.

[25] D. Meyer, F.T. Wien, Support vector machines. The Interface to libsvm in package e 1071, 28, 2015.

[26] T.A. Gomes, R.B. Prudêncio, C. Soares, A.L. Rossi, A. Carvalho, Combining meta-learning and search techniques to select parameters for support vector machines, Neurocomputing 75 (1) (2012) 3–13.

Further reading

M. Nixon, A. Aguado, Feature Extraction and Image Processing for Computer Vision, Academic Press, 2019.

A. Yang, X. Yang, W. Wu, H. Liu, Y. Zhuansun, Research on feature extraction of tumor image based on convolutional neural network, IEEE Access 7 (2019) 24204–24213.

M. Srinivas, D. Roy, C.K. Mohan, Discriminative feature extraction from X-ray images using deep convolutional neural networks, in: 2016 IEEE International Conference on Acoustics, Speech and Signal Processing (ICASSP), IEEE, 2016, pp. 917–921.

V. Chouhan, S.K. Singh, A. Khamparia, D. Gupta, P. Tiwari, C. Moreira, R. Damaševičius, V.H.C. De Albuquerque, A novel transfer learning based approach for pneumonia detection in chest X-ray images, Appl. Sci. 10 (2) (2020) 559.

H. Ravishankar, P. Sudhakar, R. Venkataramani, S. Thiruvenkadam, P. Annangi, N. Babu, V. Vaidya, Understanding the mechanisms of deep transfer learning for medical images, in: Deep Learning and Data Labeling for Medical Applications, Springer, Cham, 2016, pp. 188–196.

H. Wu, P. Xie, H. Zhang, D. Li, M. Cheng, Predict pneumonia with chest X-ray images based on convolutional deep neural learning networks, J. Intell. Fuzzy Syst. (2020) 1–15 (Preprint).

K. Suzuki, Overview of deep learning in medical imaging, Radiol. Phys. Technol. 10 (3) (2017) 257–273.

A. Wibisono, J. Adibah, F.S. Priatmadji, N.Z. Viderisa, A. Husna, P. Mursanto, Segmentation-based knowledge extraction from chest X-ray images, in: 2019 4th Asia-Pacific Conference on Intelligent Robot Systems (ACIRS), IEEE, 2019, pp. 225–230.

S.M. Anwar, M. Majid, A. Qayyum, M. Awais, M. Alnowami, M.K. Khan, Medical image analysis using convolutional neural networks: a review, J. Med. Syst. 42 (11) (2018) 226.

N. Dey, A.S. Ashour, F. Shi, V.E. Balas, Soft Computing Based Medical Image Analysis, Academic Press, 2018.

I. Kumar, J. Virmani, H.S. Bhadauria, M.K. Panda, Classification of breast density patterns using PNN, NFC, and SVM classifiers, in: Soft Computing Based Medical Image Analysis, Academic Press, 2018, pp. 223–243.

A. Badnjevic, L. Gurbeta, E. Custovic, An expert diagnostic system to automatically identify asthma and chronic obstructive pulmonary disease in clinical settings, Sci. Rep. 8 (1) (2018) 1–9.

A. García-Floriano, Á. Ferreira-Santiago, O. Camacho-Nieto, C. Yáñez-Márquez, A machine learning approach to medical image classification: detecting age-related macular degeneration in fundus images, Comput. Electr. Eng. 75 (2019) 218–229.

L.L.G. Oliveira, S.A. e Silva, L.H.V. Ribeiro, R.M. de Oliveira, C.J. Coelho, A.L.S. Andrade, Computer-aided diagnosis in chest radiography for detection of childhood pneumonia, Int. J. Med. Inform. 77 (8) (2008) 555–564.

R.T. Sousa, O. Marques, F.A.A. Soares, I.I. Sene Jr., L.L. de Oliveira, E.S. Spoto, Comparative performance analysis of machine learning classifiers in detection of childhood pneumonia using chest radiographs, Procedia Comput. Sci. 18 (2013) 2579–2582.

E. Naydenova, A. Tsanas, C. Casals-Pascual, M. De Vos, Smart diagnostic algorithms for automated detection of childhood pneumonia in resource-constrained settings, in: 2015 IEEE Global Humanitarian Technology Conference (GHTC), IEEE, 2015, pp. 377–384.

P. Simon, V. Uma, Deep learning based feature extraction for texture classification, Procedia Comput. Sci. 171 (2020) 1680–1687.

A. Boyd, A. Czajka, K. Bowyer, Deep learning-based feature extraction in iris recognition: use existing models, fine-tune or train from scratch? in: 2019 IEEE 10th International Conference on Biometrics Theory, Applications and Systems (BTAS), IEEE, 2019, pp. 1–9.

N. O'Mahony, S. Campbell, A. Carvalho, S. Harapanahalli, G.V. Hernandez, L. Krpalkova, D. Riordan, J. Walsh, Deep learning vs. traditional computer vision, in: Science and Information Conference, Springer, Cham, 2019, pp. 128–144.

S. Dara, P. Tumma, Feature extraction by using deep learning: a survey, in: 2018 Second International Conference on Electronics, Communication and Aerospace Technology (ICECA), IEEE, 2018, pp. 1795–1801.

N. Dey, Y.D. Zhang, V. Rajinikanth, R. Pugalenthi, N.S.M. Raja, Customized VGG19 architecture for pneumonia detection in chest X-rays, Pattern Recogn. Lett. 143 (2021) 67–74.

D. Varshni, K. Thakral, L. Agarwal, R. Nijhawan, A. Mittal, Pneumonia detection using CNN based feature extraction, in: 2019 IEEE International Conference on Electrical, Computer and Communication Technologies (ICECCT), IEEE, 2019, pp. 1–7.

M.F. Hashmi, S. Katiyar, A.G. Keskar, N.D. Bokde, Z.W. Geem, Efficient pneumonia detection in chest xray images using deep transfer learning, Diagnostics 10 (6) (2020) 417.

C.C. Chang, C.J. Lin, LIBSVM: a library for support vector machines, 2001. Software available at http://www. csie. ntu. edu. tw/~ cjlin/libsvm. 2012.

J. Virmani, V. Kumar, N. Kalra, N. Khandelwal, SVM-based characterization of liver ultrasound images using wavelet packet texture descriptors, J. Digit. Imaging 26 (3) (2013) 530–543.

J. Virmani, N. Dey, V. Kumar, PCA-PNN and PCA-SVM based CAD systems for breast density classification, in: Applications of Intelligent Optimization in Biology and Medicine, Springer, Cham, 2016, pp. 159–180.

J. Virmani, V. Kumar, N. Kalra, N. Khandelwa, PCA-SVM based CAD system for focal liver lesions using B-mode ultrasound images, Def. Sci. J. 63 (5) (2013) 478–486.

J. Virmani, V. Kumar, N. Kalra, N. Khandelwal, SVM-based characterisation of liver cirrhosis by singular value decomposition of GLCM matrix, Int. J. Artif. Intell. Soft Comput. 3 (3) (2013) 276–296.

S. Rana, S. Jain, J. Virmani, SVM-based characterization of focal kidney lesions from B-mode ultrasound images, Res. J. Pharm. Biol. Chem. Sci. (2016). ISSN: 0975-85852016.

A.E. Hassanein, T.H. Kim, Breast cancer MRI diagnosis approach using support vector machine and pulse coupled neural networks, J. Appl. Logic 10 (4) (2012) 274–284.

Y.H. Chan, Y.Z. Zeng, H.C. Wu, M.C. Wu, H.M. Sun, Effective pneumothorax detection for chest X-ray images using local binary pattern and support vector machine, J. Healthc. Eng. 2018 (2018), 2908517.

A.E. Hassanien, L.N. Mahdy, K.A. Ezzat, H.H. Elmousalami, H.A. Ella, Automatic x-ray covid-19 lung image classification system based on multi-level thresholding and support vector machine, med Rxiv (2020).

A. Depeursinge, J. Iavindrasana, A. Hidki, G. Cohen, A. Geissbuhler, A. Platon, P.A. Poletti, H. Müller, Comparative performance analysis of state-of-the-art classification algorithms applied to lung tissue categorization, J. Digit. Imaging 23 (1) (2010) 18–30.

J. Yao, A. Dwyer, R.M. Summers, D.J. Mollura, Computer-aided diagnosis of pulmonary infections using texture analysis and support vector machine classification, Acad. Radiol. 18 (3) (2011) 306–314.

Comparative analysis of computer-aided classification systems designed for chest radiographs: Conclusion and future scope

10.1 Introduction

The present work aims at improving the diagnostic capabilities of radiologists by designing convolution neural network (CNN) model-based computer-aided classification (CAC) systems for the binary classification of chest radiographs into Normal and Pneumonia class. For this, multiple experiments have been performed for: (a) designing end-to-end pretrained CNN-based CAC systems for chest radiographs using AlexNet, ResNet18, and GoogLeNet to identify the best performing CNN model; (b) designing a hybrid CAC system for chest radiographs using the CNN model with best performance, deep feature extraction, and adaptive neuro-fuzzy classifier with linguistic hedges (ANFC-LH); (c) designing a hybrid CAC system for chest radiographs using the CNN model with best performance, deep feature extraction, and principal component analysis and support vector machine (PCA-SVM) classifier; (d) designing lightweight end-to-end pretrained CNN-based CAC systems for chest radiographs using SqueezeNet, ShuffleNet, and MobileNetV2 to identify the best performing lightweight CNN model; (e) designing a hybrid CAC system for chest radiographs using lightweight CNN model with best performance, deep feature extraction, and ANFC-LH classifier, (f) designing a hybrid CAC system for chest radiographs using lightweight CNN model with best performance, deep feature extraction, and PCA-SVM classifier. The workflow of these experiments are discussed briefly in Chapter 3.

The conclusions derived from the multiple experiments conducted in the present work have been discussed as follows.

10.2 Conclusion: End-to-end pretrained CNN-based CAC system design for chest radiographs

In Chapter 4, the results of conducting a series of experiments to design the CNN model-based CAC systems are given, and from the results of these experiments it can be concluded that the CAC system designed using the GoogLeNet CNN model yields an accuracy of 90.00% for the binary classification of chest radiographs, which is the best when compared to other CAC system designed using the

AlexNet CNN model yielding 89.00% accuracy and the CAC system designed using the ResNet18 CNN model yielding 88.00% accuracy.

10.3 Conclusion: Hybrid CAC system design using end-to-end pretrained CNN-based deep feature extraction and ANFC-LH, PCA-SVM classifiers for chest radiographs

On the basis of the results of experiments conducted in Chapter 4, the CAC system designed using GoogLeNet CNN model performs the best; hence, it is used as a deep feature extractor in these chapters to design the CAC systems with different machine learning classifiers, namely ANFC-LH and PCA-SVM. From the results of the experiments carried out in Chapters 5 and 6, the CAC system designed using deep feature extraction by GoogLeNet and ANFC-LH yields the maximum accuracy of 93.00%.

10.4 Conclusion: Lightweight end-to-end pretrained CNN-based CAC system design for chest radiographs

Chapter 7 conducts a series of experiments to design the lightweight CNN model-based CAC systems, and from the results of the experiments conducted, it can be concluded that the CAC system designed using the lightweight MobileNetV2 CNN model yields 94.00% accuracy for the binary classification of chest radiographs, which is the best compared to other CAC systems designed using the lightweight SqueezeNet CNN model yielding 83.00% accuracy and the CAC system designed using the lightweight ShuffleNet CNN model yielding 92.00% accuracy.

10.5 Conclusion: Hybrid CAC system design using lightweight end-to-end pretrained CNN-based deep feature extraction and ANFC-LH, PCA-SVM classifiers for chest radiographs

From the results of experiments conducted in Chapter 7, the lightweight MobileNetV2 CNN model is used as a deep feature extractor to design a CAC system for the binary classification of chest radiographs. The results of the experiments conducted in Chapters 8 and 9 show that the CAC system designed using deep feature extraction by lightweight MobileNetV2 CNN model and ANFC-LH yields the same accuracy as the CAC system designed using deep feature extraction by lightweight MobileNetV2 CNN model and PCA-SM, which is of 95.00%.

10.6 Comparison of the different CNN-based CAC systems designed in the present work for the binary classification of chest radiographs

Table 10.1 shows the comparative analysis of the different CAC systems designed in the present work for the classification of chest radiographs into Normal and Pneumonia.

From the results presented in Table 10.1, it can be concluded that the CAC systems designed using the pretrained GoogLeNet CNN model yields an accuracy of 94.00%, which is the maximum when

Table 10.1 A comparative analysis of the different CAC systems designed in the present work for the binary classification of chest radiographs.

S. no.	Experiment	Network/classifier	Accuracy (%)	ICA_Normal (%)	ICA_Pneumonia (%)
1	Designing end-to-end pretrained CNN-based CAC system for chest radiographs using AlexNet	AlexNet/softmax	89.00	98.00	80.00
2	Designing end-to-end pretrained CNN-based CAC system for chest radiographs using ResNet-18	ResNet-18/softmax	88.00	100.00	76.00
3	Designing end-to-end pretrained CNN-based CAC system for chest radiographs using GoogLeNet	GoogLeNet/softmax	90.00	96.00	84.00
4	Designing end-to-end pretrained CNN-based CAC system for chest radiographs using decision fusion	Decision fusion	91.00	100.00	82.00
5	Designing hybrid CAC system for chest radiographs using deep feature extraction, GoogLeNet and ANFC-LH classifier	GoogLeNet/ANFC-LH	93.00	96.00	90.00
6	Designing hybrid CAC system for chest radiographs using deep feature extraction, GoogLeNet and PCA-SVM classifier	GoogLeNet/PCA-SVM	91.00	96.00	86.00
7	Designing lightweight end-to-end pretrained CNN-based CAC system for chest radiographs using SqueezeNet	SqueezeNet/softmax	83.00	98.00	68.00
8	Designing lightweight end-to-end pretrained CNN-based CAC system for chest radiographs using ShuffleNet	ShuffleNet/softmax	92.00	100.00	84.00
9	Designing lightweight end-to-end pretrained CNN-based CAC system for chest radiographs using MobileNetV2	MobileNetV2/softmax	94.00	98.00	90.00
10	Designing lightweight end-to-end pretrained CNN-based CAC system for chest radiographs using decision fusion	Decision fusion	95.00	100.00	90.00
11	Designing hybrid CAC system for chest radiographs using deep feature extraction, lightweight MobileNetV2 and ANFC-LH classifier	MobileNetV2/ANFC-LH	95.00	98.00	92.00
12	Designing hybrid CAC system for chest radiographs using deep feature extraction, lightweight MobileNetV2 and PCA-SVM classifier	MobileNetV2/PCA-SVM	95.00	100.00	90.00

ICA_Normal, individual class accuracy for Normal class; ICA_Pneumonia, individual class accuracy for Pneumonia class.

compared to other CAC systems designed using AlexNet CNN model and ResNet18 CNN model. Also the CAC system designed using deep feature extraction by GoogLeNet and ANFC-LH yields higher accuracy than the CAC system designed using deep feature extraction by GoogLeNet and PCA-SVM machine learning classifiers. Additionally, it yields an individual class accuracy (ICA) of Pneumonia that is the same as the CAC system designed using GoogLeNet CNN model.

The CAC system designed using deep feature extraction by lightweight MobileNetV2 CNN model and machine learning classifiers yields a higher accuracy (95.00%) as compared to the CAC system designed using lightweight MobileNetV2 CNN model.

10.7 Future scope

For future work, other pretrained CNN models, such as VGGNet and ResNet-50, and other variants, such as DarkNet and NasNet, can be used to design CAC systems for the binary classification of chest radiographs. Similarly, deep feature extraction can be used on different layers of the CNN models, and various other machine learning-based algorithms can be used. Furthermore, hybrid CAC systems can be designed using different techniques of feature fusion, decision fusion, and a combination of handcrafted features with deep features extracted. These CAC systems could be designed for multiclass classification such as the three-class classification of chest radiographs into Normal, Pneumonia, and COVID-19 classes.

Fig. 10.1 shows a schematic representation of a decision fusion-based multiclass CAC system design. This can be designed by using multiple end-to-end pretrained CNN models as decision makers and then performing different types of decision fusion to achieve a final decision. These CAC systems can be designed for binary as well as multiclass classification of the input data.

Fig. 10.2 shows a schematic representation of a feature fusion-based hybrid multiclass CAC system design. This type of CAC system can be designed by performing the feature fusion of the deep features extracted using the CNN models and the handcrafted features. These extracted features can be fused

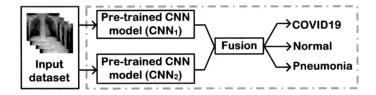

FIG. 10.1

Schematic representation of fusion-based three-class end-to-end CAC system.

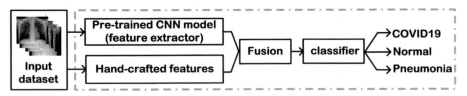

FIG. 10.2

Schematic representation of fusion-based three-class hybrid CAC system.

using various techniques, and then machine learning-based classifiers can be used to perform the final classification, either binary or multiclass.

Fig. 10.3 shows a schematic representation of a feature fusion-based hybrid multiclass CAC system design. This type of hybrid CAC system can be designed by performing deep feature extraction from multiple pretrained CNN models and then applying different feature fusion strategies to ultimately perform classification using machine learning-based classifiers.

Fig. 10.4 shows a schematic representation of deep learning-based hierarchical multiclass CAC system design. This type of hierarchical CAC system can be designed by training an end-to-end CNN model to perform classification in the manner similar to a tree structure.

Fig. 10.5 shows a schematic representation of hybrid hierarchical CAC system design. Similar to the previously discussed CAC system, this hybrid hierarchical CAC system applies the machine learning-based classifiers to perform classification.

These CAC system designs previously discussed can be implemented not only with pretrained CNN models but also with self-designed CNN models, lightweight CNN models, and other variations of deep learning-based networks. These CAC systems can be applied for binary and multiclass classification of chest radiographs as well as for other imaging modalities and different tissue diseases.

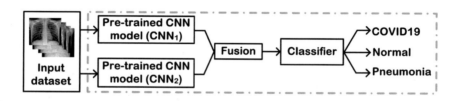

FIG. 10.3

Schematic representation of fusion-based three-class combination hybrid CAC system.

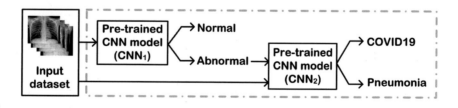

FIG. 10.4

Schematic representation of deep learning-based hierarchical CAC system.

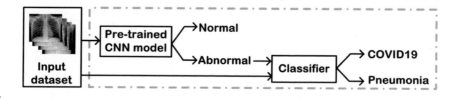

FIG. 10.5

Schematic representation of hybrid hierarchical CAC system.

Index

Note: Page numbers followed by *f* indicate figures, *t* indicate tables, and *b* indicate boxes.